RACE AND ETHNICITY IN EDUCATION

Monitoring Change in Education

Series Editor:
Cedric Cullingford
University of Huddersfield, UK

Change is a key characteristic of the worlds of business, education and industry and the rapidity of change underlines an urgent need to analyze, evaluate and, where appropriate, correct its direction. The series is aimed at contributing to this analysis. Its unique contribution consists of making sense of changes in education and in offering a timely and considered response to new challenges; the series, therefore, focuses on contemporary issues and does so with academic rigour.

Race and Ethnicity in Education

RANJIT ARORA
Education and Management Consultant

ASHGATE

Published by
Ashgate Publishing Limited
Gower House
Croft Road
Aldershot
Hants GU11 3HR
England

Ashgate Publishing Company
Suite 420
101 Cherry Street
Burlington, VT 05401-4405
USA

Ashgate website: http://www.ashgate.com

British Library Cataloguing in Publication Data
Arora, R. K. (Ranjit K.)
  Race and ethnicity in education. - (Monitoring change in education)
  1. Multicultural education - Great Britain 2. Discrimination in education - Great Britain 3. Educational equalization - Great Britain 4. Minority teachers - Training of - Great Britain 5. Minority teachers - Recruiting - Great Britain
  I. Title
  370.1'17'0941

Library of Congress Cataloging-in-Publication Data
Arora, R. K. (Ranjit K.)
  Race and ethnicity in education / by Ranjit Arora.
      p. cm. -- (Monitoring change in education)
  Includes bibliographical references and index.
  ISBN 0-7546-1441-7
  1. Discrimination in education--Great Britain. 2. Educational equalization--Great Britain. 3. Minority teachers--Training of--Great Britain. I. Title. II. Series.

  LC212.3.G7A76 2004
  371.829'0041--dc22

2004012569

ISBN 0 7546 1441 7

Typeset by Get Set Go, Bordon, Hampshire.
Printed and bound in Great Britain by Antony Rowe Ltd, Chippenham, Wiltshire

Contents

List of Figures

Foreword

Robin Richardson

'The past' said L.P. Hartley, 'is a foreign country. They do things differently there.' Another novelist, William Faulkner, said: 'The past isn't dead and gone. It isn't even past.' As we think about the subject-matter of Ranjit Arora's fine book, we are pulled backwards and forwards between these two views of history and of our times and spaces. Is Britain making progress, so far as the achievement of race quality is concerned? Or is it still gripped by the inheritance of Empire and by the vicious hostility towards not-white people that characterised the age of immigration, roughly 1945-1965?

Dr Arora's book explores these questions through discussion of the education system in general and of the training of teachers in particular. What is the role of a country's education system in combating racism and helping to build a more decent, just and inclusive society? Within this context, what is the role of initial teacher training (ITT)? These are the questions with which the book is centrally concerned.

A cynic, paralysed by disappointment and despair, would say that the education system can do little and that ITT can do virtually nothing. The key actors, a cynic would continue, are the government and media on the one hand and individual schools, and perhaps local authorities, on the other. ITT, compared with the principal actors, is marginal, even a bit of a joke.

An alternative view, articulated at length and with passion throughout this book, is that ITT is pivotal. Here is where, the book argues, extremely important changes may take place. Young people contemplating joining the teaching profession are faced here with searching questions about their own role and identity. If they are white, they probably have to question deeply-held notions of Britishness, whiteness, Empire and national identity. Helping and supporting them requires great sensitivity, expertise, sympathy and professionalism from their tutors and lecturers. If they are not white, they are faced with no less searching questions about identity, responsibility and role, and their tutors and lecturers are no less challenged to develop their understanding, courage and skill.

If personal change and commitment in young teachers preparing to enter the profession were the only achievement of ITT it would be, though substantial, not enough. For it would take 20 or more years before those young teachers were in positions of seniority and power. ITT's potential contribution is also that of a demonstration project, showing the wider education system how personal and professional change take place.

Ranjit Arora's book magisterially recalls the difficulties, dilemmas and debates that have taken place in ITT over the last 20 years or more. It notes soberly that ITT is no panacea. It shows also, however, ITT's pivotal role and the dignity and duties of those who are engaged in it.

courses of the 1970s, only address the problem in a limited way by focusing on teachers with overseas qualifications who have hitherto been unable to get qualified teacher status. Meanwhile most of the teacher-training institutions continue to recruit mainly, if not exclusively, an all white population of student teachers.

According to a CRE survey (Ranger 1988) of teacher training institutions the minority ethnic students made up 2.6 percent of all students in the relevant groups and courses compared with 5.3 percent in the appropriate age group in the population. This survey found that well over half the teacher training institutions had either none or only one Black student about to emerge as a teacher. The survey also found that despite the Swann recommendations and DES consultation papers the number of minority ethnic teachers was on the decline. A BICC survey (1988) to investigate the entry of young people into teacher education also found that teaching as a career was seen as much less attractive than many other professions by minority ethnic students, but no more than it was for indigenous White students. It was seen as less attractive as a career not so much because of the low salary/low status syndrome associated with the profession, but more because of the stress associated with the job and lack of recognition of minority ethnic teachers within the profession. The lack of clear and consistent career advice, absence of minority ethnic teachers as role models, fear of racial discrimination and racial abuse and fear of being marginalised were also echoed by most students in the survey. A group of practising Black teachers confirmed the incidence of racial discrimination and marginalisation, and also gave substantial evidence of the stress caused by their jobs.

The research for this publication was located in the context identified above and also in the context of several other recent and current studies of a similar nature (Siraj-Blatchford 1991, HEFC 1993-94). The main aim was to address the two central issues, which have been in the forefront of teacher education at least for a decade, but without a substantive body of empirical analysis. The two issues are:

- The need for Teacher Education programmes to be 'open, community informed and capable of making their students sensitive to the interaction between the local community and wider social groupings in a multicultural context' (Chambers 1981); and
- The need to recruit and train teachers from minority ethnic groups and to encourage minority ethnic youngsters to consider the possibility of entering teaching (Swann 1985).

The Swann Report (1985) had emphasised that the most important source of minority ethnic teachers in the future is the minority ethnic pupils currently in schools. However most of the published work in this field has concentrated on 'not the most important source', but on teachers qualified overseas, or adults potentially benefiting from special Access programmes to facilitate entry to higher education. There has also perhaps been an untested assumption that the introduction of 'multicultural education' to established programmes of teacher education might enhance the attraction of the profession for minorities. The central purpose of this book therefore, is to study the relationship between the preparation of all teachers through initial teacher training and actual practice in schools with regard to providing an anti-racist perspective; and to study the relationship between the established need for minority ethnic teachers and the consistent failure of LEAs and teacher training institutions to recruit and train such teachers.

Chapter 1

Quality and Equality in Education

Introduction

David Blunkett in his introduction to the consultation materials for changes to the National Curriculum in England recognised that the Macpherson Report had placed a particular emphasis on the role of curriculum in encouraging children to value cultural diversity and in combating the development of racism. He has also made a very clear statement that, 'Teachers individually and collectively have to reappraise their teaching in response to the changing needs of their pupils and the ideas and attitudes of society and economic forces'.

The rationale for this book is located in the need for the preparation of teachers through initial teacher education and practice in schools with regard to education with an anti-racist perspective. It explores the relationship between professed commitment, to increase the number of minority ethnic teachers, and the consistent failure of training institutions to recruit and train teachers from minority ethnic groups. There is considerable evidence that preparation for teaching in a multicultural society has not received adequate attention by training institutions. With some exceptions, developments of appropriate courses have often been ad-hoc and dependent more on individual enthusiasms, circumstances and locations, rather than on any systematic efforts on the part of training institutions. It is more than 15 years ago, when the Swann Report, 'Education for All' (1985) identified the growing need for research into the recruitment of teachers from minority ethnic groups. It also highlighted some teacher training institutions with a particular expertise in the preparation of teachers for education in a multicultural society. More than 15 years have passed since a CRE survey (1988), several HMI reports and DES consultation documents also noted the virtual absence of minority ethnic teachers in British schools and identified the relatively small number of institutions that positively recruit minority ethnic students on their teacher education courses.

The possible causes for such gross under-representation identified by the DES's consultation paper included fear of racial discrimination, marginalization and isolation and stress resulting from it; the prospect of good stable posts and promotion not being seen to be as good as those for white teachers; and the almost total absence of role models in teacher training institutions and in the profession at large, which also resulted in inadequate career prospects for potential young teachers from minority ethnic groups. The DfES is keen to increase the supply of minority ethnic teachers and has supported a range of initiatives, some with Section 11 funds, and by giving greater autonomy to institutions in the arrangements they make to satisfy themselves with regard to entrance qualifications. The last decade has seen the development of several employment based routes to teaching as well as part-time PGCE and B.Ed. programmes specially designed to train minority ethnic teachers. But in the main these courses, like the Induction courses of the 1960s and Access

Research into Teacher Education and Multicultural Education

'The Best of Both Worlds' (1985), a review commissioned by the Swann Committee, is perhaps the most comprehensive overview of research evidence on the educational performance of pupils of Asian origin in the UK. In considering whether Asian pupils are achieving their full potential, and whether their educational needs and aspirations are being met, the authors (Taylor & Hegarty 1985) summarised and analysed evidence from large and small-scale research studies over 20 years. They concluded that in the absence of a systematic national policy on the education of minority ethnic children, a number of adhoc, short-term, often localised educational measures led to researchers making blanket statements about the under-achievement of minority ethnic pupils. A similar review, commissioned by the Rampton Committee ('Caught Between', Taylor 1981), concerned with research bearing on the education of children of West Indian origin. Another DES funded study 'The School Effect' (1989), looked at the effectiveness of Multi-Racial Comprehensive schools, and challenged the assumption that minority ethnic groups under-achieve in secondary schools. The study showed that although starting behind White children at the age of 11, Asian and West Indian children tended to catch up between the ages of 13 to 16, and claimed that it was due to school policies rather than the qualities of the children. The media coverage of this report was predictably slanted, and led many teachers to believe that there was no longer a problem of minority ethnic under-achievement in schools and that 'race' was no longer an educational issue. However, the authors acknowledged that they were not really able to explain why differences between schools occur; and that they did not have the resources to carry out a study of classroom interactions. Another major weakness of the study is the inadequacy of data on management styles, organisational structures and teacher perspectives. (A book of more than 300 pages devotes less than 2 pages to Teachers and Schools.) Gillborn & Drew (1992) in their critique of 'The School Effect' drew attention to a number of methodological and interpretative weaknesses. They were particularly critical of Smith and Tomlinson's conclusion regarding the apparent lack of racism in schools. They pointed out that the absence of evidence of racism is not necessarily an evidence of the absence of racism, 'in fact this may simply be due to the inadequacy of the research instruments given the highly complex, and sometimes subtle, forms of racism which many Black pupils experience' (Gillborn & Drew 1992).

Over the last two decades there has been a minor explosion of studies in teacher education both in this country and in the USA. The dominant recurring themes in the 1980s have included the insistence on the centrality of practice, the need for partnership with schools, and the development of practical theories or principles. McNamara's (1982) account of research in Teacher Education makes reference to a range of descriptive and evaluative studies (Alexander & Harris 1977; Reid & Patrick 1980; McNamara & Ross 1982; Alexander & Wormald 1983) and also describes projects, which involved established teachers (Raynor 1981; IT-INSET 1978-82). He concludes that research on teacher training is unlikely to have an impact on professional practice, until teachers and the realities of the classroom are more closely associated with the training process. It does seem strange that the idea of partnership of teacher training institutions with schools seems to have been presented as something new, when it has always been practised, albeit with varying degrees of success. The fact is that no teacher education could possibly have taken place without the co-operation of schools. The only difference now is that schools, with the availability of finance, may be willing to participate more readily in the process of training, but whether they are they more able to do so, given what is required of them after the ERA of 1988, is debatable. Graves (1990) argues that they are not any more able to do so, because for teachers to become reflective practitioners they need to understand what reflection-in-action means. More practice without the opportunity to reflect, and without an adequate intellectual framework to underpin their practice and reflection, is not likely to lead to improved practice. Graves offers an interactive framework in which students derive the know-how of teaching from direct experience in schools and from research findings based on work in schools. But he argues that this learning needs to be mediated and organised by someone who is familiar both with the world of practice and that of research.

Research projects such as IT-INSET (Ashton & Henderson 1989); DES-funded School-based training in the PGCE at Cambridge and the East Anglia project (Tickle 1987) are quoted as examples of good practice. A number of other theoretical and empirical studies of teacher education, for example, Lucas (1988) Ashcroft & Griffith (1989) have also been concerned with partnership and reflective teaching. However, there have been relatively few recent studies that have looked at the relationship between 'race' and initial teacher education. The DES-funded, Keele-based research project on 'In-Service Education in a Multi-racial Society' (1981) still remains the only substantial piece of research in this area, and that too was only concerned with In-Service Education. The lack of discussion, direction and support for doing multicultural research and the paucity of multicultural education research studies is partly due to the 'marginalisation of minority intellectual thought in traditional writings on teaching' (Grant 1992). More recently, Siraj-Blatchford (1993) has examined the central role of teacher educators in reconstructing and promoting equality. The accumulated message from this publication is that there is massive evidence that discrimination and inequality continue to permeate institutions and individuals involved in teacher education, and that change is urgent and long overdue. Some small-scale individual projects have also examined the incidence of minority ethnic under-achievement in initial teacher education (Clay, Cole & Hill 1990; Siraj-Blatchford 1990) and Black students' experience of racism in initial teacher education (Siraj-Blatchford 1991). But a lot more has been written about the employment of minority ethnic teachers. With some exceptions (Ranger 1988, BICC 1988, Siraj-Blatchford 1990 & 1993), most of these accounts are not based on formal research but on personal observation and direct work experience.

Key Questions

The central issue for researchers to keep in mind is the fact that whatever their personal views, children will continue to be taught in schools 'as they are', and that the people who are most likely to have a positive impact upon schools and improve the quality of children's experiences within schools are newly trained teachers who are accepted as credible by their colleagues and achieve posts of responsibility. The purpose of my research was not to offer explanations for the under-achievement of minority ethnic children, but to draw attention to the under-achievement of teacher training institutions, and to expose the hypocrisy of policies and practices that claim to be non-discriminatory. Thus I began with the following questions in mind:

- Why is it that certain training institutions who claim to be national leaders in their provision for preparation of teachers for a multicultural society, and whose courses receive glowing reports from external examiners and inspectors, still seem to fail in meeting the needs of their minority ethnic students?
- Why is it that despite a national under-representation of minority ethnic teachers, there are significant numbers of well-qualified teachers from minority ethnic groups who are unable to find a teaching job?
- Why is it that despite central Government's professed support for training and employing minority ethnic teachers, most Teacher Training Institutions are unable to recruit minority ethnic students onto their courses?
- Why is it that even when training institutions have succeeded in recruiting minority ethnic students, they fail to recruit minority ethnic staff?

To seek answers to these questions I had to look back at the history not just of teacher education, but also at the history of educational policies concerned with 'race' and education. These two extensive literature reviews were conducted with a great deal of rigour, by going directly to primary sources and not depending entirely on existing reviews. This was seen to be an important part of my research, because much of what is already available has been selected from a particular point of view, and is subject to interpretations and inferences alternative to the ones I was seeking. Unfortunately, the use of primary sources has necessarily made this a very long book, but I am sure it has added to it a quality of depth and breadth that other reviews may not have. I also studied some of the recent developments and new initiatives related to the training and recruitment of minority ethnic teachers. Thus my research had a clear sense of being challenging, both of the assumptions and processes of contemporary teacher education. By shifting attention away from the victims (Black people) on to the perpetrators (White institutions) of racism, it tries to shed light on processes through which racism is reproduced. As a Black researcher, I believe I have been able to provide an authentic perspective on what is essential in terms of student 'need', and how minority ethnic students experience the process of teacher education in largely White institutions. As a teacher trainer, and thus as an insider, I have also been able to match this insight, due to my familiarity with the issues, with the perceptions of training providers in the institutions where the research was based. Another significant dimension of seeing myself as an 'insider' has to do with being a member of a minority ethnic group, thus being able to identify with and relate to the issues of discrimination and racism within institutions.

Equality of Opportunity in Education

It could be argued that it is an inevitable consequence of any hierarchical society that inequalities will persist. The power that the more advantaged have will enable them to determine if and when change will take place. There will be an instinctive desire to ensure that whatever change does take place, it does not put their advantageous position in any jeopardy. Inequalities are thus locked in a vicious circle. If you have the power, then you will attempt to retain that, using whatever strategies may help. The focus on an assimilationist approach of the Conservative governments has resulted in equality issues, especially from the point of culture and race, being very much marginalised. Terms such as equal opportunities, education for equality, education for cultural diversity, and education for a culturally plural society are often used as if they were interchangeable. More seriously, the terms have often become associated with certain political beliefs, with the result that support for equality policies have been dependent on what are perceived to be the political levers. The three most commonly known approaches, currently in use in the United Kingdom are described below.

Equal opportunity as equal treatment

Such an approach assumes that as long as there is no deliberate unfair discrimination against another person, there is equal opportunity. The central thrust of this approach is that everyone is treated in the same way, thus ensuring equality of opportunity. In practice such an approach could lead, for example, to treat all Black children as if they were White, consequently ignoring individual differences and varying educational needs. This approach also assumes that by forbidding unfair treatment, the existing patterns of inequality will automatically disappear.

Equal opportunity as equal access

This approach also considers it important to remove unfair treatment, but goes further by suggesting that it is not enough to remove discrimination at the point of service delivery, because there may not be equal access to the point where service is being delivered. There can be no real equality, if for example, women can't be considered for a job because of an unnecessary obstacle, or a requirement such as attendance at a residential course, which may not be possible for some women with children to attend.

Equal opportunity as equal share

This approach, whilst incorporating the notions of equal access and equal treatment, suggests more direct action. It implies that equal opportunity can only truly exist when the benfits of society or service delivery, such as education and employment, are available and held in equal proportions by the groups, which make up our society. Such an approach also suggests an equal share in the power and economy of society. In my view, an equal opportunity policy should therefore aim at positive measures to eliminate not only overt discrimination, but also conditions or requirement and practices, which are discriminatory in operation. Such a policy should also include provisions for affirmative action and measures to provide special education and training for those who would be otherwise unable to enjoy the full benefits of an equal opportunity policy. Whatever the terminology, for more people in Britain today, cultural diversity is visible and a part of life. This is not to deny or overlook the increase in racism in certain areas.

Finally, different dimensions of equality have to be seen much more as a part of the same issue, rather than as separate and divisive compartments. The proposals for a Single Equalities Bill which incorporates the issues of race, gender and disability can only be a good thing if it results in further co-operation between the various Commissions, such as the CRE and the EOC, for ensuring the implementation of equality legislation. However, the complexities of disadvantages need to be understood and managed sensitively and effectively. During the 1980s there was some notable achievements in the area of equality and cultural diversity. The need for all students to be educated with a view to being citizens of a culturally diverse society had been accepted, as well as the fact that racism was an important factor in society, and that education had to be seen in its broadest context so that the responsibilities of anyone part of the education system could be understood. Though most people accepted these principles, the implementation of policies was variable. Similar variations of policy implementation were found in schools and in institutions of further and higher education.

DES Circular 16/89 advocated the collection of ethnically based data in order to 'to help secure equality of opportunity for minority ethnic pupils'. It explains that children learn best if the teaching they receive is related to, and seeks to draw and build on, what they already know. A school is better equipped to offer each child suitable education if the basic facts about his or her cultural identity – including ethnic origin, linguistic background, and religion – are known'. National Curriculum Council Guidance Document on the Whole Curriculum (1990) stated that

> 'a commitment to providing equal opportunities for all pupils, and a recognition that preparation for life in a multicultural society is relevant to all pupils, should permeate every aspect of the curriculum'. It goes on to state that 'in order to make access to the whole curriculum a reality for all pupils, schools need to foster a climate in which equality of opportunity is supported by a policy to which the whole school subscribes and in which positive attitudes to cultural diversity are actively promoted' (NCC 1990a).

The document further specified that introducing multicultural perspectives gives pupils 'the opportunity to view the world from different standpoints, helping them to question prejudice and develop open mindedness. Teachers have a major role to play in preparing young people for adult life; this means life in a multicultural, multilingual Europe, which in its turn is interdependent with the rest of the world'. There was further reference in the National Curriculum Council Newsletter (1991) to how national curriculum contributes to multicultural education by broadening the horizons of all pupils so that they can understand and contribute to a pluralist society. National Curriculum Council Circular 11 (Linguistic Diversity and the National Curriculum 1991) promoted a supportive approach to bilingualism in the context of National Curriculum by stating:

> such linguistic diversity is an asset. It provides an opportunity for pupils to gain firsthand experience, knowledge and understanding of other cultures and perspectives. It also helps to prepare pupils for life in a multicultural society by promoting respect for all forms of language. Variety of languages is a rich resource which schools should use as they implement the National Curriculum (NCC 1991).

More recently the Qualifications and Curriculum Authority's (QCA) statutory inclusion statements for all subjects and all phases have required teachers to have due regard to responding to pupils' diverse learning needs and overcoming potential barriers to learning for individuals and groups of people. However, despite a clear guidance and plethora of government circulars, HMI Annual Report on Education in England (1992) noted that in secondary schools, among particular groups of pupils, standards remain worryingly low, and that, the less academically able pupils from some minority ethnic backgrounds and those in disadvantaged areas continue to underachieve. 'There was substantial underachievement by some groups of minority ethnic pupils in Key Stage 3 and GCSE. Of particular concern was the lack of success of Black British (Caribbean) boys and pupils of Bangladeshi origin.'

The period of Conservative government had, in general, the effect of pushing equality issues very much onto the margin. However LEAs, schools and other institutions that believed equality to be a part of good education have continued with the practices. At the same time, volumes of research have highlighted the dire consequences for certain groups of children from minority ethnic groups if there is no intervention. It is becoming clear that while there may, over the past few decades, have been an improvement in girls' level of achievement, more boys are under-performing. There is an increase in racial incidents, especially in certain parts of Britain. Another example is that of continued racism amongst employers, especially when the level of qualifications amongst minority ethnic groups has been rising. 'Words or Deeds?' (CRE 1989) found that institutions of higher education have shown a lack of understanding and progress, and that a tone of moral superiority or complacency plus ignorance of the issues was pervasive. Polytechnics and universities may have been untouched by the debate on racial equality in schools, because as institutions of higher education they may have been perceived as incapable of discrimination or unequal treatment. The current climate of increasing competition between institutions, with funding allocated on the basis not only of recruitment but of retention and outcome, should encourage students to consider themselves as consumers with the right to complain if services are not perceived to be adequate or fairly distributed.

Can There be Quality in Education Without Equality?

What is quality?

Education is perceived to serve a number of different purposes, ranging from simple transmission of knowledge, to an instigator of new ideas and developments for society as a whole. The application of a market economy in higher education, however, has been followed by changes in practices, which have in many cases revolutionalised the ethos of institutions. Internally cost effectiveness, income generation and downsizing are amongst the key words that often determine policies and practices. External pressures revolve around quality, which in turn affect funding and then practices within the institutions. Quality, it is argued, is elusive of definition. Some common definitions include, 'tradition from the past'; 'about defining the best'; 'meeting specifications'; 'fitness for purpose'; 'conforming to requirements'; 'blend of good design, efficient production and reliability'; 'above average' and 'value added'. Definitions of quality are varied; some believe the concept is an impossible one to deal with abstractly. There is no agreement about the exact meaning of quality and its application. The danger however, to quote Conrad (1994) is that 'the reasons for working with such a concept are rarely questioned; and the concept itself, is seldom defined. Nevertheless, it is employed in a variety of ways and purposes in the field of education and is usually accepted, as if we knew what it meant'.

The more common applications of quality relate to higher education institutions as business enterprises. Quality can be taken as consistency, or it can be measured in terms of the end-product, i.e. the level and percentage of passes. It could be value for money, or it could be high standards but then again the question would be who defines those standards? There are, however, other possibilities. Nightingale and O'Neil (1994) indicate a preference for quality as transformative and go on to state that the 'purpose of university education is to develop the general qualities of a personal and social kind as well as those of an intellectual kind' (1994:53). Outcomes would thus include communication skills, problem-solving abilities, inter-personal skills, planning and strategic thinking abilities etc. Current focus on quality is particularly significant in higher education in Britain as funding and status are very much linked to judgements about quality. Quality Assurance (QA) in education is a nexus of reciprocal responsibilities and rights involving every one with a justifiable interest in the courses concerned. For QA to be credible it should demonstrate its own fitness for purpose.

There are two key measures of quality that good businesses need to consider. The first is whether they are getting the best out of their staff, by rewarding them appropriately and giving them maximum opportunities to develop further. The second is whether their customers (in particular the students) are satisfied and receive the best possible education they are entitled to. As good businesses, it is the job of Higher Education Institutions (HEIs) to make sure that these two key measures are in place. Education objectives of institutions are likely to include statements about the level and extent of skills the students acquire. The skills can be very mechanistic, or they could refer to qualities such as flexibility, independent study and teamwork. In such a situation the students have to be taken from where they are to what employers may expect of them. Like school teachers, higher education tutors need to relate their education specifically to what the students bring and the levels they are at. An HEI offering teacher education is subject both to the Quality Assurance Agency (QAA) and to ITT criteria expressed in Framework for the Assessment of Quality and Standards in ITT (Ofsted 1996), developed jointly by Ofsted and Teacher Training Agency (TTA). Its aims are to provide a means of assessing the quality of ITT and the standards achieved, provide evidence to inform decisions on accreditation and allocation of student numbers, provide a means of identifying strengths and weaknesses in the training in order to help providers identify clear targets for improvement and contribute to raising standards in schools by improving standards in ITT.

The Ofsted/TTA scheme was imposed in 1996 despite widespread opposition by teacher educators. Ofsted claims that precepts of professionalism, fairness, integrity and co-operation underpin all inspection processes. Though there is broad agreement with the corporate goal of 'Improvement Through Inspection' and the underpinning aspirations of objectivity, fairness, partnership, integrity and cost-effectiveness, the different emphasis placed by each of these agencies reflect their different location in TET. Jim Graham's analysis in 'Improvement through Inspection? Quality Assessment and the Role of OFSTED in the Regulation of Teacher Education in England', offers a very succinct view from the perspective of a training provider. He has argued that inspection in education should be a cost effective, mutually consensual process based on respect and esteem for professional judgment and not just about centralised control and bureaucratic command structures promoting competition in ITT against narrow criteria. He has argued that more open and participative processes for reaching and sustaining a professional working consensus are essential to avoid dysfunctional conflicts such as that which has recently characterised the English system.

Quality and equality

The question that needs to be posed is why the narrower definitions of quality, which are based more on treating higher education as a business, pay little attention to equality? People in higher education are drawn to accept the argument that 'you know quality when you see it'. They also however accept the need to define and measure quality in ways that are understood and shared externally as well as internally. 'Equal opportunities is not just about changing people's prejudices and habits, to facilitate the discovery of increased potential in every member of a workforce' (Collins 1992). The traditional route to employment has been via paper qualifications. The modern route is integration with a network, which co-operates, which educates, trains and learns. If people are to exercise their responsibilities to a greater extent in shaping their skills and abilities, they must first be able to enter institutional training systems more easily. This implies familiarity with, broader access to them and better mobility between the different courses.

The White Paper, 'Learning To Succeed' (1999) and its plans to radically reform the management and delivery of post-16 education and training include promoting employability by developing skills that are in demand. It is also about the needs of students and requires a mechanism for interlocking learner support, curriculum innovation and credit accumulation transfer framework. Other current and recent developments have included concepts such as Inclusive Learning, Life Long Learning and Widening Participation. All of these have a very direct link with the equality agenda, a link that is not made explicit, but nevertheless expected to be implicit. However, the frameworks used to assess quality management and quality enhancements in Further and Higher education, with a few exceptions, do not include a direct reference to issues of equality, nor do they require institutions to demonstrate their commitment to equity. The concept of quality has become increasingly pervasive in the public services and as it has become increasingly elaborated in operational terms, it has become very crucial to ensure that it includes equality as one of the bench marks/performance indicator of quality. If equality is ignored and not measured and cross-referenced to educational achievement, leading to appropriate action, then injustice becomes institutionalised.

What many have failed to realise is that quality and equality are inextricably linked, and that we can not attempt to raise standards through the delivery of a new curriculum and with new methods of assessment, without using the knowledge we have gained about the differential effect of teaching style and grouping on pupil performance. Similarly, it is not possible to improve our assessment techniques if we ignore what we have learnt about differences in motivation and performance between boys and girls. How can we hope to develop productive mechanisms for appraising teacher performance without acknowledging the different ways in which women and men develop their teaching styles? The enormous amount of research that was carried out in the 1980s is still central to the task of improving the quality of education. Any school, therefore, which is aiming to raise standards and is not looking at issues of equality is bound to fail and those schools which are seemingly addressing the issues and discover that standards are not rising, may need to look again at their practices.

Higher education in Britain is currently experiencing the most profound change since the founding of polytechnics in the sixties. The abolition of the binary system by the 1992 Further & Higher Education Act has removed the divide between vocationally and technologically oriented public sector and the academically exclusive university sector. Polytechnics have to some extent helped to widen the participation from non-traditional students, specifically by encouraging mature students through Access routes and by encouraging the participation of under-represented groups such as women, minority ethnic groups and students with disabilities. Equal opportunities only became a part of the Higher Education Funding Council audit in 1993, and it was acknowledged that in relation to services afforded to non-traditional students, they were variable and in some cases will require close review and monitoring. A checklist of 'good practice' includes a belief that individuals matter and should be treated with respect and an appreciation that individuals are different and will require different approaches within a framework which is fair and based on principles of equal opportunity. The new arrangements for HEIs for courses other than Teacher Education have been developed in consultation and active collaboration and consent of the whole HE system. They have been revised in response to feedback from HE and have been trialled. Quality Assurance Agency's (QAA) declared aims are 'continuous improvement, meeting information needs of stake holders, public confidence and accountability, efficiency and economy and reduced burden on institutions' (QAA 1998 p2).

An overview of equality issues in higher education is likely to give a very patchy, almost peripheral picture when assessments in quality are made. This generally indicates equality has not been analysed and accepted as a key factor in quality maintenance and assessment. Since the introduction of Race Relations (Amendment) Act 2000, there is some movement towards an increasing emphasis on equality in issues related to Human Resources. The Equality Challenge Unit was set up to offer practical advice and guidance to HEIs. In addition to the free advice and information to all HEIs on implementing the complex and challenging framework of equality legislation, its advisory service has provided institutions with substantial consultancy to address institutional issues. The work of the Equality Challenge Unit and its advisory service has demonstrated that changes in attitudes can occur very swiftly in the context of financial rewards and legislative requirements. This has been demonstrated by the recent initiatives of the Higher Education Funding Council (HEFC), which designated funding for HR strategy of Universities and required them to introduce measures to increase the number of student teachers from minority ethnic groups, and to support students with special needs. This also coincided with the introduction of the Race Relations (Amendment) Act 2000, whereby HEIs, like most other public sector institutions were required to produce Race Equality Schemes and action plans.

There are many reasons why there has been slow progress, and in some cases, almost a reversal of an uptake of equality issues. This is partly due to the questioning of relevance of equality as an ideology, and the assumption that higher education institutions as business enterprises can only ever be concerned with economic efficiency. It is also due to lack of understanding that quality and equality are indeed two sides of the same coin, but one can not indeed be achieved without the other. There is a misguided belief in some circles that striving towards quality can somehow automatically ensure equality. However, despite the numerous quality assurance frameworks and inspection regimes, there is evidence that the participation level and achievement of students from Black and minority ethnic groups in higher education is still considerably low. There is further evidence that the experiences of students and staff from Black and minority ethnic groups in higher education institutions are of serious concern. The rest of this chapter will address these issues.

Participation in Higher Education

Though the experience of children from minority ethnic groups in British schools has been well documented and researched, there is very little information about their experiences in institutions of higher education. It may be argued that due to lower participation rates, the numbers of students from minority ethnic groups in higher education are not sufficiently significant to be the subject of separate study. However, there is evidence of a significantly higher staying on rate in post-compulsory education among black and minority ethnic groups compared to their White peers. Despite this some Black and other minority ethnic groups are under-represented among applicants to higher education. Participation rate in higher education is determined by factors such as the value of education in personal terms and in terms of the social status it accords to individuals within their own community. It is also determined by social class, the nature of schooling received and benefits expected from higher education in the labour market. It may be further influenced by the opportunities available and the ease of access into higher education. For minority ethnic groups, discrimination in admissions and assessment procedures can limit their chances of benefiting from the opportunities available. In addition to the general ethos of the institution, the nature of the curriculum can also deter some sections of minority communities from entering higher education.

The participation rate of Asians in full time higher education is higher than for any other minority group. However, it is lower amongst Pakistani women and amongst Bangladeshi men and women (Ballard & Vellins, 1985). In 1992, 11 percent of home students from minority ethnic groups entered universities (greater than their proportion in the total population). There were more Indian/Asians than African-Caribbeans in these figures. The CRE survey (Ranger 1988) of minority ethnic trainee teachers showed that overall students from minority ethnic groups made up only 2.6 percent of all students in the relevant groups/courses compared with an estimated 5.3 percent in the appropriate age group in the population. The results also showed a significant difference between students of African-Caribbean and of Asian origin in respect of the type of course undertaken. Over two thirds (67 percent) of Asian students were in PGCE courses compared with less than half (48 percent) of African-Caribbean students. There was also a marked variation of representation of students from minority ethnic groups at an institutional level. About one third of PGCE courses and a little over two fifths of B.Ed. courses had no representation of students from minority ethnic groups. At the other extreme, about one in ten courses had five or more students from minority ethnic groups The overall picture was that well over half the institutions providing initial training for teachers had either none or only one student from minority ethnic group about to emerge as a teacher. Only five percent of all institutions had ten or more students of minority ethnic groups on their courses. The figures from the GTTR and CRCH11 suggested that despite Swann recommendations and DES consultation papers, the number of Black teachers was on the decline.

The general ethos of some schools and the lower expectations of teachers for their pupils may not help to motivate children from minority ethnic groups to aim for qualifications necessary for entry to higher education. Evidence from an intensive ethnographic and statistical survey of two multiracial comprehensive schools (Wright 1986) showed that the interaction between the teachers and African-Caribbean students was frequently characterised by confrontation and conflict. One of the consequences of an adverse relationship between students and teachers was a denial of educational opportunities, with students being placed in ability bands and examination sets well below their actual academic ability. This research offered plenty of evidence that as far as the allocation to sets, streams and bands was concerned, complex processes may be involved which serve to disadvantage Black students, particularly those of African-Caribbean origin by excluding them from particular subjects or from particular qualifications.

Minority Ethnic Groups and Higher Education (PSI 1994) was based on statistical analysis of more than 500,000 applicants to UCAS and PCAS in 1992 for admissions to Universities and Polytechnics. It found that British students of Pakistani or Caribbean origin have a relatively poor chance of getting into 'old' universities; even after their 'A' Level results are taken into account. However, members of other minority ethnic groups, especially Chinese, are more likely to get admission to an 'old' university than white candidates with similar 'A' Level scores. The results confirmed that variation in ethnic groups' entry to higher education couldn't wholly be explained by differences in performance at school. After taking academic and social class related factors into account the following significant differences existed:

- Pakistani and Black Caribbean applicants were less likely than White candidates to have gained admission to the 'old' universities.
- Black Caribbean and Indian applicants were more likely than White applicants to have gained admission to polytechnics (new universities).
- Chinese and 'other Asian' applicants were more likely than White applicants to have gained admission to 'old' universities, but less likely to have gained admission to 'new' universities.
- Bangladeshi applicants were less likely to have gained admission to 'new' universities than their White counterparts.

However, the report confirmed an existing general trend for minority ethnic groups to enter the new universities. In 1990 the proportion of mature students in polytechnics was 25 percent, female students just fewer than 50 percent and students from minority ethnic groups was 16 percent. In the same year the admission figure for students from minority ethnic groups in the university sector was eight percent. Although the profile of students in higher education has changed considerably over the last twenty years, African-Caribbean and African students, even with qualifications similar to other groups were less likely to achieve university places (UCCA 1990). Since UCCA did not cross-reference ethnic data with gender, it is difficult to know whether the same applied to Black women. However PCAS data shows that twice as many Black women were admitted as men not because the acceptance rate was higher but because twice as many applied. In the case of Bangladeshis and Pakistanis, it was twice as many men who applied. As for choice of subjects, compared with the UK students as a whole, South Asians are over-represented in the fields of Medicine and related subjects, fairly strongly represented in the fields of Engineering and Pure Sciences, but under represented in Arts and Languages (Vellins 1982).

'Minority Ethnic Attainment and Participation in Education and Training' (Bhattacharyam, Ison, & Blair 2003) summarises recent research and statistics on the position of different ethnic groups in education and training. The focus is on the participation and attainment of minority ethnic groups living in England. The evidence in this chapter reaffirms the need to understand the very diverse experiences of the minority ethnic population in England, which are in part explained by differences in socio-economic status. The requirements of the Race Relations Amendment Act (2000) specify that monitoring and evaluating the attainment and progress of minority ethnic groups are an essential component of achieving race equality in education. The combination of improved data collection and new statutory duties should lead to improved research and practice across educational provision. The Key findings of this research indicate that seven percent of trainee teachers and staff in further education colleges are from minority ethnic groups, mainly of Black heritage, and that there are very small numbers of minority ethnic staff at higher grades in Higher Education Institutions. The report also indicates that the greater proportion of minority ethnic young people in post-16 education is mirrored by the smaller proportion following work-based routes (i.e. a job or government supported training). Only four percent of minority ethnic young people reported following a work-based route at age 16/17. It is also worth noting that the representation of minority ethnic students in Higher Education has increased in recent years from 12 percent in 1996-1997 to 13 percent in 2000/01.

Experience of Students from Black and Minority Ethnic Groups in Higher Education

Black people applying to courses in higher education have found themselves excluded by admission requirements, which have been based on a White experience of education. The admission criteria ignore the experience of discrimination, which initially prevents Black people from getting onto the academic ladder. Many Black students feel they are unfairly treated at the interviews. Some of the issues they raise are linked to lack of clarity in procedures for recruitment. The Ethnic Monitoring Research Project (Leeds) offered case study evidence on the experiences of Black students on degree courses at Leeds University. Because of the low number of Black students, the staff at the University had no experience of working with multiethnic groups. Most fellow students had no experience of communication or friendship with people from different ethnic groups. The isolation felt by Black students on arrival may persist throughout the course, especially if there was lack of contact with other students. The general feeling seemed to be one of a solitary figure in lecture halls crowded with White students: It was reported to be particularly difficult for students from London who had been used to mixed groups in schools and who found it really difficult to be the only Black student in large groups of White students.

Similar experiences have been reported by students from Black and minority ethnic groups studying for other disciplines such as the Law, Medicine, Management and Social Work. The admission procedures at St. George's Hospital Medical School were found to be discriminatory on racial grounds (CRE 1988). The Medical School is an institution with a respectable student profile and with every intention of improving it. Yet its admission procedures revealed practices, which were discriminatory against both students from Black and minority ethnic groups and against women. The Central Council for Social Work Education and Training (CCETSW) made tremendous progress in encouraging higher education institutions to make their courses more accessible to minority ethnic groups and recruit more Black staff by implementing equal opportunities policies. Though this has helped Black students to get on to courses, their experience during their training and subsequent employment tells a different story. Even those who have succeeded in obtaining undergraduate degrees have found entry to post-graduate social work courses elusive because their practical experience has not been sufficiently grounded in 'mainstream' social work, i.e. their experience has been acquired in Black community settings and has therefore been discounted as irrelevant.

The legal profession requires a command of English, which enables practitioners of Law to think, speak and write simultaneously in both technical and vernacular English, to be able to convert one into the other with ease and have credibility in both. This credibility, rather than the skill itself, is a subjective and tacit element of assessment, both for recruitment into courses and entry into the profession. This area of judgment is prone to personal, social and cultural assumptions, which are usually unknown to the candidate, and sometimes, even to the assessor. The need for proficiency at high levels of reflection and analysis is related to linguistic and cultural background. Language difficulties do not necessarily mean lack of competency, because the process of articulating competency is a skill in itself. But it is this process that is used to assess transferability of skills and the ability to deal with unpredictable situations. Oral questioning by White assessors may rest on false assumptions about competence, if students' use of English is not deemed to be 'standard' or 'intelligible' (phrase used by the Bar Council). In Management, too, written reports and oral questioning are used extensively for assessing and accrediting professional standards. The candidate's ability to infer action, reflect on experience and to hypothesize is acknowledged to be a vital backup to observation of his/her performance. Despite high levels of written and spoken English, this level of reflection might be an unfamiliar and difficult process for speakers of English as a second language. Multilingual and cross-cultural skills of candidates, which were crucial to their effectiveness, could not be accredited by traditional professional standards.

When it comes to assessment Black students have found themselves failing both the written and practical work in disproportionate numbers (Willis 1987). Many Black students argue that tutors do not apply the assessment criteria universally to all students. Vague guidelines are indeed fertile grounds for discrimination. Lecturers have also been accused of using the setting and marking of essays as a tool to control students. Those who take the initiative to seek out material, which reflects multi-cultural backgrounds, have often been marked down for using 'unrecognized and non-academic sources'. A comment on one Black student's essay sums up this attitude: 'Good description, but what about considering traditional material'. There is a tacit and subjective element in assessment and recruitment into the professions, and one where bias can occur. The relative importance of standard English as distinct from logical ability is also regularly reported to be the experience of students from Black and minority ethnic groups on teacher training courses. But clearly non-standard forms of English should not be penalised and should be distinguished from grammatical errors (Arora 1994).

Difficulties experienced by students on placement are one area where educational institutions may unwittingly collude with racial discrimination by employers. Work Placement Project Special Interest Groups (Downs 1993) found that it took significantly longer to place students from Black and minority ethnic groups. They had to go to more interviews and had greater distances to travel. Employers have been known to put tutors and institutions under overt pressure to provide a student of a particular racial group; either it is a case of 'we want a Black student to cope with our difficult Black clients' or 'we want a White student because a Black student would not be able to cope with the racist atmosphere'. Widening Access to Higher Education (1992) found that access to work experience and sponsorship may be particularly important for black students because of discrimination in the labour market and the higher incidence of unemployment among Black graduates. The main issue for Social Work students was that Black students felt that their life experiences and their learning needs were not being validated or taken into account when a placement was sought. Others felt that they were being seen as the 'honorary White' in the team where the practice teacher does not accept that Black students bring specific life and work experiences on placement that are both valid and relevant.

Role of Teacher Education

In Teacher Education too there are barriers operating in recruitment on to teacher training courses and these include recognition of overseas qualifications and/ or of previous experience of teaching, cultural bias in interviewing, lack of institutional commitment to equal opportunities, reluctance to recognise and challenge incidence of racism and inability to change practices that have proved to be discriminatory and thus damaging to the profession. It would appear that the disproportionately low number of teachers from Black and minority ethnic groups in schools and on teacher training courses has been not entirely due to ambivalence on the part of minority ethnic groups and within the institutional structures of the educational system, as was suggested by Taylor & Hegarty (1985), but also due to a consistent failure to encourage youngsters from black and minority ethnic groups to enter the teaching profession. The very experience of schooling and the visible lack of teachers from their own ethnic groups may discourage young people from seriously considering teaching as a profession. Though the key points of the Swann report are indirectly accepted by the TTA documents. The implications that all the teachers need to be aware of the issues such as interaction of different cultures, teacher attitudes and expectations in relation to pupil performance have not entirely been understood.

However, it is important to take note of the standards that the TTA has been setting. Anne Wadsworth's report, 'The Review of the Promotion of Teaching as a Career' (1994) emphasised that raising the profile of teaching, and emphasising professionalism, was very important. Geoffrey Parker, Chairman of the TTA (1994) also gave an important message in his statement that 'we intend to be pro-active in forging close links with career specialists, including the institutions providing initial teacher training, with professional associations and with those who could assist us in widening access to teaching, including, from the minority ethnic groups'. Any institution that takes up these points needs to be able to combine quality with diversity of entrants.

The TTA's 1996 Corporate Plan clearly stated what effective teachers should be capable of doing. Within this statement a wide range of equality issues are implied. Teachers need to be knowledgeable about, and sensitive to the children as individuals, and as affected by characteristics such as their cultural, religious, linguistic backgrounds, their gender, mental and physical levels of development etc. Thus when the TTA documents are examined carefully, it is clear that the task of teachers and thus teacher educators would be to ensure that the professionalism of the teachers acknowledged these tasks. What the documents do not do is to indicate the extent to which these points must encompass the implications of cultural and sexual diversity.

There is some movement, however, towards an increasing emphasis on equality. Examples of recent policies to tackle these issues have not been supported by adequate backup for effective implementation. The target of having more men, more people from black and minority ethnic groups and more disabled people as student teachers may only work if there are adequate policies and strategies to ensure success at every stage from application to the training courses to the final assessment. At the same time, unless action is taken to educate more employers, like many other people from such disadvantaged groups, an increase in student numbers could remain unmatched by an increase in the number of teachers. Similarly an assertion that there will be government policy to tackle the low achievement of many children from Black and minority ethnic groups may end up being hollow if the proposed curriculum for teacher education remains virtually devoid of personal and professional development to both understand and develop appropriate teaching strategies.

The reports from the 18 Special Initiatives to Encourage Widening participation of students from Minority ethnic groups in Teacher Training (HEFCE, July 1995) have illustrated the type of work that needs to be done by the providers from the point of marketing, recruitment procedures, as well as support being given to the students once they are accepted. The experience of students, however, has included academic and social isolation, which was often compounded by inadequate support systems within institutions. Ten of the projects raised racism as one of the main issues encountered. Teachers commented that they felt they were not valued as a professional and put down by fellow staff. Others had experienced abusive language from parents. Student teachers had experienced isolation and intimidation from white teachers. Although there were no specific examples of overt racism within higher education institutions, students had felt uncomfortable at jokes made by staff about Black students.

The isolation experienced by minority ethnic students in higher education became much more apparent when alone on a teaching placement and, together with the stresses of teaching practice, caused too great a strain for some students. Evidence indicated that currently there was a lack of support for students on placements and some inappropriate placements were arranged. Students and institutions expressed concern at the difficulties of challenging the racism encountered in schools. Five of the HEFCE projects reported success in increasing the participation of students from Black and minority ethnic groups. Whilst not directly increasing participation, many projects were confident that their work had made a positive impact on encouraging participation and/or improving support during training and entry to the teaching profession.

Summary

Despite several examples of recent initiatives to ensure equality of opportunity in education, there is still evidence from labour market surveys that, individuals from certain sections of Black and minority ethnic groups are still at a disadvantage, and while there has been some progress, discrimination still plays an important part in both recruitment for training, and obtaining jobs after qualifying. Schools and higher education institutions need to develop well thought out policies and practices to ensure that people from the disadvantaged categories are recruited, that they are of the right level (this could mean special/access/foundation courses), and that they perform well (this has implications for the nature of student support services), in an academic as well as personal framework. Achievement of students from minority ethnic groups has been an ongoing issue but some aspects are very pertinent at the moment. An area of great concern to teachers and many Black and minority ethnic communities is the number of children from Black and minority ethnic groups being excluded, in proportion to their overall numbers; for example, The 1996 OFSTED Report, includes frightening evidence of this, particularly in relation to Black boys.

The inspection frameworks for schools and for further and higher education are a very important tool for ensuring the quality agenda, but until recently they have failed to show any consistency of approach towards monitoring or assessing equality issues. Education Inclusion is now part of the OFSTED inspection framework and inspectors will be looking for evidence on materials and teaching that cultivates pupils' personal, spiritual, moral and cultural development. However, lack of involvement of minority ethnic groups in the inspection teams can still allow the process to completely bypass the issues or pay a very superficial attention to issues of equality if they happen to surface in the self-assessment documents.

Finally, the need to place equality at the heart of quality assurance is not widely understood. Even when the recruitment of students from minority ethnic groups is high, their retention is often low, and their achievement is never measured. All too often quality and equality are seen to be contradicting rather than complementing each other. There are still only a very small number of lecturers from Black and minority ethnic groups in further and higher education in mainstream positions and fewer still in senior management positions. The indispensable element needed for the implementation of full-blooded equality assurance is leadership from funding organisations and from senior management of higher education institutions. This is not yet forthcoming.

Chapter 2

Literature Review – Race and Education

Introduction

The educational response to the arrival and settlement of minority groups in Britain cannot be considered separately from the politics of 'race' and race relations and indeed the way in which 'immigrants' and immigration policies were viewed. There are several useful and early detailed accounts of the politics of race in Britain – Ben-Tovim & Gabriel (1979); Rose (1969); Rex & Tomlinson, (1979); Sivanandan (1976). There has also been considerable literature, which has described the development of the educational responses to the changing ethnic composition of Britain over the last three decades. Britain has moved through what can be described as three overlapping phases of assimilation, integration and cultural pluralism. However, there is a danger of over-simplification in describing this process as a neat and regular progression from one stage to another. The reality of practice is very different indeed. Some policies have been based on aspects of all three ideologies interacting with each other. Some policies have been designed with one ideology in mind, but implemented by people who believed in a different ideology, thus adapting the policies to fit their principles. There are several useful reviews of this process published in the 1980s and these are well rehearsed in Jeffcoate (1982); James & Jeffcoate (1981); Troyna (1982); Stone (1981); Carby (1982); Madan Sarup (1986); Troyna & Williams (1986); Mullard (1982) and Davies (1981). Although most of these authors have very different philosophical and political perspectives, there is a surprising degree of consensus in their analysis of the shift in educational policy from assimilation of an explicit kind in the 1950s, to a psuedo-pluralism in the 1980s, via Roy Jenkins' brand of integration in the 1960s, and cultural diversity of the 1970s. This chapter offers only a very brief examination of principles underlying these ideologies and the attitudes engendered in turn. This may help in analysing and understanding current educational practices, as they affect minority groups in this country. The purpose of this review is to examine the relationship between the development of race relations legislation, and the educational responses of successive Governments as well as responses from other related agencies.

Assimilation

The ethos of absorption, of assimilation, and of making them disappear out of recognition had, as its central tenet, a commitment that a nation is a single and indivisible entity, both politically and culturally. Consequently, there was an expectation that all people living in that nation, irrespective of colour, race and/or cultural background, will become part of one homogeneous culture, where the only visible difference between people will be one of their colour, and perhaps certain minor unobtrusive cultural patterns. This ethos was given a particular focus in relation to educational provision. Carby's Marxist perspective characterises the initial educational policy as embodying the philosophy of assimilation. It describes schools as the primary site for successful assimilation and Black parents were referred to only as potential, or actual inhibitors of this process. In common-sense terms, the system was seen as capable of absorbing Black children, and it was thought that race problems would literally die away with the older generations (Carby 1982).

Educational responses underpinned by assimilation

In terms of educational practice the assimilationist policies of the 1960s gave rise to Immigrant Education, a model that was based on a number of racist assumptions and beliefs. It was thought that Black pupils would concentrate in, swamp and racially over-power some inner-city schools; that their presence would arouse latent tensions and conflicts of a racial kind; that their numbers, if uncontrolled, would present a threat to the normal educational life, stability, order and discipline in schools; and that they would (DES 1965) hamper the scholastic progress of White children, as their presence would demand the undue preoccupation of the teaching staff with linguistic and other difficulties. With the problem securely defined as one of Black 'immigrants', and their different (by implication deficient) cultural and linguistic traditions, the specific educational response to it was expressed in a way that reflected a class-stratified, mono-cultural, monolingual concept of society. It was assimilationist in the sense that schools were expected not only to actively encourage Black children to accept the dominant class-based culture being transmitted to them, but also to prepare Black pupils to take up their social, though racially excluded, positions in society, thus helping to maintain and procreate racist policies and practices of the institutions. The funds made available under Section 11 of the Local Govt. Act (1966) were also aimed at providing 'immigrants' the skills (mainly through ESL and remedial teaching) to be assimilated into the British society. Although policies and practices of the 1960s were influenced by Plowden, they made little if any concessions to the cultural and experiential learning of Black and minority ethnic pupils.

This model of Immigrant Education, the child of assimilationist ideology, thus developed characteristics which required no modifications to the traditional ethnocentric curriculum, placed a great deal of emphasis on the learning of English and organised buses to move 'immigrant' children around, so that the English children could get on with their learning. Surprisingly enough, all this was done within an ethos of 'treat them all the same', but make provision for special needs. It really meant that the minority groups were expected to be absorbed into a homogeneous society, and that challenges associated with backgrounds of 'immigrants' and their cultural adjustments were assumed to be short-term. Teachers, on the other hand, continued to exclude from the curriculum any knowledge about pupils they taught, and continued teaching a mono-cultural curriculum, which by definition gives a version of the truth acceptable to authors of books and to teachers who use them. Such a selective approach to curriculum inevitably leads to teachers teaching half-truths thus upholding the values of a dominant group within the education system and perpetuating the myths of racial, cultural and religious superiority of one group over another. It can only be assumed that they believe no knowledge about Black people to be valuable enough to be included in the curriculum, and regard the experiences of Black people to be totally irrelevant for White children. By accepting the ideology inherent in the selections made by publishers and other media sources, teachers continued to perpetuate not only the existing racial and cultural bias in materials but also the notion of racial and cultural superiority of particular groups in society. Since the assimilationist perspective continued to define the Black people as the 'problem' and failed to challenge negative views about Black people, the racist ideology of White superiority, which underpinned such a perspective, actually promoted and strengthened such views in society. By reflecting an inaccurate and inadequate view of Britain's position in the world, the education system has done a great disservice to all children and has consistently mis-educated both White and Black people.

Integration

The policies of the early 1960s thus defined the needs of 'immigrant' children essentially in terms of learning English. However, events outside the school gates and in the wider world were increasingly indicative that a strategy of assimilation was not a viable one, not least because of the racist responses of the indigenous white population. This ethos of focusing on the ethnicity and culture of the 'immigrants', rather than examining racism and power structures, was also reflected in the work of social science researchers studying race relations in the 1960s and 1970s and is well documented in Bourne (1980), Gilroy (1980), and Lawrence (1981, 1982). Thus the concern for the education of 'immigrant' children, which 'must involve social, cultural and emotional adjustments of a special kind' (DES 1971), was not based on an understanding of their historical and contemporary position in British society, but on an understanding that their difficulties, apart from the linguistic and cultural differences and culture shock of being in a strange land, were no different than those of native-born children living in socially and culturally deprived areas.

   The first and a remarkably early acknowledgment of the failure and deficiencies of assimilationist philosophy came in 1966, when Roy Jenkins, Home Secretary at the time, defined integration as, 'Not a flattening process of assimilation but as equal opportunity, accompanied by cultural diversity, in an atmosphere of mutual tolerance' (NCCI 1966). The integrationist perspective with room for cultural diversity and equal opportunity had a sound of idealism about it that was hard to resist. It certainly represented a decisive departure from the explicit racism of the assimilationist ideology. The central features of this perspective still had a focus on the minority groups, with the belief that contact with minority groups will reduce prejudice so they should be accommodated and tolerated; that teaching about culture will promote a positive self-image among Black people and 'tolerance and sympathetic understanding' amongst White people. The educational models that emerged during the 1960s and the 1970s were compensatory for the disadvantage of being coloured, and for the linguistic deprivation of being bilingual or multilingual. Teachers saw the need to become more informed about the cultural and religious backgrounds of their pupils (but not their own), with a view to assist their integration into the unchanged culture of the school and British society. Although the issues addressed included a consideration of functional equivalence of languages other than English, their maintenance was left to the voluntary sector. English as a second language continued to be taught separately to second class-citizens with second-rate teachers. The curriculum of schools continued to be mainly euro-centric with some concessions, such as the inclusion of black studies and a celebration of cultural diversity of the festive kind.

The rhetoric of integration failed to make any substantial impact on the educational policy. The late 1960s saw the beginning of several new initiatives, promoted by a series of reports and papers published by the Schools Council, a plethora of books and articles on multicultural, multiethnic and multiracial education, and a mushrooming of courses and conferences to inform teachers about the home-lands of British-born children of minority groups. The shift from the special needs of 'immigrant' children to special characteristics of their backgrounds helped to maintain the status quo of educational institutions. At the same time it was recognised that many 'immigrant' children have to meet the shock of immersion in an entirely different culture,

> of exposure to a completely new environment, to a strange climate, to other habits, attitudes and behaviour and to a language they can only speak and understand imperfectly – if they can understand or speak at all. They may thus experience a more complex form of deprivation....as they stand bewildered between two cultures (DES 1971).

But the assimilationist hangover continued to cloud the process and direction of change. Though the 1973 Select Committee on Race Relations and Immigration noted that the exceptions (newness, language and culture) would justify a serious advisory and support effort, and also recommended the establishment of a central fund to meet the special educational needs of 'immigrant' children and adults; it also suggested that those who come to settle must, to some extent, accept the ways of the country in which they are going to live. The crucial phrase in such a statement is 'to some extent' and how far the extent was a matter for negotiation, or to be determined by people in power. In the face of an indigenous society that believed strongly in making the strangers 'invisible', cultural integration was accepted merely as a modest tokenism. The 'extent' was determined by accepting the quaint aspects of minority cultures, but rejecting those aspects which seemed threatening, mainly because they were too alien to be accepted and understood, or because they were in some way in conflict with the values of the indigenous society. Such a limited view of integration was seen by many members of minority groups as assimilation with a new label, and therefore rejected. As Gus John put it:

> To wish to integrate with that which alienates and destroys you, rendering you less than a person, is madness. To accept the challenge to join it and change it from within, when it refuses to accept that you are there in your fullness and refuses to acknowledge the results of interaction between you and it, is double madness (John 1976).

The Government White Paper of 1974 further stressed the essential similarity of urban deprivation for black and white people, but also 'taking account of the distinct needs of different ethnic groups and of individuals, whatever their origin' (DES 1974); thus avoiding the political embarrassment of setting up any special provision for minority ethnic groups. The focus on the cultural problems of the minority ethnic groups enabled institutions to continue unchanged and helped perpetuate a pathological view of minority groups within society at large. Carby argued that in the development of educational policy, 'the pluralistic model acknowledged the existence of different cultures, different ways of life, but ignored the way in which these cultures were produced and existed in social relations of power, of dominance and subordination' (Carby 1982). Thus the mismatch between the ideal of integration expressed by Roy Jenkins and the practical implementation of such an ideal in educational practices was clearly visible throughout the 1970s. Though teachers saw the need to become more informed about the children they taught, the prime motivation to do so was to assist their assimilation into the unchanged culture of the school and society. An abundance of in-service courses and advisory posts were created to deal with what was still termed as the problem of Immigrant Education. Despite the official denouncement of dispersal policy and expressed concern about West Indian children in Educationally Sub-Normal schools, the stark reality of the under-achievement of minority ethnic children and the disillusionment of their parents was on the increase.

Educational responses underpinned by integration

A number of authors (Mullard 1981, Davies 1981, James 1981) have described three different but complementary models of education that emerged in the 1970s. Several graphic representations of comparative ideologies, of issues addressed and methodologies involved have been produced and reproduced by academics and practitioners. Sometimes these models have been described as developmental stages in the life cycle of institutions and sometimes they have been presented as conflicting views, which have only served to polarise the issues. In essence all three models have emerged from the same ideology of tokenistic integration and reluctant tolerance of cultural diversity. It is worth summarising the rise and demise of each of the models to appreciate the debate surrounding 'Education For All' and to understand the arguments for Anti-Racist Education.

Multiracial education
The advocates of multiracial education, in rejecting the assimilationist philosophy of Immigrant Education, found solace in Roy Jenkins's vision of society in which Black groups have equal opportunity in 'an atmosphere of mutual tolerance accompanied by cultural diversity'. The conceptual basis of this racial form of education and the policies and practices emerging from it were, like Immigrant Education, concerned with the protection of social and educational order. It embraced rather than questioned built in inequalities of class and power and ignored the racist effect of social policies (The Immigration Acts of the 1960s and 1970s), and educational practices such as dispersal. Also by concentrating on the racial distinction, thus reinforcing the disadvantage of being coloured, having low self-esteem, belonging to a different religion and speaking languages other than English, Multiracial Education failed to address the issue of racism in our society. The educational practices of this model may have attempted to ameliorate and soften the blows of racism by overtly accepting religious and cultural differences, but they have not made any changes in the content and process of education to take account of the power relations reproducing racism in our society. Its advocates saw society in terms of a two-tier multiracial system of class, status and racial groups, a society with a culturally-diversified value system in which Black groups were an integral part.

The only difference between the model of Immigrant Education of the 1960s and the Multiracial Education of the 1970s was that its practices were more concerned with the integration of different racial groups rather than their assimilation. It was still the perceptions of the white middle class and their interests that defined the problem. The acknowledgment of the multiracial nature of our society did not change the racial structure of power that tends to reproduce and legitimise white perceptions of the 'Black problem'. Furthermore by concentrating on the racial distinctiveness of groups, it was only able to consider the educational needs of Black and minority ethnic pupils in terms of racial disadvantage, low self-esteem and consequent under-achievement. The success of such a model depended not only on the assumed neutrality of all teachers but also on the open-ended classroom strategies with outcomes negotiated between the teachers and the learners.

Multiethnic education

Multiethnic Education evolved in the late 1970s as a kind of antidote to the notion of assimilation and integration. Based on a concept of pluralist society with often competing but never integrating, class, ethnic and cultural groups with different values and beliefs, it was a form of education that developed largely within urban, racially mixed schools and was completely ignored by rural and white inner-city schools. This only confirms that it was the ethnicity and culture of Black people that was considered to be problematic. It was still believed that Black and minority ethnic pupils constituted a problem and that their difficulties were peculiar to them as members of specific, ethnic, racial, cultural and linguistic groups. The attempt to stress the educational importance and social significance of ethnic and cultural distinctions, over and above those of class and gender (Bullivant 1981), only resulted in institutionalising ethnic differences as the basis for making educational decisions and creating policies for Multiethnic Education. In Sivanandan's words 'ethnicity was a tool to blunt the edge of black struggle... ethnicity de-linked black struggle, separating the West Indian from the Asian, the working-class black from the middle-class black' (Sivanandan 1983).

The educational practices associated with this model of education were the ones described previously as compensatory; for example, curriculum with additive elements such as Black studies, multi-faith assemblies, festival celebrations, cookery demonstrations and exhibits of ethnic dress. The recognition and affirmation of minority ethnic groups' cultures and languages was seen to be necessary, not because of their inherent value but because it was thought that a diet of culture might help improve the so-called low self-image of Black and minority ethnic children. In fact the introduction of special courses for Black and minority ethnic children was nothing more than an attempt to pacify the parents. It was as though 'black children were being compensated for being deficient white children' (Davies 1981). This model of education led many teachers in multiracial schools to develop a form of cultural apartheid, whereby Black pupils were encouraged to bring in a 'bit' of their culture, such as different kinds of food or modes of dress. Unfortunately such contributions were only seen as exotic or strange preliminaries before getting on to the task of talking about 'normal' food or dress. Teachers retained and taught the same White euro-centric knowledge and depended on the children to provide the multiethnic variations or 'asides'. Since the children were either diffident about which aspects of their culture were really of interest, and/or wanted to avoid being labelled as strange or different, the examples offered were those that were part of the English culture, because that is what was given value in the classroom. Consequently, children were seen to have adopted the English way of life to such an extent that teachers saw no need to change the curriculum. Though there is nothing wrong with a model of multiethnic education that aims to promote a positive self-image, the divisive nature of this approach was extremely dangerous. By using the term ethnic as a euphemism for disadvantaged and by emphasising differences, pupils of minority ethnic origin tended to be channelled away from academic subjects, thus further reinforcing stereotypical judgments. This also led to some White teachers building stronger walls around their knowledge and themselves. It was seen by many as a form of cultural racism, which diverted the attention away from the real issues.

Multicultural education
Several assumptions that formed the basis of conflicting interpretations of what constitutes Multicultural Education have been the subject of many conferences and seminars and have led to numerous publications (Milner 1983; Nixon 1981; Craft 1983; Cohen and Manion 1983; Jeffcoat 1982; James 1982; Tierney 1982; Arora and Duncan 1986; Sarup 1986). The common theme that runs through most of these publications is that since contemporary Britain contains a wide variety of social, racial and ethnic groups, the school curriculum should reflect that and prepare all children for a society that is multicultural. It has been demonstrated that education models derived from the social ideology of assimilation, separatism and integration mostly ended up being either compensatory to counterbalance the linguistic and cultural disadvantage of not being white, or tokenistic to add on bits of other cultures but without changing the essential nature of the core curriculum. Consequently, multicultural issues, even in multiracial areas, have tended to be regarded as matters for the specialist adviser or the teacher 'expert' rather than as having implication for the staff and school as a whole. It is therefore suggested that Multicultural Education is not just for 'them' (black and minority ethnic groups), but is for the good of all our children. The atmosphere and ethos of schools is considered to be crucial in determining equality of relationships and expectation of high standards of attendance, work and behaviour is deemed important for creating high morale.

Multicultural Education was thus intended to be part of the education of all pupils and aimed to promote inter-cultural understanding and respect by giving the pupils knowledge about similarities and differences between various cultures in Britain. Ethno-centricism was recognised to be theoretically unsound and it was acknowledged that cross-influence of various cultures can only enrich pupils intellectually and spiritually. One particular definition that was well received and used as a blue-print came from a school in Manchester, an authority which has also been the subject of a major inquiry with reference to racial violence in schools, (Burnage School Inquiry 1988). A working party of Birley High School defined Multicultural Education, as 'as much an attitude and a relationship as it is a pack of materials or a set of ideas'. They further described it as a 'whole curriculum which involves an attitude to life. It aims to promote positive self-image and respect for the attitudes and values of others' (Birley High School, 1980). The working party expected such an education to improve academic attainment. Thus the libertarians, in the late 1970s, did make a conscious effort to redefine Multicultural Education as a permeation of all aspects of the curriculum and as a concern for all teachers and all pupils. This led the researchers to examine the strengths and intrinsic value of minority languages, religions and cultures and of their importance for all children, whatever colour, race or creed they may be. Teachers too began to see the racial/cultural bias inherent in their curriculum and concern about bias in texts began to appear firmly on the educational agenda of many schools and publishers.

However in spite of the 'permeation' approach gradually replacing the mono-cultural curriculum with added extras many teachers were unwilling, or perhaps unable, to address the question of racism inherent in their knowledge base. Those who claimed not to discriminate and treat every one equally, had not yet faced the crucial question, 'How can you treat all individuals with equality of respect and consideration, if you are not prepared to treat knowledge of and about them with equality of respect and consideration?'. So despite a critical examination of curriculum content, text books, visual aids with a view to remove negative stereotyping, and the positive addition of resources to represent other cultures in our schools, teachers who had not made the effort to personally encounter knowledge about the areas of life that are meaningful to children from minority groups were likely to remain at the mercy of the received misunderstandings and prejudices about the minority groups to which their children belonged.

Mal Philips-Bell (1981) summed up the range of meanings and approaches attributed to Multicultural Education by suggesting that practices that emphasise education through many cultures raise fundamental questions about which aspects of many cultures are logically, psychologically or morally necessary or even acceptable. The practices that emphasise education in many cultures could include a simple acceptance and understanding of other cultures or it could involve a necessary understanding of one's own culture to know and understand other cultures. The practices that are aimed at education for a multicultural society have a very different aim of making explicit changes in society and have greater implications for classroom practice. It is because Multicultural Education as an umbrella term has incorporated so many different approaches that its critics emerged from a whole range of educational and political thought. The Hillgate group (extreme Right) have claimed that multicultural curricula are 'both intellectually vacuous and politically motivated', and suggest that to adopt such a curriculum is to fail to transmit either the common culture of Britain, or the high culture that has grown from it, and if no other culture is put in the place of those, the result is nothing more than a void, existing in the child's consciousness (Scruton 1986).

Multicultural Education has also had its critics from the Black communities and has been identified as being relevant only for certain minority groups. It could therefore only be provided through special courses and by specialist teachers. Salman Rushdie described it as 'the latest token gesture towards Britain's blacks, it ought to be exposed like "integration" and "racial harmony" for the sham it is'. (Rushdie 1982). Faroukh Dhondy (1978) attacked multi-culturalism because it has been taken over by the state, and has become respectable and is therefore suspect. He argued that there is no such thing as Black culture to incorporate in the curriculum; that the current mixture of colonial history, working class culture and high culture is too diverse and will not be recognised by the examination system; and most important, Black school students are concerned with far more important issues than their own boredom at school. To them, identity means political identity and a campaign focusing upon political injustices would not be tolerated inside school. Sivanandan (1976) had also argued that the processing of a docile labour force via the schools has been challenged by an explicit anti-school, anti-work ethic among Black youngsters.

Multicultural Education has been also criticised for its emphasis on cultural dimensions, for its indifference to the phenomenon of racism and for either relegating racism to cultural misunderstanding or for completely ignoring it. Since the paradigm of multi-culturalism does not include the concept of dominant and subordinate cultures, it fails to recognise the existence of racism and its relationship with the political and economic control. Consequently it also fails to recognise the need to challenge racist practices and resist the power of dominant social groups. The Government at the time eventually began to notice the apparent failure of its policies and the alienation of Black children in British schools. The West Indian Community offered a new interpretation to the essentially common experience of disadvantage, shared by Black and White youth, and recognised the racial disadvantage experienced by Black youth. This led the Department of Education and Science to set up a Committee of Inquiry (Rampton Committee, 1981) to identify 'any weaknesses in the educational system affecting the achievement of West Indian Pupils'. But when the committee submitted its report in 1981, the publication was delayed by the Tory Government. The chairman was asked to resign and replaced by Lord Swann, because the under-achievement of West Indian Pupils was being explained in terms of racism amongst teachers and in the schools. Nearly a decade later the publication of The Burnage Inquiry was held back because it may upset head teachers. The Schools Council report, Multiracial Education: Curriculum and Content 5-13, was also held back in 1976 because it exposed racism amongst teachers and pupils in schools. It seems that nothing much has changed over the last 20 years.

Meanwhile the minority ethnic communities began to wake up to the discriminatory practices of education authorities and the consequent under-achievement of their children. The publication of Bernard Coard's book (1971) 'How the West Indian Child is made Educationally Sub-normal in the British school System' led to the formation of the Caribbean Teachers' Association (1974) and the establishment of African Caribbean Education Resource Centre (ACER 1976). The setting up of Saturday schools, initially to teach children their first language, and to acquire knowledge about their own religion also led to serious debates about setting up separate schools.

On the whole, the ideology of integration and educational responses emerging from it, proved to be as inadequate and unacceptable as its predecessor ideology of assimilation. The assimilationist phase was about encouraging Black people to absorb and be subsumed in the British society, forget about their linguistic and cultural heritage and disappear out of recognition at the bottom of scoio-economic and occupational ladder. The ideology of integration, despite its rhetoric of recognition of different, cultures, languages and religion, was primarily concerned with maintenance of status quo. Since there was no acknowledgment of cultural bias, ethno-centricism, or racism in institutional procedures and practices, any failure on the part of social policy was attributed to the failure of 'immigrants' to integrate. In 1977, both the ILEA report 'A Multiethnic Education' and The Green Paper (DES 1977) recognised that the education appropriate to Britain's imperial past could no longer meet the needs of a culturally plural Britain, but managed to skirt around the problem of existing racism. The notion that if isolated from the social and economic functioning of the state, the classroom can become 'a microcosm of a happy and co-operative world' (DES1977) and this harmonious microcosm can then be translated into the outside world has proved to be a false one. It took nearly a decade before cultural pluralism as an ideology formed the basis of any significant development in education.

Cultural Pluralism

In a sense that pluralism simply means a co-existence of different groups with diverse features, cultural pluralism has existed in Britain for centuries. But the cultural pluralism of the seventies and eighties implied the existence of a range of homogeneous cultures with shared interests and interaction by a system of negotiation resulting in consensus. When these distinctions are predominantly cultural, a truly plural society should ensure that each group can preserve their own traditions and can still participate as citizens within a wider society. In contrast to the assimilationist and integrationist ideologies, which emphasised the supposedly homogeneous nature of Britain, advocates of cultural pluralism maintain that our society consists of culturally distinctive groups, which exist without conflict under the political authority of a neutral state. However, in practice there are several problems with such a concept. For a start the political authority of this state is not neutral. It favours the rich and powerful by making them richer and more powerful. Secondly, it implies the right of each group to define their own identity, work out solutions to problems on an equal basis when they are clearly not equal. It also means respecting and accepting lifestyles of groups that they may disagree with fundamentally and most of all it means giving up some long standing and familiar privileges. For many people cultural pluralism is in fact no different from out-moded ideologies of assimilation and integration. Madan Sarup (1986) described it as a more refined version of both and points out the ludicrousness of the assumption that all groups within a plural society possess roughly equal amounts of power and that all groups are equally able to assert pressure on the state and negotiate with its agencies for the maintenance of cultural equilibrium. It is abundantly clear that Black and minority ethnic groups within Britain do not possess any thing like the same amount of power nor could they 'develop their cultural traditions without the unconditional approval and encouragement of white society as a whole and of white power groups in particular' (Sarup 1986). Many members of minority ethnic communities, especially the young, also reject the commonly accepted notion of cultural pluralism because its ideals are neither obtainable nor acceptable.

There is also a widespread fear that cultural pluralism of the kind described above may also lead to political pluralism and consequently to separatism or apartheid. In the field of education such a separatism could mean the development of separate schools for minority group children at one extreme, and at the very least major changes in the way provision is made for minority groups at the other extreme. The beginnings of a concern to maintain children's mother-tongues, to develop their bilingualism, and to include aspects of their home culture in the everyday life of the school have been with us for several years, but only as a concessional rather than as a natural part of the education process. The notion of equal opportunities under-pinning the ideology of cultural pluralism should ensure that this happens as a natural part of the education process and children have access to education in their home languages as a matter of right.

Equal opportunities

The notion of equal opportunity in a culturally plural society is open to various interpretations. The existence of legislation against discrimination has not done a great deal to change the patterns of race and gender inequality. Lack of clear definition and inadequate shared understanding of this concept has only partially contributed to the ineffectiveness of anti-discriminatory legislation. There is a range of possible, but not mutually exclusive, interpretations of equal opportunity as equal treatment, equal access and equal share/outcome. In terms of education the kind of policies that are going to make it possible for all concerned to have equal access, equal share and equal treatment is the only goal to aim at. This would mean an education system in which all students would enjoy equal chances to maximise their educational potential. It would mean that education system should be free from discriminatory practices, which reduce the chances of educational success of certain students. It would also mean providing additional resources to support those in need of additional help.

Equality of opportunity could only have meaning if those who began with unequal chances had unequal (greater) support from the educational system. For equality of opportunity to become a reality it is necessary to compensate those who started at a disadvantage by positively favouring them in the educational system. In Halsey's words, 'The aim of equal opportunities is not only the liberal one of equality of access, but equality of outcome for the median member of each identifiable non-educationally defined group' (Halsey 1972). Peter Foster suggests that inequalities of outcome are the result of many complex factors, some of which may relate to cultural and material disadvantage of home backgrounds (Foster 1992). The aim is essentially one of competitive equality of opportunity, in which all enjoy an equal chance to compete in a system which recognises the differences in talents and abilities of individuals and achieves a fair and just allocation of social positions and rewards.

Educational responses to cultural pluralism

The educational responses of the 1980s have included significant developments to promote appropriate educational provision for a culturally plural society. These have included a clear move away from the integrationist policies and multicultural approaches of the 1970s towards the 'good educational practices' highlighted by Arora & Duncan (1986) and the Education for All model offered by the Swann Report (1985) with a hope to achieve racial equality. Tory discourse on race and education (Hatcher 1989) occupied the same rhetorical terrain as the new multiculturalism, situated between the terms of the pluralist dilemma, social cohesion and cultural diversity. However, it articulated them in a different way, not social cohesion through cultural pluralism, but social cohesion despite cultural pluralism. This does not entail exclusion of ethnic cultures but their incorporation and de-radicalisation as subordinate and peripheral elements. This complex process of incorporation in practice meant that Section 11 money, or what was left of it, continued to fund multicultural support services, DES courses promulgated multi-culturalism, ESG projects were set up to improve race relations, but in terms of the Education Reform Act (1988) and the National Curriculum, multicultural education did not get a mention anywhere, nor did it figure in specific curricular objectives. The extent to which educational responses of the 1980s were influenced by the ideology of cultural pluralism and underpinned by the concept of equal opportunities is discussed through a brief overview of major research reports and government publications.

Research and Government Inquiries

The White Paper 'Better Schools' (DES 1985d) acknowledged that the 'principles of freedom, justice and tolerance will be most effectively applied in our national life if they are soundly established at school' (p62). The section on general school objectives included the need 'to help pupils to develop... tolerance for other races, religions and ways of life' (p14), but in the more detailed subsequent sections on primary and secondary schooling, there was no mention of multicultural objectives. The government accepted, and was concerned about, the findings of the Swann Committee that minority ethnic pupils were continuing to achieve below their potential. The Education of Minority Ethnic Pupils (Better Schools 1985) states that 'all pupils need to understand and acquire a positive attitude towards the variety of ethnic groups within British society, and that these objectives will be embedded in the statements of curriculum objectives', but an analysis of DES curriculum documents does not bear out this claim. Education For All (1985) defines and conceptualises pluralism in democratic and ideal terms, as 'enrichment through cultural diversity'. The emphasis is on maintaining social cohesion and on pluralism, which enables, expects and encourages members of all ethnic groups; both minority and majority, to participate fully in shaping the society as a whole within a framework of commonly accepted values, practices and procedures.... 'whilst also allowing and, where necessary, assisting the minority ethnic communities in maintaining their distinct ethnic identity within this common framework' (DES 1985). But the report also noted that there is an obligation on the Government to ensure equal treatment and protection by the law for members of all groups, 'together with equality of access in education and employment, equal freedom and opportunity to participate fully in social and political life, both locally and nationally, equal freedom of cultural expression and equal freedom of conscience for all' (DES 1985).

   Even though it seemed to move on the debate considerably by arguing for the maintenance of ethnic identity and by implication culture and language, the Swann Committee failed miserably to address the vital issue of bilingualism as an asset, and ended up by offering a very wishy-washy compromise which advocated the maintenance of and respect for languages other than English in the early years, but only in so far as it was beneficial for the learning of English and the possibility of community languages being offered as part of modern languages in the secondary schools. This is despite the recommendations of the Bullock Report (1975) that 'their bilingualism is of great importance to the children and their families, and also to society as a whole. In a linguistically-conscious nation in the modern world, we should see it as an asset, as something to be nurtured and one of the agencies which should nurture it is the school'; and that 'No child should be expected to cast off the language and culture of the home as s/he crosses the school threshold, nor to live and act as though school and home represent two totally separate and different cultures which have to be kept apart' (Bullock Report 1975). The bilingualism of non-European children in British schools is still regarded as a problem rather than as an asset, something that may interfere with the learning of English, even though the research evidence available refutes such suggestions. The bilingualism of thousands of British children is a liability in their lives, not because there is something inherently wrong in the nature of bilingualism, but it is to do with society's attitude and treatment accorded to bilinguals within our education system.

However, Education for All sought to blend the best of multicultural and anti-racist perspectives into a coherent and detailed criteria to help teachers critically evaluate their curricular strategies. Some of these had already been published and used (Schools Council), but the last two were the redeeming feature of Education for All. These were that all children should be encouraged to see the cultural diversity of our society in a positive light; and the issue of racism, at both institutional and individual level, should be considered openly and efforts made to counter it. The Swann Committee believed that 'for schools to allow racist attitudes to persist unchecked, in fact constitutes a fundamental miseducation for their pupils'. It also concluded that all youngsters need to be provided with the necessary knowledge and the ability for reasoned and rational thought and judgment and that 'Whilst schools therefore may not be able to lead change directly, they should be capable of leading to change by creating an overall unity of purpose, which will encompass the concept that to be British you do not have to have a white skin nor to have family origins only in this country' (DES 1985).

It is quite clear that the committee recognised that the central and pervasive influence of racism, in our educational institutions at least, has to be acknowledged and recognised it as being morally wrong. However, the committee did not recognise, or at least did not vocalise it, that any strategies to oppose racism and counter it with positive action must be informed by a Black perspective. This may mean developing a more effective consultation and communication network involving people who are at the receiving end of racist practices. To remove discrimination from educational institutions not only requires reorientation and training of all staff but also a fundamental change in the content and process of educational courses at all levels to ensure that all students learn to identify, resist and combat racism wherever they meet it. As for the question of under-achievement the Swann Committee argued that differential performance for all children was associated with differences in scoio-economic status, but accepted that racial discrimination and prejudice were responsible for the additional disadvantage experienced by minority ethnic children. The committee further argued that a programme of Education for All could help overcome the disadvantage experienced by minority ethnic children. Such a programme should include an international dimension of education; education against racism; political education; elimination of racist procedures in school practices; use of cultural variety of Britain for educational purposes; programmes to meet specific needs of minority ethnic children; systematic reviews of the curriculum to eliminate racism and encourage multi-culturalism and that all schools should incorporate such a programme not just the ones in inner-city areas or with a substantial population of minority ethnic children.

Swann's brand of racism suggests that racism is not accounted for in historical and structural terms of colonial, imperial and capitalist dimensions, but is redefined in psychological and personal terms of prejudice. Roots of racism are astonishingly linked to white natives' legitimate reaction to refugees and to the economic success of Blacks. The notion of institutionalised racism was also deemed 'confused and confusing'. State institutions are 'in no way racist in intent' (Swann, 1985: 28), just racist by accident. The best way of stopping the state from enacting all racist legislation, it would seem, is by changing individual attitudes. So, contradicting Rampton, the Swann Committee removes the responsibility for under-achievement from the teachers, schools, LEAs, DES and the State and gives it back to Black parents. It then uses racist stereotypes to explain the relatively better performance of Asian children, i.e. 'Asians keep their heads down' and that the 'tight knit of Asian communities and families helps the children to do well' (DES 1985: para 86). Incidentally the same tight-knit family structure was supposed to be holding the Asian children back in the 1960s.

Thus the Swann Report appeared to have argued for equality of opportunity, even though it was mainly in terms of under-achievement issues; and accepted the need for multicultural education, but only of the kind where all children must learn about other cultures; and even acknowledged the existence of racism, both within schools and in society, and argued for political education with explicit inclusion of racism and Anti-Racism as topics. The Committee also rejected the arguments for separate schools on the grounds that all pupils need to share a common educational experience. However, it did take a strong stance for a change in the teaching of religious education in schools, even if it was only to avoid the threat to the cohesion of the educational system by those advocating separate schools for separate religions. In their argument, the Committee sought to establish fundamental principle concerning cultural pluralism, thus making a distinction between religious instruction and religious education. The Secretary of State's refusal to accept the Committee's recommendations for the reform of 1944 regulations on religious education effectively negated the Committee's pluralist paradigm for educational and social change. On the other hand, Saturday schools, unlike separate schools, offering religious education and mother-tongue teaching outside school hours, have no legislative implications and as such are seen to offer no threat to the social cohesion especially if they require no resources from the state.

'Education For Some' (1986), most commonly known as the Eggleston Report, provided a different perspective on the issues of race and education. Though funded by the DES, it was not published by the HMSO, but appeared as a book almost two years after the research was completed. It was based on the educational and vocational experiences of 15-18 year old children of minority ethnic groups and focused on the part played by schooling in influencing the future education and employment of young people of minority ethnic origin. This study was not about the failure of minority ethnic pupils but about the failure of the system, the failure of teachers, head teachers, career teachers and educational institutions in general. It showed that even though the students and teachers did not perceive institutions to be acting in a racist manner, the outcome of certain forms of actions in institutions was in fact racist. One of the key chapters in this book was an ethnographic study of two schools with minority ethnic populations of 25 percent and 60 percent. Cecile Wright, the author of this section of the report provides a telling account of the perception and treatment of Afro-Caribbean pupils by teachers in these two schools, and the pupils' responses characteristic of the powerless defiance of the victims of institutional racism. The report emphasised the active resistance by some pupils to racism in institutions which was no different from that identified in the previous decades by Coard in 1971 and Stone in 1981.

The 10 pages of recommendations of Education For Some are addressed to schools and teachers, to Further Education Institutions, to LEAs, to the Manpower Services Commission and to the Department of Education and Science. The recommendations for schools included attention to careful planning of the curriculum for the 16+ that takes full account of pupils' ambitions, motivations and uncertainties; attention to procedures of allocation to sets, streams and bands; and to procedures for examination entries and allocation to examination groups to ensure that individual pupils are given the fullest opportunity to attain the highest level of qualification possible. Schools were asked to make efforts to develop the capacities of their minority group pupils, but not to ghettoise by providing them with a soft option curriculum in which they can easily succeed. It was also suggested that schools should take anti-racist guidelines seriously, and that racist teachers should be given a clear opportunity to consider whether or not they are suitable to be members of the profession. Schools were asked to recognise that there are many ways in which teachers' responsibility for guidance and encouragement and support may be shown; and that children should not be held back because they are not able to utilise standard varieties of English usage. Attention was also drawn to the evidence of students with a relatively modest initial command of English completing higher degrees successfully in colleges and universities (Eggleston et al 1986). Thus Education For Some provided the empirical data, which both Rampton and Swann neglected. It was recognised as mould breaking and demonstrated beyond a per-adventure that racist attitudes and practices are currently doing much to hinder the education of Afro-Caribbean pupils. It identified the point at which the problem intensifies (the third year of secondary school), and it lays bare the cycle which often begins, with prejudice on the part of the teachers becoming a self-fulfilling prophecy, so that Black pupils lose interest in work and accordingly get themselves assigned to the lowest streams.

Three years later, The School Effect (1989), a Study of Multiracial Comprehensives challenged the assumption that minority ethnic groups under-achieve in secondary schools. It also showed that the academic level at which a child is expected to compete depends more on the school policies than on the qualities of the child. The study followed a group of 3000 children in 20 multi-racial comprehensive schools over the five years up to the age of 16. It concluded that, 'measures that will promote the interests of racial minorities in secondary schools are the same as those that will raise the standards of education generally' (The School Effect). However, it did not single out racism as a factor in educational performance, mainly because neither the parents nor the researchers raised the issue. Yet around the same time, several major publications such as 'Racism in Schools' (Kelly & Cohn 1988), 'Learning in Terror' (CRE 1988), 'The Burnage Report' (MacDonald et al 1989) and Bullying in Schools (Tatum & Lane, 1989), offered substantial evidence of bullying and racial harassment in schools and colleges, including a racial murder. Kirp (1978) suggests that Britain, unlike USA, has consciously attempted to diffuse the significance of 'race' in determining policy and embedded racial issues in a broader educational context, thus subsuming the needs of minority children under a plethora of 'racially inexplicit categories: language, urban deprivation, educational disadvantage, cultural adjustment and so on'. Kirp however regards this phenomenon as 'doing good by stealth' which is clearly not acceptable to many educationists in Britain. Dorn (1980) in particular argued that the absence of coherent national policy is a political strategy and that such inaction with reference to racial issues indicates a lack of political will to confront the racism experienced by Black communities in Britain. In the absence of overt policies on multiracial education which could result in explicit measures to combat racism and tackle inequality, 'doing little will be doing nothing' (Dorn 1980). It is this deliberate indifference to the phenomenon of racism that gave rise to the notion of anti-racist education, a characteristic of the social and educational developments of the 1980s.

The Rise and Demise of Anti-Racist Education

An understanding of why racism is so powerfully rooted in British society is essential to the concept of anti-racist approaches. Hatcher & Shallice (1983) argue that if racism is primarily an ideological anachronism from the days of Empire, then the task of eradicating it is primarily an educational one. But if racism is being newly generated at the political, social and economic levels of a society in crisis, then it has wider implications. Stuart Hall (1977) pointed out the need to confront the 'specificity of a British racism....which has a real life at the base of the society'. The major task of an anti-racist programme in education should be the elimination of conscious and unconscious discrimination in provisions of allocation and selection, that is to say a fight against what sociologists used to call racialism. Such a programme would deal, not with thoughts and ideas, but with actions, which were to the detriment of minority children. Of course it might be shown that stereotypical thinking was one of the causes of discrimination and that a process of teacher education in racism awareness was necessary, but it is essential to emphasise that the object of anti-racist policy is ultimately the control of actions and not the control of thoughts. Mullard (1984) and Carby (1982), who dismissed multi-culturalism as a superficial irrelevance and a 'right wing inspired sop' to communities who are suffering injustices, talk about a form of anti-racist education that goes far beyond the essentially emotional empathy with other people's life styles. They pointed out the irrelevance of teaching the four Cs (costume, calypso, carnival and cricket) or the three Ss (saris, samosas and steel bands), which may generate some positive feelings towards other cultures at an individual level, but cannot do anything to influence the power structures that perpetuate the most basic injustices that really matter. They argue that making other cultures acceptable merely dampens down the legitimate anger. Further, as Paul Zec (1980) points out, any understanding gained through multicultural education is unavoidably superficial and presents cultures in so positive a spirit that it is difficult to see why they should feel alienated at all. Most importantly, an emphasis on other peoples cultures implies that it is the existence of these, rather strange and presumably inadequate, cultures that are the cause of social problems. Consequently, attention is diverted from the basic issues of power, inequality and racism, and some see it as a deliberate political tactic to maintain the '*status quo*'. The ineffectiveness of multicultural education has also been cited in the growing harassment of black individuals and families by young whites during the last two decades. It is also evident in the lack of preparation of Black pupils to come to terms with and challenge constructively, social and economic injustices.

Anti-racist education that is currently being demanded by Black parents and academics is a political challenge to teachers, who need to recognise that racist assumptions and values permeate many text books and courses and unless actively condemned and questioned they continue to perpetuate a racist ideology. To embark on that questioning process needs a political decision. Banks (1984) suggests that many practitioners hope to take education out of that context and 'palliate social rage' by so doing. The conflict between multiculturalists and anti-racists is not so much in what they hope to achieve through education, but more in terms of their starting points and very different social and political philosophies reflecting different racial, economic and political experiences. Banks refers to this conflict as, 'the radical scholars criticise multicultural education for not doing what the conservatives are afraid it will achieve; i.e. a significant reform of the social structure' (Banks 1984). It is not surprising therefore that even amongst its supporters, both Black and White, there is a great deal of hesitation and conflict in implementing anti-racist strategies, even when there is an agreement as to what needs to be done.

For some, like Brandt (1986), the aims of anti-racist teaching are concerned with examining the pattern of institutional racism in public services and to give students competence, skills and the knowledge necessary to change the situation. For others, it is about creating an atmosphere of rational debate about issues of injustice and social inequalities. The methods and strategies advocated for anti-racist teaching range from open political discussions in the classroom using a political vocabulary, to an oppositional stance in relation to the power structures represented by society, schools and organisations. Some suggest that anti-racism teaching has to be of matching complexity to the racism it challenges, and as permeative of the curriculum as the racist education it replaces. In the words of Stuart Hall:

> We have to uncover for ourselves, in our own understanding, as well as for the students we are teaching, the deep structural factors which have a tendency persistently not only to generate racial practices and structures, but to reproduce them through time; and which therefore account for their extraordinarily immovable character (Hall 1980).

Thus two positions that are significantly different in nature have to some extent been pushed towards a synthesis by academics, who want to appear not too radical, and those who are desperate to shake off the liberal cloak, but are afraid to join the ranks of so called radicals. It is important to acknowledge that multicultural education without an anti-racist perspective is superficial, tokenistic and inadequate both in educational and social terms, and that anti-racist permeation of the curriculum at all levels is only possible with critical awareness of cultural implications. According to Jeffcoate

> the proper aim of multi-cultural curriculum is to furnish children with the knowledge and skills to come to a critical understanding of the different cultures impinging on them, including their own, in order to decide for themselves which culture or which bits of which culture are worthy of respect, allegiance and adoption (Jeffcoate 1979).

The contrast between the two positions cannot be more obvious and is very aptly described by Robin Grinter:

> one is descriptive, the other analytical; one confirms the established structure, the other questions and seeks to change it; one looks for appreciation of other cultures, the other for criticism of one's own; one appeals primarily to the emotions, the other to the intellect; one emphasises the social and cultural aspects of life, the other economic and political. In terms of educational practice, similar distinctions apply: one is indirect, the other direct; one persuades, the other challenges; one is an extension of existing practice, the other, at least on surface, a challenge to it (Grinter 1985).

Grinter further argues for an anti-racist multi-culturalism, which is more a matter of approach, emphasis and a choice of examples and a question of sensitivities to issues and perspectives that might otherwise be omitted. Information about other cultures and minority ethnic groups is an important part of anti-racist education but only when it is not presented as a simplified caricature or tokenistic gesture. In a broad sense the content and process of teaching needs to be determined by what we want students to learn and that derives from a view of the particular qualities we wish to see developed in students as anti-racists and for them to be able to work towards a just and equitable non-racist society.

An effective strategy to educate all children in a multicultural society has to be anti-racist, but in order for it to provide equal opportunity for all, it has to promote sensitivity to social issues of gender, race and class. Banks identified the 'expanded concept of political and cultural democracy' as an essential aspect of effective education for equality. Some have argued that such expansion may result in diffusion of energies and a blunting of the cutting edge of anti-racism, whereas others like Chris Mullard insist that if multi-culturalism were to be taken seriously, 'it would inevitably include class based, gender based as well as race based culture......and be concerned with the relationship of class and gender groups over and above the concern for race groups' (Mullard 1982).

By setting race and gender in its class context, educational initiatives of an anti-racist nature can begin to address issues of wider political education and gain the sympathy and involvement of a large number of people who wish to dismantle discriminatory practices in favour of a just society. For anti-racist multicultural teaching to have academic and professional credibility, it has to take on board the notion of good education and address issues of the contradictions, distortions and inhumanities associated with ethnocentric thinking. Grinter suggests that Anti-Racism is implicit in multicultural strategies, because it is difficult to avoid the issue of racism in a discussion about cultures in schools where children are experiencing prejudiced behaviour, racial harassment and violence every day both within and outside schools. Mullard believes that anti-racist education is the only racial form of education that can, in combination with anti-sexist and anti-classist education, lead to a redefinition of what education should be. Mullard also characterises multicultural education as microscopic in that its advocates tend to have a narrow focus on issues of culture, they are concerned with formulating policies to eradicate ignorance of other cultures, undermine the prejudice and discrimination which stems from ignorance, and develop greater understanding and tolerance of members of minority groups. The site of change is the school; the nature of change concerns the removal of ethnocentric materials from the classrooms, and replace them by more culturally sensitive and educationally appropriate materials. In contrast anti-racist education is defined as periscopic, that is to say it deliberately seeks to make a connection between institutional discrimination and inequalities of race class and gender. Troyna (1987) considers anti-racist education as a radical example of political education, as it demands a critical examination of those explanations and practices, which misinform and oppress people. In that process it calls for collaboration and co-operation and demands greater recognition of students' rights. All this is likely to threaten established modes of behaviour and relationships within educational institutions, especially when it includes collaboration with Black communities and self help organisations. But as Dhondy (1978) puts it, 'To be professionally anti-racist and not to be influenced by the actions and interests of the population that faces the brunt of racism is racist' (Dhondy 1978).

Thus the main ideology underlying anti-racist education is that power structures within society are at the root of social inequality, and that education has a role to play in removing such inequalities, and that equal opportunity does not mean the same opportunity, but also equal access and equal share. The issues addressed in the educational models resulting from such an ideology have been identified by the Swann report as those of personal, institutional and structural racism and the effect of teacher attitudes on the education received by all children. More recently, and as a direct consequence of attacks on anti-racism, a more acceptable face of change has emerged in the form of a move towards 'education for racial equality'. Some people would argue that such an education should include a positive attitude towards bilingualism as an essential component because it signifies an equal status for languages spoken by different groups. The other essential components of education for racial equality could include Black perspectives on education, social, political and moral education of all children, positive action to provide equal opportunities and awareness training to include an analysis of how racist practices operate at a personal and institutional level. (For further discussion see chapter 6.)

To prepare teachers to challenge the existing practices requires a fundamental change of ethos in our educational institutions. Teachers are ideally placed to play a leading role, both as educators of children and as agents of change, acting to combat racism within schools and outside. It is even more important with greater involvement of parents under the new Education Act, that teachers are clear about their understanding of the issues and confident about the support they can get from colleagues, head teachers and local authorities. Those opposed to anti-racism and indeed to education for racial equality have been able to exploit ambiguities associated with the terminology itself, and in some respects some of its allies have also discredited the kind of anti-racism that trivialises Black peoples' lives as nothing more than a response to racism. The recent assaults on anti-racist social work and the practices of multicultural and anti-racist education have not really been responded to in a collective way by professional unions with clearly defined policies for equal opportunities and anti-racism, nor indeed, with few exceptions, have they been counteracted by academics and researchers with a clear ideological and professional commitment to anti-racism. It is this very antipathy that gives further credence to the critics of anti-racism.

The Education Reform Act

The educational responses of the 1980s included significant developments to promote appropriate educational provision for a culturally plural society. In addition to the national and regional policy initiatives, the 1980s also witnessed major national reports such as The Rampton Report (1981), The Swann Report (1985), The Schools Council Report and the Report of House of Commons Home Affairs Committee (1981), major research reports such as Other Languages of England, (1985) Education For Some (1986), FEU reports on research in the field of multicultural education and local and national priorities for INSET work on curriculum issues have all made a valuable contribution to making education for all a reality. On the other hand, controversial issues and debates have also occupied the minds of many schools, teachers and LEAs. Ray Honeyford in Bradford, Maureen McGoldrick in Brent, parents in Dewsbury ('The School Above the Pub', Naylor 1989), the murder of an Asian pupil in Manchester (The Burnage Report, 1989), and Rushdie affair in Bradford have all contributed to the polarisation of educators and public alike.

The Education Reform Act of 1988 (ERA) was the most controversial piece of education-based legislation in the 20th century. The debate generated by the GERBIL (Great Education Reform Bill) prior to the ERA is characteristic of the way in which education has been used as a tool in the hands of politicians to score points during elections or has been blamed for all kinds of social and economic deprivation and for numerous other ills of society that can't be explained away. It has also been frequently referred to as some miracle to compensate for society. In some respects the fundamental reform in our education system was long overdue and on the whole a new Education Reform Act was to be welcomed. It certainly raised a lot of expectations and was indeed the subject of extensive speculation. Some thought that with the provision of 'open admissions', greater parental choice, 'Local Management of Schools' and the opportunity for schools to become grant maintained and indeed a National Curriculum, it will improve the prospect of a decent education for all children. However, there was also a concern that it will create further divisions within society, thus recreating the elitist system of selecting 'la creme de la crème', for respectable careers and university education, and relegating the failures at 7, 11, 14 and 16 to service the professionals. It was also feared that some LEAs might choose to abandon their equal opportunities policies, because the Education Reform Act had chosen to ignore the cultural, religious and linguistic diversity of our schools.

At the same time it was hoped that some of the more progressive and the liberal LEAs might continue to review the content and process of our education system and not abandon their policies for equal opportunities. Unfortunately, but not surprisingly, the Education Reform Act aimed to provide a popular education within an ideological framework, which is individualistic, competitive and racist. It did not take the development of educational policy and practice in a multiethnic society forward on a statutory level. There was no mention anywhere in the Act of multicultural, non-racist education or of education appropriate for a multiethnic society. The strong resistance to attempts made by the opposition to amend the legislation, as it passed through the Parliament, was a clear indication that the Government did not want the act to be explicit on issue of race and ethnicity.

Overall the response of the profession to the Education Reform Act seems to have been one of benign resignation, and in some circles the National Curriculum was being used as an excuse to discard successful policies and practices, simply because they did not fit the straitjacket designed by Kenneth Baker, the Secretary of State for Education at the time. The interesting thing is that the major proposals of the Education Reform Act were intended to reform our education system, not deform it. The curriculum for schools was expected to be 'balanced and broadly based, which promotes the spiritual, moral, cultural, mental and physical developments of pupils at the school and of society; and prepares such pupils for the opportunities, responsibilities and experience of adult life'. The proposals of ERA had significant implications for various sectors of education. But this is clearly not the place to discuss these. However, it is important to examine some of the proposals concerned with Open Enrolment, Local Management of Schools, National Curriculum, Testing and Religious Education and their implications of education for racial equality.

Open enrolment

The proposals were intended to ensure that parents would be able to send their children to the schools of their choice, as long as it was not physically full. It also meant that parents were supposed to have a real choice and could send their children to schools other than those in their near vicinity. If the events in Dewsbury and Cleveland were anything to go by, we may have seen many more ethnically segregated schools, and that cannot be good for harmonious race relations or good educational practices. The economic ability of some parents to send their children further away from home could also lead to the movement of good teachers, thus stripping ethnically mixed inner city schools of valuable resources. The biggest concern was that 'popular' schools are likely to be selective, perhaps with a social, religious or racial bias. The choice they offer is not real, because it is the schools that pick and choose the parents, not the other way round. Less popular schools end up with pupils whose parents had no choice, either because of economic constraints or for lack of informed guidance. The notion of an equal choice for every individual in an unequal society is purely ideological. In practice only those with means to transport their children to alternative schools have the choice, and this could mean closure of inner city schools, thus weakening the links between schools and communities. The Cleveland decision (1988) also raised fundamental philosophical and ideological issues that characterise the debate about individualism and collectivism; about the extent to which, and the circumstances in which, individual choice and preference can be curbed in the interest of the alleged collective good.

Local management of schools

The Act required LEAs to submit details of the authority's arrangements for delegating financial responsibility to school governors. The governing bodies with delegated budgets were responsible for deciding, within the total resources available to them, how many teaching and non-teaching staff should work at the school and have greatly increased powers in respect of appointments, suspensions and dismissals. Such an arrangement can be helpful if it means that parents and teachers as governors have a more effective share in the running of schools. In schools, where there is an established policy for education for all, and issues of equal opportunities are on the agenda, this could mean a fairer allocation of resources in line with their priorities. But in schools and local authorities, in all-white areas for example, the concern for anti-racist education may well depend on the existence of highly influential and skilled advisory teams, and strongly dedicated anti-racist teachers. Otherwise schools may tend to ignore local councils' initiatives on race equality in education.

Another consequence of financial delegation may also be in the form of all-Black schools, especially in areas with large minority ethnic populations, with schools containing 90-95 percent minority ethnic children. Ideally, a balanced governing body should seek to ensure that centrally run services in schools and colleges continue to get adequate resources as the health of some institutions may depend on them. But the likely effect of this shift of financial responsibility could be that the gap between LEA policies and the policies and practices of individual schools will be widened. Individuals and organisations concerned with promoting equal opportunities and anti-racist education may find it more difficult to influence individual schools than LEAs.

Religious education

All pupils in maintained schools are required to attend an act of collective worship in each school day, unless withdrawn at their parents' request. This can be provided at any time of the day, must continue to be non-denominational, but is likely to be 'wholly or mainly of a broadly Christian character'. However, there is provision for schools with a large majority of non-Christian pupils, to seek approval for other acts of worship. The Standing Advisory Council for Religious Education (SACRE) was set up by all LEAS, each reflecting the principal religious traditions in its area. So, theoretically, it was possible for schools to offer religious education that takes account of principal religions of the world. In practice, an NFER survey found that not many authorities were likely to go to SACRE for a waiver of an act of worship, which is mainly Christian. The emphasis on religious education, which ignores the religions of some of its pupils, may in fact be another impetus for minority communities to opt out for separate schools.

National curriculum

Curriculum documents produced by the DES throughout the 1980s asserted the importance of curriculum in helping all pupils to come to terms with a multicultural Britain. The School Curriculum (DES 1981a) talked about how learning should specifically 'help pupils to develop pastoral, moral values, respect for religious values, and tolerance of other races, religions and ways of life' and should 'help pupils understand the world in which they live and the interdependence of individual groups and nations'. It also insisted that a major purpose of learning was to give pupils 'the ability to question and to argue rationally'. However, the 5-16 Curriculum (DES 1985) spoke of the need not to include a multicultural dimension in 'the important elements of the curriculum' but to 'become familiar with the broadly shared values of our society' and the only mention of bilingualism was with reference to Welsh. Better School (1985) promoted the view that curriculum should be a major vehicle for recognising the need for social change. It required that 'all pupils need to understand and acquire a positive attitude to the variety of ethnic groups within British society' (p61) and that this should be a major curriculum objective both in specified subject areas and in permeating the ethos of all schools. The document also noted that multicultural curriculum objectives were embodied in the national criteria laid down for the GCSE examinations and in the criteria for initial teacher training. Within the provision of the Education Reform Act (1988), the purpose of the National Curriculum was to 'develop a broad consensus about what children are taught, accepting of course that children differ in what they learn and in their rates of learning' (DES 1988). In terms of race issues, initially there was some hope that the National Curriculum, despite all misgivings, does offer one major advantage that schools will not be able to differentiate between curriculum delivery on grounds of race, gender, language or any other discriminatory criteria. But the hope was misplaced and the absence of multicultural issues in the core subjects, for which statutory documents were issued, was alarming.

The guidance documents issued from the National Curriculum Council (NCC) made no specific reference to existing inequalities of race, gender and class or indeed to the existing legislation for equality. As a cross-curricular theme multicultural education was not subject to statutory control, and consequently LEAs with established models of good practice may or may not feel obliged to continue to work along those lines. This was despite the fact that the NCC was instructed to 'take account of the ethnic and cultural diversity of British society, and of the importance of the curriculum promoting equal opportunity for all pupils regardless of ethnic origin and gender'; and members of the council were broadly sympathetic with the issues. The subject-specific focus on curriculum was seen to be unhelpful for cross-curricular approaches currently in use in primary schools. It was also seen to act as a barrier for cross-curricula permeation in respect of anti-racist education. The responsibility of interpreting programmes of study, arrangements for assessment and designated attainment targets usually lies with the class teachers and head teachers, who will have an explicit responsibility to ensure the delivery of 'broad and balanced curriculum which promotes the spiritual, moral, cultural, mental and physical development of all pupils'. It can therefore be argued that the amount of time devoted to each component and the way in which the school timetable operates, teaching methods, selection of books and materials will still remain in the hands of teachers and a matter of professional concern. Consequently, the treatment of cross-curricular issues, concern for anti-racist education and delivery of good 'education for all' does not have to be in competition with the delivery of core subjects and foundation subjects as identified by the National Curriculum.

Assessment

With regard to the new assessment procedures, the report of the Task Group on Assessment and Testing demonstrated sensitivity to the dimension of multicultural issues and recommended that the assessment tasks be reviewed regularly for evidence of bias, particularly in respect of gender and race. The report also recommended that children who speak English as a second or third language should be exempted from tests in English if their present level of competence in English is likely to make the task of assessment meaningless. They recommended that schools should take this as an indication that the child requires help in acquiring English and should not lead to damaging assumptions about his or her level of competence in other aspects of learning. The use of children's first language in testing was also recommended. The agencies planning to develop standard assessment tests were advised by SEAC that they make every effort to ensure that the SATS, which they produce, avoid ethnic or cultural bias, that their use would not be inhibited by translation into a foreign language, and that they do not contain material which would disadvantage pupils from minority ethnic groups.

Theoretically, a combination of assessment by teachers who are familiar with their pupils, and by standard tests used nationally should improve objectivity and regular comparisons between schools locally and nationally should facilitate continuous monitoring for equal opportunities. In practice, however, greater reliance on subjective assessment by teachers coupled with nationally standardised tests, which expect a uniform performance at the age of 7, 11, 14 and 16, could lead to greater disadvantage for minority ethnic children, especially those who may be competent in English at one level, but may not understand the subtle nuances of language sufficiently to perform in certain assessment tasks. Moreover uninformed teacher expectations have a habit of perpetuating the vicious circle of self-fulfilling prophecy.

Equality Assurance

It was in the light of this vacuum that the Runnymede Trust set up a working group to produce guidelines to support the implementation of new legal requirements affecting the curriculum in schools, including the requirements of the National Curriculum. 'Equality Assurance in the School Curriculum' (1992) identified three key themes of Equality Assurance, Quality, Identity and Society. These were explored in conjunction with ways of making these themes operational through the National Curriculum, thus offering guidelines and examples for practice in schools. The three key objectives were how to ensure quality education for all pupils; how to support the development of cultural and personal identities; and how to prepare pupils for full participation in society. Each one of these themes was further developed with reference to knowledge and understanding, skills and attitudes required in the context of whole- school issues including the treatment of each area of the National Curriculum and cross-curricular issues.

'Equality Assurance in Schools' (1992) demonstrated that the degree to which the practitioners have to comply with the written and unwritten guidance, offered by government documents, depends very much on the commitment of the individual teachers, of schools and of the LEAs. It has the potential to rekindle the issues of race equality placed by ERA on the back burner of educational, political and financial priorities. It also has the potential to enable teachers to organise curriculum experiences, which foster and support pupils' sense of their personal and cultural identity, and foster a sense of value for each individual. The fact that this document was sold out in months could suggest that it proved to be very popular and has helped many teachers to offer a truly balanced and broadly based curriculum. However, despite the lengthy responses from the Commission of Racial Equality and the publication of Equality Assurance by the Runnymede Trust, the issues of cultural diversity and racial equality did not find a place in The Dearing Report on the National Curriculum and Assessment.

The 1992 White Paper, Choice and Diversity: A New Framework For Schools' repeatedly emphasised the overriding aim of government policy 'to raise the standards achieved in schools by all pupils of all abilities' and offered a theme of excellence as the basis for all monitoring, evaluation and inspection. Although there is no explicit reference in the White paper to issues to do with cultural diversity and race equality, Kenneth Clarke, in his speech, did refer very directly to the under-development and under-use of talent in Britain's minority ethnic communities. 'I am sure that barriers remain to full opportunity for people from minority ethnic groups and to a fully integrated society. The most obvious and obnoxious barrier is racial discrimination' (Clarke 9th June 1992, House of Commons).

Runnymede Trust and the CRE highlighted their concerns in responding to the proposed legislation. These included a concern for upholding the anti-discrimination legislation; the need for a clear and explicit statement to promote equality of opportunity; the need for formal guidance to schools to ensure that their policies for admissions and exclusions are non-discriminatory; the need to ensure adequate representation of minority ethnic communities in the membership and staffing of bodies for curriculum guidance and assessment and the need for continuous and rigorous monitoring of all aspects of the education system to identify the effects on minority ethnic communities. An HMI Consultation Paper 'Framework For the Inspection of Schools' (1992a) also failed to take account of the need to ensure that inspectors are aware of the unlawful discrimination in the education system. The Commission For Racial Equality, in the light of evidence from its own investigations (Secondary School Admissions, Lessons of the Law, & Ethnic Monitoring in Education), urged the DfEE to re-examine this framework. The CRE's main concern was to ensure that all Inspectors are fully aware of the Race Relations Act (1976) and its implications; that they are fully conversant with how unlawful discrimination and harassment operates in the education system and how it can be eliminated; and that appropriate inspectors from minority ethnic communities are appointed at least to the inspection teams for multiracial schools.

Racial Equality in the New Millennium

The position of race in education has shifted considerably in recent years. This has been largely due to two major catalysts for change. The first is the Macpherson Report (1999), report of an inquiry into the death of Stephen Lawrence, and the second is the introduction of the Race Relations Amendment Act (2000). The following paragraphs include a brief overview of these two developments and the educational responses resulting from them.

The Macpherson Report

The Stephen Lawrence Inquiry, commonly known as the Macpherson Report, was a milestone in being the first acknowledgement by the British State of the existence of widespread institutional racism. Sivanandan argues that through the course of the Inquiry, 'the gravitational centre of race relations discourse was shifted from individual prejudice and ethnic need to systemic, institutional racial inequality and injustice'. The following definition of institutional racism offered by Macpherson has been the subject of many academic and political debates:

The collective failure of an organisation to provide an appropriate and professional service to people because of their colour, culture or ethnic origin. It can be seen or detected in processes, attitudes and behaviour which amount to discrimination through unwitting prejudice, ignorance, thoughtlessness and racist stereotyping which disadvantage minority ethnic people (Macpherson 1999).

The report also included 70 wide-ranging recommendations, three of which recognise the key role of education in combating and addressing street and institutional racism. Recommendation 67 called for a national curriculum aimed at valuing cultural diversity and preventing racism. The report created huge waves of guilt and recrimination in all sections of public services and led to a number of Government departments taking steps to create structures and frameworks that will assist schools and educational professionals with the preparation and implementation of race equality work. The following is a summary of some of the initiatives resulting as a direct consequence of Macpherson Report.

The White Paper 'Schools Achieving Success' includes, for the first time, a very specific commitment to raise standards for pupils from minority ethnic groups. Whilst acknowledging that there was some evidence that standards were rising among some minority ethnic groups, the document stated that it is 'unacceptable that children of Caribbean, Pakistani or Bangladeshi families have been half as likely to leave school with 5 good grades of GCSEs as children of some other ethnic backgrounds'. The White paper also indicated that the Ethnic Minority Achievement Grant would be monitored and targeted to support schools to break down the barriers to equality of opportunity and tackle the cycle of disadvantage. According to the QCA Guidance document 'Respect For All', the statutory inclusion statements for all subjects at all phases will require teachers in the planning and teaching of the curriculum to have due regard to the principles of: setting suitable learning challenges; responding to pupils' diverse learning needs; overcoming potential barriers to learning for individuals and groups of people. However, the guidance itself is non-statutory and schools are not obliged to follow it. 'Learning for All' – a document issued by the Commission for Racial Equality (CRE) also sets out standards for race equality work in seven core areas of education. By working towards these standards schools will be implementing the recommendations of the Stephen Lawrence Inquiry Report. The CRE has also issued codes of practice to enable public authorities to comply with the RRA. 'Learning For All' was consistent with the Ofsted Inspection Framework. This has also helped some LEAs (for example, Stoke on Trent, Greenwich) to build racial questions in the Self-evaluation Framework.

New improved arrangements for Ofsted inspection came into force in September 2003. Educational Inclusion (addressing race, gender, SEN) is now part of the inspection framework and Ofsted will be looking for evidence on e.g. materials and teaching that cultivates pupils' 'personal, spiritual, moral and cultural development'. It is worth mentioning that following the Stephen Lawrence Inquiry; the inspectors were offered extensive and compulsory training to improve their awareness of equality issues. However, there is still evidence that through some inspections do include issues of inclusion, there remain a significant number of teams with no members who can make more than a superficial judgment on fundamental equality issues. The Teacher Training Agency (TTA) has published a document – 'Raising the Attainment of Minority Ethnic Pupils', which includes Guidance and Resource

Materials for providers of initial teacher training. It also includes a number of sections with very useful guidance for schools. It describes what inclusive schools should do:

> Inclusive schools review the curriculum to ensure that it includes appropriate subject content, language materials and resources which 'recognise and respect the cultural differences of all pupils; recognise the contribution to knowledge of a wide diversity of human groups; promote an understanding of cultural, religious and linguistic diversity and do not ....reinforce misconceptions about others' (TTA 2000).

It also emphasises the importance of inclusive education by stating that 'An inclusive education cannot be achieved by treating all pupils in the same way. To be effective schooling has to take account of the often very varied life experiences, assumptions and interests of different pupils and different groups, including sometimes their differing responses to schooling itself' (TTA 2000).

Race Relations (Amendment) Act (2000)

Following the Stephen Lawrence Inquiry Report, The 1976 Race Relations Act has been amended. The RRAA is a significant step forward in the history of anti-discrimination legislation in Great Britain. It provides schools and other public authorities with a new and important framework for promoting racial equality. The new duties place clear responsibilities on teachers to play a full and active role in helping their schools to promote racial equality. The Act places a Statutory duty on local education authorities and educational institutions to have due regard in the functions they carry out to eliminate unlawful discrimination; and promote equality of opportunity and good race-relations. For the first time in many years, the educational institutions will genuinely have the potential to develop and implement sound race equality policies. The CRE will be working with Ofsted to get the requirements of the positive duty integrated into inspection frameworks. (For further information read Samidha Garg in MCT Vol. 20 No. 3.) However, it does not take account of the changing nature of race relations and the role played by cultural diversity and does not recognise fully the significance of religious identity. The introduction of European Employment Directive (2003) which requires all EU member-states to legislate against religious discrimination and discrimination on the basis of sexual orientation (useful account is to be found in an article by Robin Richardson in MCT 20.2.2002).

Comments and Summary

It is clear that the policies and initiatives promoting multicultural education in the 1980s were not always supported by the Government. The politicians, writers and academics from the extreme right were always opposed to multicultural education and did not welcome the proposals of the Swann Committee. For example, the recorded opposition to 'promote foreign tongues, customs and religions' (Pearce 1985) in a Monday Club paper soon after the publication of the Swann Report; Margaret Thatcher at the Tory Party conference in 1987, 'Children who need to be able to count and multiply are learning anti-racist mathematics – whatever that may be. Children who need to be able to express themselves in clear English are being taught political slogans'; and John Major's speech in Brighton (1992) about 'Primary teachers should learn how to teach children to read, not waste their time on the politics of race, gender and class'. suggested that racism has played a crucial part in the development of the new Right's ideas on education. Scruton and Honeyford have appealed to popular racism of the kind that thrives on myths and ignorance.

The ideological climate, in which ERA was created, was one of the radical Right dictating the market forces and the centralisation of more power to the Secretary of State for Education. At one level, the Act was about decentralisation of power, a shift of power away from the LEAs to school governing bodies. Whilst the management of schools was devolved to school governors, the curriculum was taken away from the schools to the government. In LEAs where equal opportunities and anti-racist education still remains on the agenda it might still be possible for schools to negotiate curriculum development initiatives on these lines. The changes in the structure of funding for local government meant reduction of finance for schools. The new arrangements for INSET and the new regulations for section 11 funds did not made any specific allocation for work concerned with race equality. As Whitty and Menter (1989) noted, the very emphasis on the National in the National Curriculum, the centrality of a notion of national testing with all the cultural and linguistic bias which that implies, the failure to recognise languages other than Welsh and English as pupils' first language, and the omission in any of the consultative papers, let alone in the Act of any reference to the Swann Report of 1985, suggests that race equality was not on the agenda.

The ideology of equality of opportunity, which was important in the structural development of comprehensive education, and in progressive curriculum reform, was overtaken by a greater emphasis on the economic functions of education in preparing pupils for the world of work in an increasingly unequal society. The narrowly White and English concept of the Nation in the National Curriculum is not only visible in subjects like History, but is also evident in the regulations governing the teaching of Religious Education and school assemblies which are supposed to be mainly and broadly Christian acts of worship. Whilst the Act provides the opportunity for schools to apply to opt out of this regulation through application to SACRE, they are not required to opt in to the provision of a single-faith act of worship in a multi-faith society (Hardy & Porter 1992). Similarly, whilst Welsh has been recognised as a core curriculum subject in Wales, the other living languages of Britain are relegated to Schedule 2 as options to be offered as an alternative to the required Schedule 1 of European Languages.

Since the Education Reform Act was based on a political and economic philosophy of individualism and consumerism and introduced a curriculum based on a narrowly defined notion of the nation, it is visibly contradictory to the principles of justice and equality, which underpin the anti-racist movement. It offers very limited opportunities to improve educational opportunities for minority ethnic groups but creates further barriers in the implementation of equal opportunities policies. The open enrolment offers a risk of segregated schools. Financial delegation and the opportunity to opt out offers some advantages and may improve parents' participation in the running of schools. Schools with a substantial number of minority ethnic children can certainly recruit more Black parents as governors but equally a majority of White parents can keep them out from schools with fewer

Black children. On the whole parents have more power to determine the allocation of funds to a particular school, as 75 percent of funds are related to the number of children in school. The significant shift in the balance of power is in the role of parents, changing from parents as voluntary helpers to parents as clients, who have to be told how their children are likely to be assessed and how they are performing.

The Education Reform Act also offered another significant opportunity for teachers to review, qualify and enrich much of their work. Teacher appraisal, though much resisted, is perhaps the only way to ensure quality education for all our children. The effect of national curriculum will depend on the skills and common sense of teachers in schools. The need to challenge stereotypical attitudes and discriminatory practices remains urgent, even if they don't figure on the central Governments agenda. The responsibility of delivering good education for all is very much that of teachers and head teachers, but the role of teacher trainers, advisers, the NCC and the SEAC is equally crucial, as indeed is the responsibility of parents and governors to ensure that schools are working efficiently and effectively. The Education Reform Act established, as an entitlement for all children, a curriculum which is balanced and broadly based and which 'promotes the spiritual, moral, cultural, mental and physical development of pupils at the school and of society; and prepares such pupils for the opportunities, responsibilities and experiences of adult life'. Teachers need to ensure that a balanced and broadly based curriculum is made available to all pupils, including those from minority ethnic backgrounds, many of whom are bilingual and may arrive at school needing extra support to learn English to ensure full access to curriculum.

Teachers also need to ensure that all pupils learn through school experiences values, which reflect respect for different cultural, linguistic and religious traditions of ethnic groups, which are part of our society. The NCC (1991) did acknowledge that multicultural education is the professional responsibility of all teachers in all schools, and that NCC did not see Multicultural Education as a subject but as a dimension, which permeates the entire curriculum. As such it should be at the heart of curriculum planning, development and implementation. However, it chose not to issue guidance to make this a reality, despite having commissioned a working group to produce such guidelines. The statutory orders did not actively encourage this permeation approach, nor did they offer any help to teachers in implementing these twin aims.

The onset of a Labour government has done little, despite the rhetoric of 'an inclusive society', to challenge the fundamental injustices and inequalities faced by Britain's minority ethnic groups. Gillborn (2001) points to a few cosmetic changes, such as the funding of some Muslim schools and the retention of Section 11 funding (now Minority Ethnic Achievement Grant), as disguising the lack of commitment of the Labour government to tackle the real issues which confront minority groups in Britain. Labour policy, he argues, is, like the policies of predecessor governments, informed by a deficit view of minority peoples and cultures, an obstacle, which prevents real understanding of social justice issues and prevents any attempts to tackle them.

The introduction of the Race Relations Amendment Act (2000) following on from the aftermath of the Stephen Lawrence Inquiry has helped to put race equality back on the agenda. But the new Right has also been very active in the last 10 years. Most teachers may never have read the Black papers, the Salisbury Review or books like Anti-Racism – an Assault on Education and Value (Palmer 1987), or heard of the Hillgate group. But the writers of this ilk are swiftly adopted as folk-heroes by the popular media and are used to discredit anti-racist education. The 'discourse of the new Right is primarily that of anti-anti-racism' as it is seen as a threat to national identity and traditional values. The neo-liberals refuse to accept racism as a cause for under-achievement and inequality. In the light of such vociferous opposition it is even more important that the cause of race equality and anti-racism is pursued vigorously and with equal rigour. The discourse of the anti-racists has to be about condemning racism not only because it leads to under-achievement but also because it is unethical and leads to an incredible waste of the intellectual and economic resources of our society.

Recently, the British Home Secretary, David Blunkett, suggested that 'institutional racism' was a slogan that let individual managers 'off the hook' in tackling racism. He said that it was important that the government's 'diversity agenda' tackled the fight against prejudice but also took on the long-standing need to change attitudes:

> That is why I was so worried about people talking about institutional racism because it isn't institutions. It is patterns of work and processes that have grown up. It's people that make the difference. It's not the structures created in the past but the processes to change structures in the future and it is individuals at all levels who do that (Blunkett 2003).

Blunkett's intervention represents an attempt to turn back the tide; to trivialise institutional racism by describing it as a 'slogan'; indeed to deny its existence and to revert back, in Blunkett's own words, to 'individual prejudice' as being the major problem. If it is the case that managers in the police and elsewhere are using the acceptance of the existence of 'institutional racism' as an excuse for inaction, then this should, of course, be challenged. What is problematic in Blunkett's remarks is the shift in focus from 'institutional racism' to a conception of racism as an autonomous personal problem – a move from 'institutional racism as collective failure' to the 'rotten apple theory' of racism. There are two main problems with this. First of all, the psychological concept of prejudice divorces discriminatory practices from wider structural factors: institutional racism usually refers to racism permeating major institutions, e.g. the police force, the education system, the political system, and so on, at the local level, the national level and/or beyond. Second, in stressing individual blame, the need for structural change at local, national, and international level is negated. Acknowledging structural and institutional injustices opens up the possibilities for institutional and structural change, whereas the accentuation of personal prejudice does not.

Chapter 3

Literature Review – Teacher Training Provision

Introduction

The National Commission on Education (1993) outlined a vision of a teacher in the 21st Century who 'will be an authority and enthusiast in the knowledge, ideas, skills, understanding and values to be presented to pupils, will have the capacity to think deeply about educational aims and values... will be willing to motivate and encourage each and every pupil, assessing progress and learning needs in their widest sense'. This chapter argues that for teachers to deliver that vision, they need to be trained to do so effectively. Teachers have not always been prepared adequately to motivate and encourage each and every pupil to realise their individual potential and achieve as well as they should. It will demonstrate that two major aspects of teacher education in relation to minority ethnic groups, namely the preparation of all teachers to work in a multicultural society and the recruitment, training and employment of teachers from minority ethnic groups in the British education system have not been given adequate attention in the last three decades. Both these strands have an important bearing on the understanding of the intricately woven tapestry of the British education system. The issues that need exploring relate to the development of specific programmes of teacher education for a multicultural society, and subsequent research reports and surveys on their implementation and the mismatch between policies and practices of educational institutions. Other relevant issues are barriers to implementing equal opportunities policies in the recruitment, training and employment of minority ethnic teachers; their participation in schools and in teacher training institutions and how far their presence within the system is likely to make a difference to the way children with minority ethnic backgrounds are being taught within our schools.

This chapter is not a historical review of the last three decades in the history of teacher education. It is an attempt to give readers a flavour of some of the recent and current practices, with regard to the preparation of all teachers for a multicultural society. It will begin with a summary of teacher training Provision in the eighties and will consider the effects of the Education Reform Act (1988) and the attacks on teacher education and on anti-racism by the extreme Right. It will also include a brief discussion of the barriers to implementing well-intentioned equality policies; explore the mismatch between policy and practice, and between supply and demand. Finally, there will be a discussion of Schools Based Teacher Education including the developments of shorter training courses and the recruitment of teachers from the overseas, in terms of their implications for minority ethnic groups and their participation in the teaching as a profession.

It seems that it was only towards the end of the 1960s that teacher-training colleges began to pay some attention to the needs of minority ethnic pupils and it was later still when the preparation of all students to teach in a multicultural Britain came to be considered. The efforts of teacher training colleges in translating the thinking of the DES into action were intensified by a series of local and national conferences and by opportunities to undertake a systematic examination of the content of courses. They also focused attention on the difficulties experienced by what was then described as 'immigrant' children in some schools and on the recruitment of tutors with overseas experience. On the whole the picture that emerges for initial teacher education during the 1970s is consistent with the general ideology of assimilation and tinkering with the curriculum that was the theme of the 1970s. It is painfully obvious from the plethora of research reports and government publications of this decade that there was a basic concern for the education of minority ethnic children and a realisation that teachers were not being adequately prepared through initial education or through in-service for the challenging task of educating all children for life in a multicultural society. HMI report of an inspection undertaken during 1979-80, to investigate the coverage of multicultural issues during initial and in-service training of teachers, revealed an overall picture, which was: 'not a particularly bright one' (Annex B of The Swann Report), and revealed a visible lack of minority ethnic teachers in the profession at all levels. It is also clear that the reasons for people from minority ethnic groups not taking up teaching as a profession included the lack of clear and consistent career advice, the absence of minority ethnic teachers as role models; fear of racial discrimination and racial abuse and the fear of being marginalised. These were certainly echoed by minority ethnic students and groups of minority ethnic teachers, who further confirmed the incidence of racial discrimination and marginalisation and also gave substantial evidence of the stress caused by their jobs.

Summary of Provision in the 1980s

The beginning of the 1980s saw the two dual themes of multicultural aspects of teacher education firmly on the agenda of training institutions, that is the preparation of some teachers (those who wish to teach in multiracial schools), with provision designed to give the students particular knowledge and skills to teach in multiracial schools; and the preparation of all student teachers to teach in a multiracial society, irrespective of whether the students concerned will be teaching in an 'all-white' school or a 'multiracial school'. To some extent the confusion between the two kinds of needs began to be clarified in the mid 1980s and there was some acceptance, especially since the Swann Report, that both these complementary elements are crucial to the effective education of all our teachers through initial and in-service training. A third dimension that has also been on the agenda for some time is related to the recruitment, training and employment of teachers from minority ethnic groups. The record of training institutions and indeed of LEAs in this respect is not impressive and the change in attitude and practice has been even slower than in the education of all teachers for a multicultural society (see chapter 4). The Home Affairs Committee (1981) acknowledged that it was no longer acceptable to wait for the complex administrative structures of teacher education to come to terms in its own good time with the challenge presented by the multiracial classroom. Although the Home Affairs Committee thought it was desirable that all teaching should be as broad-minded as possible and teacher education courses should be permeated by this understanding, it did not wish to say that multicultural education should be a compulsory part of initial teacher education, as that might give an impression that it should be something extra tacked on to each and every course. The Committee therefore recommended that 'every initial teacher training course should be examined by the Council for National and Academic Awards (CNAA) or other validating body to ensure that it accurately reflects the society in which those who follow the course will be working' (Home Affairs Committee 1981).

The Committee also applauded the initiative shown by some colleges, in areas without multiracial schools, in giving students the opportunity of direct experience of teaching in such schools elsewhere, and recommended that other colleges should follow this example. The Committee felt that although there had been some progress over the years, the claims made by the DES that about half of the training institutions appear to be offering relevant compulsory or optional studies of some kind in this field were unduly optimistic. The Committee was concerned that the multicultural dimension in teacher training remained partial, often optional, and only in colleges in areas of minority ethnic concentration, rather than permeating all teacher education courses. The Committee recommended that all teachers should have at least some initial specialised training to enable them to perform effectively in a multiracial classroom. The Home Affairs Committee was also anxious that initial teacher education should provide more specialised instruction in the skills needed for teaching English as a second language and offering second-stage support, especially as most young teachers would be teaching in a multiracial school within five years of their induction and might be unprepared to teach pupils of Asian origin. The Government's reply to this report was generally positive in recognising that members of minority ethnic communities have an important part to play in shaping the Britain of the future, and that they represent an important source of talent but their full potential will only be realised within a society free from prejudice and discrimination. The Government's response to particular recommendations concerned with teacher education was not so encouraging, but it promised to consider carefully what further part it might play in encouraging teacher education to take account of the multiethnic character of our society in other ways than at present.

A View of the Curriculum (DES 1980) and The School Curriculum (DES 1981a) both drew attention to the fact that British society had become multicultural, and ministerial speeches also indicated the need for teachers to be better equipped to respond to the problems and challenges raised by education for life in a multicultural society. Similarly a seminar organised by CRE's Advisory Group on Teacher Education concentrated on the Task for Teacher Education to prepare teachers to teach in a multicultural society. The Nottingham seminar was a gathering of experienced, knowledgeable and committed specialists, and it generated a lot of constructive discussion of the central issues, such as leadership from the DES, validating bodies and senior managers in institutions; the complexity of the field and the issues involved; need for a wider and more comprehensive dialogue between providers and policy makers; available expertise, the knowledge base and the need for research and development work as well as the practical issues, such as the why, what and how of multicultural education.

The key messages emerging from this seminar identified the need to define, quite explicitly, the essential professional characteristics required by those who teach, or wish to teach, in a multicultural society. It was agreed that they need to be adequately prepared to teach children from diverse backgrounds and that they needed greater awareness of their own levels of intercultural prejudice. The need for a centralised information agency in a decentralised system was highlighted, but the suggestion for a new specialised agency for initiating curriculum development and staff development in multicultural education was not well received, as it might have threatened the established practices of white liberal professionals. The strategy of permeation through existing agencies and professional unions and a strategy of linking innovative teachers with teacher educators were thought to be more effective (Craft 1981).

NATFHE (1982) took the view that an institution concerned with teacher training can adopt two main complementary approaches of promoting such awareness among all its students, and of giving some students the opportunity to explore relevant academic and professional options in greater depth. The evidence submitted by the Association suggested that the greater professional orientation of the new B.Ed. provided an opportunity to incorporate multicultural studies for all student teachers, and that to avoid fragmentation and superficiality of content, there should be a logical relationship among the elements within the modules to develop a coherent approach to multi-culturalism. The evidence also pointed to the need for all colleges, no matter where they are situated, to play their full part in developing a wide range of multicultural studies. Similarly the evidence submitted by NUT (1982) pointed to the need for improvements in the multicultural perspective of teacher education. The NUT's own survey of Teacher Education for a Multicultural Society confirmed the need for a compulsory element in all teacher education courses of preparation for teaching in a multicultural, multiracial society and the need for validating bodies to ensure that courses measure up to criteria laid down by them.

The overall picture emerging from The New Teacher In School (DES 1982c) was a mixed one. Nearly a quarter of the teachers in the sample felt that they were poorly or very poorly equipped for the task of teaching. A significant finding of the survey was that the personal qualities of the teachers were in many cases, the decisive factor in their effectiveness. About 52 percent of the teachers in the sample (55 percent Primary and 50 percent Secondary) considered themselves not at all prepared to teach children with different cultural backgrounds. In the words of one of the respondents, her training had prepared her, 'adequately for teaching in a small suburban primary group in a middle class area', but not 'for the Special Priority Area, urban multicultural mixture' that she was now experiencing (DES 1982c). In the same year Education 5-9, an illustrative survey of 80 First Schools in England, concluded that all children should be made to feel like members of the school community and that their cultural backgrounds and practices should be valued in the school. The survey's findings revealed that although nearly half the schools in the survey had pupils from Asian and Afro-Caribbean backgrounds, there was little awareness in schools of the changing nature of the community or any recognition of the diversity of cultures and faiths represented and there was no reference to the need for, or presence of, minority ethnic teachers.

The main recommendations of a discussion paper on 'Teaching in Schools: the Content of Initial Training' (DES 1983a) stressed that the initial training of all student teachers should give them an awareness and understanding of the broader context of their work and the responsibility of the schools in catering for the aspirations and expectations of society at large. The only reference to the issues concerned with minority ethnic groups was rather implicit, in a recommendation (pp16-17) which emphasised the need for greater differentiation in the education and deployment of teachers to reflect the variety of tasks that teachers face with different age groups. This White Paper was clearly about improving the quality of teaching and included several proposals intended to achieve this end. In summary, the ideal teacher was required to be enthusiastic and well qualified, to feel secure in teaching a subject specialism, to have adequate professional and class room skills, to be professionally and socially aware, and to be adequately prepared to deal with the different learning needs of all children.

Since the White Paper made very little, if any, specific reference to the issues concerned with the needs of minority ethnic groups or to those concerned with equipping all teachers for education in a multiracial society, it was left to the staff and managers in teacher training institutions to interpret the proposals in such a way so as to avoid implementation of potentially harmful and undesirable statements of policy direction. Like most of the Government documents, this White Paper was written in a language which was open to interpretation. The teacher trainers were expected to strike a delicate balance between the political-legal constraints, implied in these documents, and the wider needs of educational philosophy and development. The proposals in the Teaching Quality 'Good teachers need to have a mastery of the subject matter they teach and the professional skills needed to teach it to children of different ages, abilities, aptitudes and backgrounds' (Teaching Quality 3.26) and 'The teacher training system must continue to be responsive to changes in pupil numbers, the school curriculum and the society served by the schools' (Teaching Quality 4.52) were thus open to a positive interpretation by those with a particular concern for promoting education for a multicultural society.

However, it does seem strange that despite overwhelming research evidence, and despite the progressive statements in official documents indicating an urgent need for teacher education to take on board the needs of minority ethnic groups, the Teaching Quality did not think it appropriate to concern itself with these issues. The fact that there was so little time for professional debate before the drafting of centrally determined criteria for the approval of initial teacher education courses did cause some concern in the profession. NASUWT and NUT both made extensive responses to the Government White Paper on Teaching Quality, but neither of the unions made any specific reference to or commented about the need for preparing teachers to teach in a multicultural society. Guidelines for the Voluntary Colleges for 'Teacher and Higher Education in a Culturally and Racially Diverse Society' did recognise that all students needed to be given some background knowledge about the nature of multicultural Britain and the role of education within it. It also recommended that all students should follow appropriate professional courses which examine the implications of linguistic diversity and bilingualism; that they should be made aware of the implications of cultural and racial diversity for the subjects they teach; and recognise the need to consciously counter race prejudice and racism through their teaching.

NAME (National Association for Anti-racist Movement in Education) issued a policy statement on Teacher Education (1984), which included recommendations for implementation. The NAME policy statement rested on the twin beliefs that all teachers in Britain should adopt an anti-racist approach throughout their professional activities; and that to do so effectively demands as full an understanding as possible of the context within which they work, and of the educational, cultural, social, moral and political issues, on which their decisions will depend (NAME 1984). The NAME proposals for implementation included reference to changes in institutional management, staffing, recruitment and assessment of students, provision of courses and staff development opportunities, course content, evaluation and resources, so as to ensure adequate representation of minority ethnic groups and an anti-racist approach in curriculum content and processes.

By the mid 1980s although the enunciation of multicultural aims had moved in from the periphery of educational debate to become integral to expressions of DES policy, reports from the Schools Council, Home Affairs Committee and the Rampton Committee indicated that progress in schools had been limited. The Rampton Committee (1981) found that by the end of the 1970s, no institution of teacher training appeared to have succeeded in providing a satisfactory grounding in multicultural education for all its students, and that the great majority of students were thus entering teaching having receive little or no guidance on how to adopt a broadly-based approach to education which takes full account of the presence of minority ethnic groups in our society.

On the whole teacher education for a multicultural society during the 1980s had been characterised by exhortation rather than systematic provision. The response to ethnic diversity had been varied, inconsistent and slow. Where courses had been developed they were marked by lack of clarity of purpose, rational planning and adequate implementation. For example, a national survey of Initial Teacher Training Institutions in 1982 (Craft and Atkins 1983) revealed that even though 70 percent of institutions claimed to convey an awareness of dialect and language differences, the existence and main characteristics of minority community languages, and issues such as mother-tongue teaching, only slightly more than 50 percent sought to develop even minimal competence in language support across the curriculum in linguistically diverse schools or skills for working in multi-lingual classrooms.

It had become clear that strategies of introducing specialist optional provision in selected institutions of teacher training, however helpful in developing some awareness of cultural diversity, had not succeeded in 'permeating' general teaching programmes for all student teachers. As Richard Willey (1983) pointed out, the emphasis needed to be on ensuring that specialist optional provision is an extension of work undertaken in mainstream courses and not a substitute for it. He also stressed, as did the Rampton Committee, that teacher education institutions need to formally consider the implications of cultural pluralism for the professional training they provide and should institute a fundamental reappraisal of their policy towards multicultural education. It had also become clear that until the central government was really interested in promoting issues of cultural diversity and equal opportunities, no amount of individual or institutional effort and commitment was likely to result in true 'permeation' of all teacher education courses.

Circular 3/84 – A Significant Shift

DES Circular 3/84 'Initial Teacher Training: Approval of Courses' was the outcome of heated debates, which began when HMI advised the Advisory Committee on the Supply and Education of Teachers (ACSET) about the diversity within the teacher education system. Awareness of this diversity led to intensified discussions about the elements and characteristics, which should be part of every initial teacher-training course. ACSET advised the Secretary of State, who at the same time produced 'Teaching Quality', the White Paper, which included his own views of the improvements, which should be made in the initial education of teachers. Circular 3/84, unlike most other DES circulars, had lasting significance, firstly due to its trans-binary nature, affecting both university-based and public sector initial training, and secondly, because it was a directive from the Secretary of State with a startling innovation in the notion of centralised course approval and accreditation. The circular's main thrust was in the following four areas.

CATE (Council for the Accreditation of Teacher Education)
A single Council was established whose terms of reference were to 'advise the Secretaries of State for Education and Science on the approval of Initial Teacher Training courses in England and Wales'. The members of the Council were appointed by the Secretary of State for Education and were drawn mainly from practising school teachers, teacher trainers and elected members and officers of the LEAs, so that they could give the Secretary of State the benefit of the advice of 'experienced professionals with a broad knowledge of the best practice in teacher education'. As a central part of the information required by CATE, HMIs visited teacher-training institutions in the public sector and also visited some University departments of education by invitation (HMI 1988). The Council's approach to Accreditation was subsequently explained in CATE NOTE I (January 1985). The message in this document was that the improvement of teacher education could only be assured by co-operation among those concerned with all stages and aspects of the professional preparation and development of teachers. The Council also gave an assurance that its procedures and practices will be consistent with this commitment.

Local Professional Committees
In response to the proposals in the White Paper 'Teaching Quality', Circular 3/84 set out the broad framework for such committees. They were not sub-committees of the CATE, their membership and terms of reference were to be determined locally and they were to discuss all aspects of initial teacher education and play an important part in promoting links between training institutions, schools and the communities in the region. CATE NOTE 2 outlined the purposes and procedures for such Local Committees. The appointments of individuals from outside the education service were expected to be especially responsive to local situations. The work of these committees was expected to facilitate the developments and strengthening of links between the institution, schools and the community; arrangements for practising teachers to participate in the selection, training, supervision and assessment of students; opportunities for teacher training staff to maintain and refresh their knowledge and experience of classroom teaching; and students' work with classes, small groups and individual pupils in ways that relate to their studies. The Circular linked the new arrangements of course approval with the existing systems for the award of QTS (Qualified Teacher Status), by indicating that this award in future will, 'specifically draw attention to the phase and subjects for which the course of training was intended and for which it was approved'. The Circular hoped that this will act as a guide to employers and schools in improving the match between formal qualification of teachers and the teaching programmes assigned to them in schools, but it did specify that teachers will not be formally

limited to teaching the age range and subjects indicated in their awards. The criteria for judging courses were grouped under four headings, namely Links between training institutions and schools, Subject studies and Subject method, Educational and Professional studies, and Selection and admission to initial teacher training courses. The criteria required institutions to develop and run their initial teacher training courses in close collaboration with practising schoolteachers, and for teacher trainers to have recent and relevant experience of teaching in schools. In a document which had much to say about partnership between school, training institutions and 'community', and which suggested that 'students should be made aware of the wide range of relationships......which teachers can expect to develop, and of the role of the school within a community' (Circular 3/84), such training and sensitisation were viewed as taking place exclusively within the training institutions and within the school, but not necessarily in consultation and partnership with minority ethnic groups.

CATE NOTE 3 (1985) dealt with the requirements of subject studies and clarified their relationship with other criteria included in the circular. Other aspects of the criteria that caused a lot of institutions to change their practices were related to the entry qualifications (minimum grade C in 'O' level Mathematics and English and a restriction on mature students intake (maximum 25 percent). The section on subject studies offered a view of the curriculum as something fixed and determined by the school or as agreed by the DES, but not as something to be negotiated between teachers, pupils and parents. Paragraphs 10, 11 and 12 dealt with Educational and Professional studies, the core element of all teacher training courses, and as such offered some opportunity to interpret statements such as 'ways in which pupils can be helped to acquire an understanding of the values of a free society, and its economic and other foundations'; and 'opportunities should be provided for students to place their role as a teacher within the broader context of educational purposes'; in a way that anti-racist perspectives could, despite the ethos of 3/84, be introduced by institutions with clear commitment to implement their policies on equal opportunities. Guidelines for links between initial teacher training institutions and schools were issued in the form of CATE NOTE 4 (1986). These aspects of the criteria reflect a long-standing concern (James Report DES 1972, Education in Schools DES 1977a, ACSET 1983) for the close involvement of teachers in the training process.

The Circular sent ripples through the initial teacher education system as never before. The age specificity of courses had never been so clearly spelt out and never before had a DES Circular attempted to regulate the length of university courses. For LEAs too, the secretary of state expected them to meet the additional expenditure of releasing schoolteachers and teacher trainers from within the existing provision. The establishment of CATE and the spelling-out of the criteria for course approval also offered unprecedented opportunities to improve the quality of teacher education. However, the practitioners were less than happy with the Circular, in particular, the demand for 'recent and relevant experience' and for 2 full years of subject studies were criticised by practitioners who argued that there were better ways of gaining relevant school experience than taking a class for a few weeks in a school and appealed for judicious flexibility from CATE. At another conference (SCETT) the chairman of CATE defended the requirements of 'recent and relevant experience', and assured the conference that the criteria were not set in concrete for all time. They may well be revised in 10 to 15 years. The teacher training institutions were caught in the contradictions and confusions between the establishment of CATE, and the sudden closure of National Advisory Body (NAB). The TES described this contradiction as: 'If your music department is praised by CATE, it will be closed down by NAB (as at Rolle College); if the NAB decides not to close you down, you will be threatened by Sir Keith, and if you are damned with faint praise by HMI and NAB recommends closure, the DES will offer a tentative reprieve, as at Hertfordshire College' (TES Nov.1985). As far as the minority ethnic groups are concerned, DES circular 3/84 on Approval of Initial Teacher Training Courses was the culmination of a trend which facilitated a degree of technical change in the field of teacher education, but which also provided no explicit direction or commitment about educating teachers capable of a comprehensive and equitable consideration of the interest of every single child growing up in Britain in the 21st century. Like the White Paper 'Teaching Quality', Circular 3/84 gave a token acknowledgment to the presence of minority ethnic groups within the education system, without accepting and addressing the implications of their presence or indeed of the fact that society and the education system are structured by class, race and gender, and that schooling underpins and perpetuates the power relations that these dynamic factors embody.

In summary, Circular 3/84 projected Britain as a society unified in terms of class, history and economic and political relations, with a predominantly White population whose culture has the advantage of being enriched by people from other cultures. The concept of education, which underpins those criteria, is one, which pays little regard to the ways in which society and the education system are structured by class, race and gender and the power relations that such structures generate. The absence of an anti-racist perspective in Circular 3/84 was neither an accident nor an oversight. It was a blatant refusal on the part of the DES to recognise the fact of British racism and the relationship between institutions such as schools and consumers (both Black and White). It thus projected a view of knowledge and of the schooling, which sees teaching as a non-ideological, non-political and neutral process in which learning is designed to meet the objective quantifiable needs of the children. However, in reality the power relations of the classroom reflect those of the society. Student teachers need to be trained to recognise and challenge the inequalities that operate within their classrooms and schools and not merely to preside over and regulate those power relations. Paragraphs 11 and 12 of the Circular 3/84 demonstrated the extent to which the entire document gave a nodding acknowledgment to the presence of minority ethnic groups within the education system, but refused to accept and address the implications of the fact that the society and education system are structured by class, race and gender and that schooling underpins and perpetuates the power relations that these dynamic factors embody (ARTEN Occasional Paper I).

The major responsibility for breaking this cycle of perpetuation thus fell on to teachers in the classroom. The preparation of these teachers therefore needs to be in the hands of people who had the skills and courage to carry out this responsibility. The ideological position and practice of staff should reflect at least a positive attitude towards minority ethnic communities and their views of the structure and content of the course provision. Sir Keith Joseph, in his speech at North of England Conference (January 1984), emphasised the role schools play not only in developing personal qualities, skills and competence but also in the transmission of values. Four years later, after all the fuss about the need to inject rigour and relevance into teacher training, the

Secretary of State announced that from September 1989 people could walk straight into a classroom and start teaching before they begin their training on the job. The introduction of the Licensed Teachers Scheme, primarily intended for graduates from overseas, was not to be the subject of scrutiny before CATE. The remit for CATE was to scrutinise every course of teacher education offered as the main route into teaching. Its impact was measured by the rate of rejected submissions. The wholesale rejection of the first submissions (only 1 out of 9 was successful) did nothing to alleviate the suspicions that the creation of this Secretary of State's watchdog (described by some as the college of the inquisition) had bred in the first place. The criteria was challenged by several very influential teacher educators and national conferences, even leading to the Select Committee's (1986) recommendation to phase CATE out. Later in 1988, two leading educationalists (Professor Paul Hurst of Cambridge University & Dr. Preston of Rolle College, Exeter) seriously questioned the Government's ability to conduct an independent review of CATE and the criteria by which it assesses courses (TES May 1988). A detailed critique of CATE is to be found in 'Recent and Relevant Experience: How CATE legitimates narrowly defined concepts of teacher education' (Boxall & Burrage 1989).

However, CATE was reconstituted in 1989, with wider brief and revised criteria to enforce. As well as vetting and monitoring courses in the light of DES criteria, it was to advise the Secretary of State on changes to the criteria and teacher training in general. Local Committees, each covering a minimum of three training institutions, were to do the detailed review of new courses against the criteria. The new CATE criteria (Circular 24/89) stipulated, amongst other things, that experienced teachers must be involved in course planning and evaluation, the selection of students, and the supervision and assessment of practical work. CATE's experience over the years would suggest that accreditation is a powerful instrument, able to secure changes and compliance with national criteria throughout education courses within the system. However, issues of relationship between accreditation and validation and the assessment of quality remain unclear and need to be seen in the wider context of moves within the system towards the establishment of a General Teaching Council and the Teacher Training Agency.

Education for all – The Swann Report

The Swann Report (1985) clearly recognised that teachers are the key figures in the education process and that changes and practice in the classroom practice and in the overall ethos of schools depend to a very great degree on the co-operation and support of individual teachers and therefore placed particular responsibilities on the teaching profession. The CRE (1985) welcomed the Swann Committee's view that racist or prejudiced attitudes on the part of teachers should be regarded as unprofessional and endorsed the view that it is the responsibility of all teachers in all schools to prepare pupils for life in a pluralist society. The CRE also shared the Committee's view that teacher education had a crucial role in equipping teachers with the necessary skills, knowledge and attitudes. However, the changes proposed by the Committee were seen to be inadequate by the CRE as it felt that it would be insufficient for teacher education to confine its course development to the issues of cultural diversity, and that attaining the objectives of 'Education For All' will also require an examination of teacher attitudes and behaviour and the development of an anti-racist ethos and practice.

The Association of Polytechnic Teachers expressed concern with regard to the role of higher education in removing racial prejudice in society, the need for attention to multicultural diversity and the need for widening access to higher education for students from minority ethnic groups. The thinking in this document lacked any understanding of issues such as racism and under-achievement. It gave no credence to the work of the Swann Committee and seemed to challenge the basic premise of the Swann Report. The White Paper 'Better Schools' (1985) accepted, and was concerned with the findings of the Swann Committee, that many minority ethnic pupils are continuing to achieve below their potential. It also recognised that racial prejudice in our society directly or indirectly affects the achievement of many minority ethnic pupils. The White Paper further claimed that, the Government's policies were designed to reduce under-achievement wherever it occurs, to remove the educational obstacles, which hold back particular groups of pupils, and to support the work of the education service in preparing pupils for an ethnically mixed society and in working towards racial harmony (DES 1985d).

HMI surveys and reports

The Initial Training of Teachers (HMI Survey 1983-85) began at the end of a decade, which had seen radical changes in the size and nature of the teacher training system. This survey of a sample of 30 institutions reported that all the institutions recognised the need to give students an understanding of the implications for primary schools of the ethnic diversity in British society and that a substantial number were reviewing their policies and revising their course content and structures with this in mind. About one-third of the institutions were reported to give considerable time and emphasis to multiethnic issues, though there was marked variation in the amount of time allocated to a compulsory core and to options. Some institutions, which offered only a slender compulsory component, claimed that this was compensated for by a policy of 'permeation' whereby multiethnic aspects were covered as appropriate in many parts of the B.Ed. and PGCE courses. Although in about half the institutions multiethnic education was given some measure of attention, there was little evidence to support this assertion. These various arrangements resulted in some areas covering a good deal of ground in multiethnic issues and others very little (Quality in Schools, DES 1987).

Some of the best work was reported to have occurred where a combination of compulsory and optional components was available and in inner-city areas where the ethnic diversity of the population heightened the students' awareness. The policy of 'permeation' was least successful in institutions where the tutors accord it low priority and where this was sensed by the students. A few institutions in areas, which lacked minority ethnic groups, made good use of urban study centres where students were able to gain experience of multiethnic communities during residential weeks. The HMIs observed that institutions increasingly recognised the need to prepare students to educate all children for life in an ethnically diverse society and also to introduce them to the particular needs of children from minority ethnic groups (DES 1987). The survey also found that in the majority of institutions there was considerable dependence upon outside speakers. In most of the valuable sessions referred to in the survey, it was the presence of a speaker or a teacher from minority ethnic groups that made these sessions successful. The survey recognised that too heavy a reliance on visiting speakers meant that a systematic development of understánding was very difficult to achieve. Again, there was no mention of minority ethnic teachers.

Primary Schools: Some Aspects of Good Practice (HMI 1987) also found evidence of teachers' sound knowledge of their pupils' social and cultural backgrounds. But again there was no reference to the need for or presence of minority ethnic teachers. During 1988-89 the media attention focused quite sharply on initial teacher education. The PGCE courses were being criticised in the media, their value was being questioned and there were proposals to base the training of teachers in schools, involving teachers as mentors and regarding students as apprentices. The New Teacher in School (1988), an HMI Survey of 300 probationary teachers revealed a lack of clarity and agreement about what trainee teachers in general might reasonably be expected to know and be capable of doing by the end of their courses, and therefore what they might need during their induction and thereafter. The survey found a disturbing proportion of all new teachers emerged from training feeling less than adequately prepared for important areas. This survey also showed up the conflict between the direction CATE wanted to take and the nature of criticism from the trainee teachers and probationers. Some teachers in the survey were critical of 'superficial coverage of areas such as self-assessment, class control, English as a second language, equal opportunities, multi-ethnic dimensions, provision for the more able and mixed age teaching' (HMI 1988).

With regard to preparation for teaching in a multicultural society, nearly half the new teachers in the survey thought they were well prepared to teach pupils of different cultural backgrounds. Nearly three-quarters felt that they were adequately prepared to promote equal opportunities for boys and girls, and one quarter felt less than adequately prepared. Some specific comments from teachers who felt well prepared to teach children with different cultural backgrounds revealed that though they felt well prepared in theory, they felt that they lacked relevant school experience. HMIs commented that it was encouraging to see higher (compared to a 1981 survey) proportions of new teachers expressing satisfaction with a number of aspects of their training. Example of these aspects were in the preparation to teach children with different cultural backgrounds, for which the proportion feeling well trained, as opposed to merely adequately trained, increased from 29 percent to 49 percent between the two surveys, and in classroom management where the increase was from 49 percent to 66 percent (HMI 1988). However, it was also considered unacceptable that a quarter of all the teachers in the survey felt less than adequately prepared to teach children with different cultural backgrounds. Another worrying factor commented on by the HMIs was in relation to the performance of the new teachers compared with their own assessment of the effectiveness of their training. This was clearly visible in their understanding of the importance of language in learning, an area that has clear implications for teaching children with different cultural backgrounds. Despite a good understanding of their own need to use appropriate language, the new teachers did not demonstrate such a clear understanding of the ways in which their teaching might contribute to the pupils' language development. The survey also reported that schools expected new teachers to be aware of child development and of 'multiethnic matters'....'an appreciation of different social backgrounds and of multicultural issues' (HMI 1988), but no specific comments were reported in terms of how far these expectations had been met and yet again, no reference was made to minority ethnic teachers. It was partly in response to the Swann Report and partly as a result of HMI findings (Quality in Schools 1987), that the government had stressed the need to take account of the ethnic diversity of our society in Circular 24/89. The need for training with regard to equal opportunities was also made a national priority (1986-87) for INSET grants and money was made available to LEAs to encourage in-service training of teachers to respond to ethnic diversity in schools.

CNAA (Council For National Academic Awards)

CNAA, a validating body for Teacher Training Courses in the public sector, had set up a working group (1981), to produce guidelines for institutions with regard to 'Multicultural Education and the Professional Preparation of Teachers'. This working group came about as a result of deliberations by the members of the CNAA Education Committee, following on from two surveys of multicultural education in Initial Teacher Training Courses validated by the Council. The Committee members were convinced that account must be taken of the needs of minority ethnic children, and that a multicultural approach was necessary throughout education. They believed that all teachers, irrespective of the areas in which they train and the schools in which they will practise, should acquire greater sensitivity, by specific attention to the nature of multicultural society in their courses of initial training. (CNAA 1982). The Council, whilst endorsing the view of the Committee, was reluctant to prescribe criteria against which courses submitted for validation could be assessed. Initially a suggestion to appoint a panel for multicultural education was not favoured by the Council on the grounds that these concerns should be integrated with other components of the course and not treated separately. However the Council agreed to set up a working group to consider ways of making progress. The working group produced a paper for consultation in 1982. This paper, 'Agenda for Multicultural Education', was based upon a premise that all education should be multicultural, reflecting the ethnic complexity of our society. It was also recognised that without a clear understanding of the central importance of equal opportunities for all children, multicultural education will be of less value. It was acknowledged that in designing courses of teacher education institutions need to bear in mind the needs of schools, pupils and society that teachers have to meet. These were defined as being equipped to prepare all pupils for life in a multicultural society, to be able to teach in multiethnic classrooms, and to have an awareness of the issues of inter-cultural relations. The strategies for meeting such needs were defined as permeation of all courses of teacher education through core elements and through special options. Though the appointment of an individual member of staff to act as a change agent and to permeate the consciousness of all staff was recommended, no reference was made to the need for minority ethnic staff.

This paper was welcomed by some members of the Council and led to 18 months of debate within the group and consultations with the CNAA boards and panels. Further amendments to the paper resulted in several drafts and subsequent revisions, incorporating changed titles from 'Agenda For Multicultural Education' (1983), to 'Multicultural Education: Discussion Paper' (1984) to 'Notes on Multicultural Education and the Professional Preparation of Teachers' (1985). The 1985 version was a more concise set of notes outlining the objectives for multicultural and anti-racist education and drawing attention to important educational and professional considerations as well as to institutional and administrative structures and resource considerations. This paper was basically in the form of a list of questions institutions were expected to address in the design of their courses and in the arrangements for their delivery. Dr. Gerald Grace (CNAA working group) resigned under protest when the Committee of Academic Affairs at the CNAA did not endorse this paper. He resigned because the Committee had been subjected to political influence and did not wish to see too many references to the phrase anti-racism in the document. Dr. Kerr the chairman of the CNAA Committee for Academic and Institutional Policy confirmed that the DES had objected to the words 'anti-racist' and that he had to be careful that the document does not appear prescriptive and lead institutions to believe that unless they adhere to the notes in the design of their courses, these will not be validated (THES March 1986).

The actual notes were in fact not prescriptive, but sought only to put the onus on institutions to respond in ways consonant with their own policies through proper academic and professional practices, and the use of the word 'anti-racist' seems to be fairly anodyne. For example, in the section headed Educational and Professional Considerations, it asked questions such as, 'how can permeation of all elements of initial and in service courses with multicultural and anti-racist considerations, including attitudes, skills and knowledge best be achieved'? (CNAA Notes 1985). Whilst welcoming the document in principal, members of both Anti-Racist Teacher Education Network (ARTEN) and National Anti-Racist Movement in Education (NAME) felt that the CNAA document offered an inaccurate view of modern Britain by not recognising the existence of racism and its pervasive influence in educational institutions. Malcolm Frazer, the Chief Executive of CNAA, in his address at an ARTEN seminar in 1987 accepted that the CNAA did not see it as its responsibility to check the anti-racist policies of member institutions, but suggested that if the validators did not raise the matters (issues of anti-racism) then individuals and those being visited could and should, because that would help to educate panel members (ARTEN 1988). The subsequent demise of CNAA has led to courses being validated either by the Universities or the Polytechnics (now called the new Universities).

Universities and teacher education

HMI review of Initial Teacher Training in Universities in England, Northern Ireland and Wales (DES 1988), concluded that much of the teaching in the University Departments of Education was of high standard, but that much of that was due to individual excellence and that the quality of the courses on the whole needed to be improved through better management, co-ordination and monitoring. However, the report made no reference to the issues concerned with preparing teachers for a multicultural society. Does it mean that 32 University Departments of Education (visited between May 1982 and November 1987) did not prepare their teachers for a multicultural society and did not have any minority ethnic students on their courses? It could also mean that the HMIs did not consider the issues concerned with the needs of minority ethnic children or indeed of all children to live and learn in a multicultural society important enough to warrant their attention. It is worth noting that traditionally the 32 University Departments of Education could only be visited by HMIs after an invitation and that too was infrequent. With the relative increase in the University based Primary PGCE courses, HMIs felt increasingly anxious to include UDEs in their reports. The Committee of Vice-Chancellors and

Principals wished to strengthen the informal links between the HMI and University Departments of Education. The University Council for Education (UCET) was alarmed and wrote to its members stating that full inspections by HMI may put at risk the autonomy hitherto enjoyed by the University Departments of Education. Yet several UDEs did take a somewhat different view and invited HMI to visit and be more fully aware of the quality of initial training being offered in the university sector. With CATE looking to HMI reports of an institution before examining the courses, the visits became more frequent and more acceptable.

With regard to the issues concerned with education for a multicultural society, UCET produced some guidelines in the form of UCET NOTE 1 (1986), which set out some of the general principles in respect of multicultural and anti-racist education for courses of initial and in-service professional education of teachers in schools and in colleges of further education. This was based on the CNAA document of 1984 (Multicultural Education: Discussion Paper) and reflected the view that all education should be multicultural, appropriately reflecting the cultural, social, political and economic complexity of the modern world. It also recognised that it is important to acknowledge the significance of various sources of cultural diversity arising from ethnicity, race, class, gender, religion and region. The paper offered specific objectives to be considered in designing courses for teacher education. These were described as five distinct areas of professional preparation, which could be achieved by a range of strategies for designing appropriate courses, such as permeation, core course elements and special options.

UCET NOTE 2 (1986) was intended to assist University Faculties and Departments of Education to discuss institutional change and professional development in more detail with special reference to the recommendations of the Swann Report. The UDEs were asked to consider the role of admission interviews in establishing the suitability of students for teacher education courses, so that they do not have negative attitudes towards minority ethnic groups; and to consider what sorts of procedures and evidence are required for making judgments about temperamental unsuitability to teach. The question raised was about the balance between fairness and justice to the pupils and fairness and justice for the students. The paper also raised questions about the role of supervising schoolteachers in forming judgments about professional suitability related to issues of alleged racism in the classroom.

The UDEs were advised to take steps to ensure that all their existing provision of in-service courses showed appropriate permeation of multicultural and anti-racist considerations and that they should also consider the best means for undertaking their own in-service training, some of which could be in-house. The UDEs were also asked to develop closer working links with minority ethnic groups. In addition to the involvement of students in community activities, and the involvement of minority ethnic communities in the professional education of teachers; a crucial area of involvement was seen to be in the constitution of Local Professional Committees. There is also related evidence from an EOC report, 'Initial teacher training in England and Wales', EOC (1989), which revealed that over 75 percent of teacher training institutions had an equal opportunities policy, but there was a disturbing lack of evidence that these policies were being implemented in an effective and meaningful way. Amongst the many recommendations of this Commission, there were several references to the concept of 'permeating equal opportunities' and emphasis on the need for comprehensive evaluation in order to prove the effectiveness of permeation.

One of the aims of the EOC investigation was to discover the effect of criteria introduced through Circular 3/84. The report found that although the criteria had encouraged some institutions to address gender issues in a positive and coherent manner, it had not provided sufficient guidance for institutions to raise gender issues in an effective way. The Commission also found that three-quarters of courses failed to show students how to assess equal opportunities in schools and only half asked them to report back on gender issues in the classroom. The Commission therefore recommended that DES guidelines should make explicit reference to the need to teach professional equal opportunities as an integral part of all initial teacher education. It also recommended that Teacher Training institutions should be required to formulate an equal opportunities policy with an associated programme of action and monitoring. A report on equal opportunities should be made annually to the governing body and forwarded to CATE, or its successor body. (EOC 1989). Although the focus of this investigation was on gender issues and not on 'race', the recommendations made have a bearing on the central issues of adoption of policies concerned with equal opportunities and of monitoring their implementation. The findings of EOC and their recommendations with regard to permeation, assessment and monitoring have a direct relevance to the concerns expressed elsewhere about the preparation of all teachers to teach effectively in a multicultural society.

Circular 24/89 – another shift in accreditation

Initial Teacher Training Approval of Courses (Circular 24/89) replaced Circular 3/84 and introduced new criteria and new arrangements for the accreditation of courses of initial teacher training and their approval. The Circular made provision for the reconstitution of CATE from January 1990, with a wider remit and a more substantial and consistent role for Local Committees whose main task will be to consider in detail new and existing courses against the criteria. The revised criteria were more directed towards output and towards statements of what students should be able to show they know, understand and can do by the end of their training. The criteria did include (Educational and Professional Studies) a reference to equal opportunities and multicultural education (6.2) and the need to learn to 'guard against preconceptions based on race, gender, religion... and the need to promote equal opportunities' (6.3) and a reference to the need for institutions to ensure that equal opportunities are given to every candidate irrespective of race, nationality or gender. The commentary in Annex B also made it clear that responsibility for assessing candidates' suitability for admission to courses lies with individual institutions and directed the institutions to seek further guidance on equal opportunities from the Codes of Practice of the CRE and the EOC.

However the Circular did miss an opportunity to make several significant changes, which were recommended by practitioners and the CRE. The CRE, while welcoming the positive references to race-related issues in the criteria, expressed concern that the revised composition of CATE and its local committees was no more likely than the existing committees to include people from minority ethnic communities and/or those with direct experience of teaching in a multicultural society. It urged the secretary of state to take account of its previous representations over this matter so that local committees at least could reflect the reality of multicultural society. It had recommended, amongst other things, that staff involved in interviewing students should receive training in identifying unsuitable candidates, particularly those with negative attitudes towards minority ethnic groups and also drew attention to aspects of selection criteria and entry requirements that may be unlawfully discriminatory.

Comments on the 1980s

The developments in the 1980s have been described by some as 'reform', radical modernisation of an inward academic system, and by others as 'continuity', as a story of the evolution of trends in higher education policy that go as far back as the 1940s. Then there is a third story of 'reaction', the abandonment of the liberal agenda prepared by the Robbins Committee and revised by Crosland's binary policy. For teacher education and for issues of 'race' it is perhaps the story of 'reaction' that seems to ring true. In the words of Peter Newsam, 'we have a Department of Education and Science with the brakes of a juggernaut lorry and a motorcycle engine and that...it had by the end of the 70s finally perfected the art of stopping things from happening'. In reviewing the eighties, he also said that:

> for every 10 hours of talk about equal opportunities, there were about 5 minutes of action. But at least more black head teachers took up posts and came to the top in several education authorities. The decade illustrates the strange phenomenon that legislation often has the opposite effect to the one intended. In the eighties the legislation designed to disperse power concentrated it; and legislation intended to reduce bureaucracy vastly increased it. The legislation of curriculum entitlement was certainly not intended to increase expenditure (Newsam TES Dec. 1989).

According to Peter Newsam that curriculum entitlement embedded in statute is the decade's best gift to the nineties. The developments during the decade have been significant in terms of a change of direction in Government policy and in the mechanisms for accreditation and validation of courses of initial teacher education. There has also been a significant shift in the funding arrangements for in-service training and in the determination of national and local priorities. But there seems to be very little evidence of any significant shift in policy with regard to preparation of all teachers to teach in a multicultural society. The impact of the recession of the 1980s on working class people, minority ethnic groups and on trade unions and the impact of the policies of the extreme Right on anti-racist initiatives has also meant that teacher education has been under constant scrutiny and teachers have been blamed for everything from inner-city riots, lager louts, drugs and disrespect for authority to cultural relativism, anti-racism and anti-sexism. The next section of this chapter will consider the reforms proposed for Teacher Education in the 1990s and year 2000 and examine the obsessive phobia amongst the extreme Right which regards teacher training institutions as arenas of socialist indoctrination and totalitarianism.

The Reform of Teacher Education – The 1990s

Recent reforms of teacher education in England and Wales tend to demonise teachers and revile them. These reforms, started during the Thatcher government in the 1980s and continued by the present Labour government, are undermining teachers' emotional and intellectual strengths by portraying them as failures. Through the establishment of two quangos, Ofsted (Office for Standards in Education) and the TTA (Teacher Training Agency), in the early 1990s, the government has been pushing for ceaseless changes imposed without adequate teacher consultation or consent and turning the majority of them into bureaucrats. Although teachers welcomed the New Labour government, as they expected it to remove some of the worst excesses of the preceding Conservative government on educational matters, they find that the Labour government is continuing the previous policy on teacher education in privileging a competence-based model in contrast to the reflective practitioner, the preferred model of the teacher educators.

Alexander, Craft and Lynch (1984) noted that in the 1980s there was no longer quite the same consensus about the knowledge, behaviour and attitudes to be transmitted to the young as there was in the 1970s. This consensus was even less in the 1990s. While teachers may have become more aware of their assumptions about 'race', class and gender, ethno-centricism still prevailed and the need for social cohesion seemed to override the celebration of diversity. The HMI report of The New Teacher in School (1988) is cited as evidence of the improved quality of initial teacher education courses. This report highlighted that 25 percent of teachers were inadequately prepared and dissatisfied with their training. The report concluded that one in four schools inspected was rated as unsatisfactory, one lesson in three was deemed to be unsatisfactory and only one school in four set expectations which were appropriate for all their pupils, not a picture of schools likely to inspire great confidence in parents. Predictably, the authors (all white men) did not make any reference to the issues concerned with equal opportunities and minority ethnic groups.

Hargreaves *et al* (1989) suggested that the system of teacher training needs to become much more flexible, with more varied recruits, more varied forms of training and more varied patterns of qualifications. They also suggested greater agreement about the standards by which teacher competence is judged and a greatly enhanced partnership between schools, LEAs and teacher training institutions. Select Committee Reports to the House of Commons are looked upon as a source of cross-party and relatively objective advice in the process of policy formulation. The extent to which The Supply of Teachers for the 1990s was objective is still a matter of debate. The constraining effects of dominant political interests were too explicit in the case of this report. The Labour members voted against this report because it failed fully to reflect the evidence which the committee received about the dire state of the profession, and also as a mark of their concern about the constant unacceptable pressure applied to the committee by government ministers. The Committee made a total of 47 recommendations but despite the detailed evidence received from the CRE and from ARTEN, none of these recommendations made any reference to the shortage of minority ethnic teachers in schools or to the need for institutions to recruit more students of minority ethnic origin onto initial teacher training courses. The evidence submitted to the Committee by the CRE (TS66) and by ARTEN (TS83) was reported in the list of memoranda received but not published. Both of these documents drew attention to some of the key issues that had been widely debated within the profession and/or had been the subject of consultation by the DES namely, Overseas Qualifications, Student Grants, Criteria for Accreditation and Validation of Initial Teacher Training courses, the ethnocentric nature of the National Curriculum, recruitment of minority ethnic students on to teacher training courses and the employment of minority ethnic teachers.

The CRE evidence (1989) described in detail the significant under-representation of minority ethnic teachers (2 percent) in schools compared with the minority ethnic proportion of the population as a whole, and the under-representation of minority ethnic students (2.6 percent) on initial teacher training courses (Ranger 1988) and the virtual absence (0.06 percent) of minority ethnic lecturers in teacher training institutions (ARTEN head-count 1987). The CRE believed that there was unlikely to be a significant increase in the supply of minority ethnic teachers in the 1990s until education administrators and teachers provide a service based on equal opportunity principles, free of racial discrimination, stereotyping and harassment and training institutions preparing student teachers to implement such a service. To quote from the CRE submission:

> In effect the issue is circular; minority ethnic pupils may experience racial discrimination and harassment at school and often perceive their minority ethnic teachers to be similarly treated. They are reluctant to be teachers themselves so institutions providing teacher education have few such students and may ignore any needs that they may have, leading to their isolation and a failure to consider the issue of 'race' within the curriculum or in the institution generally. Thus white student teachers are not adequately prepared to counter racial discrimination or to recognise the damaging effect of stereotyping and low expectations. And so the cycle is perpetuated (CRE 1989).

The ARTEN submission drew attention to the role teacher education can play in breaking such a cycle and have a pivotal influence in addressing the under-representation of minority ethnic groups in the teaching profession. It also suggested that the DES should help by recognising and legitimising qualifications from overseas and by providing greater support for Access courses and for institutions offering these courses. The DES could also help by ensuring that the agencies charged with the responsibility for inspection (HMI), for accreditation (CATE), and for validation of courses (CNAA & UDEs) include in their criteria a clear commitment to equal opportunities and positive action to redress the imbalance of ethnicity in their student population and in the curriculum delivery; and by ensuring that the guidelines issued by National Curriculum Council take on board full recognition of the needs created by the ethnic diversity referred to in the Secretary of State's initial guidelines to subject working parties. However, the failure of Government reports to take on board such long-standing concerns did little in breaking such a cycle. On the contrary such neglect only served to perpetuate the belief that equal opportunities and minority ethnic groups are a marginal issue, and not deserving of serious consideration.

Reform of Initial Teacher Training, a DES consultation document (DES 1992) included new proposals under which schools should play a much larger part in initial teacher training; the accreditation criteria to require higher education institutions, schools and students to focus on the competencies of teaching; and institutions rather than individual courses to be accredited for initial teacher training. The consultation document was initially directed at the reforms for secondary school teachers, but proposals for changes in the training for primary school teachers were introduced after considering the report from Three Wise Men (Alexander, Rose & Woodhead). The consultation document outlined the content of guidelines to be issued for equal partnership between schools and training institutions and included draft criteria for the Secondary Phase of Initial Teacher Training. The CRE response to the DES consultation was informed by two main concerns. One was to ensure that students from minority ethnic groups will not only be recruited without unlawful discrimination but also that positive steps will be taken to encourage people from minority ethnic groups to apply for teacher training places. The second concern was that the training delivered would equip all teachers to undertake their duties to meet the needs of all children in a multilingual and multiracial Britain without unlawfully discriminating. Whilst supporting the concept of an equal partnership between schools and teacher training institutions, the CRE expressed a hope that both the schools and the teacher training institutions should be able to demonstrate a commitment to equality of opportunity, both in their procedures and practices as well as in the content of training courses. The CRE was concerned that despite the specific requirements outlined in Circulars 24/89 and 59/89, many teacher-training institutions had failed to address these issues. Their concern was further heightened by the absence in the consultation document of these issues from the list of competencies used to assess the students.

The CRE, therefore recommended to the DES that all teacher training institutions should be required to demonstrate that student teachers are being trained to cater for the needs of multiracial and multilingual schools, and are equipped for their responsibilities to implement equal opportunities and that their recruitment and selection procedures are fair and non-discriminatory. They also recommended that schools chosen as partners in training should equally be required to demonstrate, through policy and practice, their commitment to equal opportunities and to the delivery of a curriculum responsive to the needs of multilingual and multiracial communities. The CRE urged the DES to ensure, that no matter where teacher training is located, 'all trainee teachers are able, where possible, to experience work in multiracial schools with a proven accredited commitment to equality of opportunity'. Given that the CRE considers such experience to be essential, the inclusion of 'where possible' in their recommendation does offer a way out for those who do not consider it essential. With reference to para 5 of the consultation document suggesting that 'the best teachers' be given responsibility for training new members of their own profession, the CRE recommended that 'teachers given this responsibility are identified by their ability to demonstrate a range of competencies including an understanding of, and/or record of work, in implementing equal opportunities, and/or curriculum development of relevance to multiracial and multilingual needs'.

With regard to competencies required of all teachers, the CRE welcomed the consultation document but suggested a range of further competencies to be included. These were suggested against a background of CRE publications such as 'Set to Fail' (1992); 'Secondary School Admissions' (1992) 'Referral and Suspension of Pupils, Birmingham LEA and Schools' (1985); and reporting practices which had resulted in direct and indirect discrimination against pupils from minority ethnic groups. The guidance offered by the National Curriculum Council to Schools (1990) advised that, 'a commitment to providing equal opportunities to all pupils should permeate every aspect of the curriculum' and also stated that 'equal opportunities are concerned with ensuring that all pupils are educated in an awareness of their rights and responsibilities with respect to equality....' and that, 'Rights include civil, political, social and human rights, and how these may be violated by various forms of injustice, and discrimination, including racism' (NCC 1990a).

Of the ten recommendations for additions and amendments proposed by the CRE, the Department of Education only took note of one, and that too in a very unspecific manner. This was under the category of subject application (2.3.6) and it reads, 'contribute to the development of pupils' language and communication skills', but no reference is made to the specific needs of ESL pupils as was recommended by the CRE. The CRE also recommended that selection of students for teacher training courses is made without unlawful racial discrimination, and that staff in teacher training institutions are fully aware of their legal responsibilities in this respect. The CRE supported the continuation of shortened under-graduate courses and part-time PGCE courses, some of which had been developed specifically to enable minority ethnic students and those with overseas qualifications to obtain QTS. Whilst welcoming the commitment of the DES to ensure that teachers have high levels of literacy and numeracy, the CRE urged that 'English tests should be designed to avoid cultural bias' as what needs to be tested is literacy skills, not a particular set of culturally specific knowledge; and that the requirement for GCSE Mathematics, Science and English should be spelt out very clearly, so that students understand that equivalents and institutional tests are available as appropriate alternatives (CRE 1992). With regard to recruiting teachers from the minority ethnic groups, the CRE believed that minority ethnic groups were under-represented in the teaching profession (Ranger 1988), and was concerned that in 1986 only 2.6 percent of students in their final year of teacher training were of minority ethnic origin. It was also concerned that the largest education authority in Britain with 23,000 teachers in post, had a total of 23 teachers of minority ethnic origin.

The new Labour policies

The policies of the current Labour Government consider it vital that teachers should be equipped to understand the issues confronting them in the classroom, and reflect constructively on their practice. They also promise to incorporate training on equal opportunities as one of the nine key competencies. However, there is no other mention of power of schooling in contributing to a socially just and egalitarian society. Though Labour's proposed policies were progressive, they were not explicitly radical. However, they recognised the value of developments and improvements in initial teacher training since the CATE criteria was introduced in 1984, and rejected the potential over-loading of the school staff by increasingly school-based models of teacher education, and believed that it would disrupt children's education. They also rejected the overloading of trainee teachers by regarding them as 'beginner teachers' instead of 'student teachers' who need time to reflect individually and collaboratively on their theoretical and practical experiences during the training. Labour policies accept some alternative routes into teaching (with proper piloting), but wish to support an all-graduate profession not differentiated or stratified by entrance qualifications that may lead to a two-tier teaching profession. Some examples of the way Labour policies have resulted in encouraging developments are given below:

DfEE Circular 4/98 – Teaching: high status, high standards

In 1997, the TTA worked closely with teachers, teacher trainers and others with interest and expertise in the field, to develop national Standards for the Award of Qualified Teacher Status (QTS). The QTS standards aim to ensure that all new teachers, wherever and through whichever route they train, are able to teach effectively from their first day in the classroom, so that all pupils benefit from high standards of teaching, have access to the curriculum and are motivated to achieve their full potential. Those achieving QTS will have the knowledge, understanding and skills necessary to secure high standards of achievement for all pupils, as well as improving the quality of their education and their experience of schooling. Some QTS standards are key to raising the achievement of particular groups of pupils, including minority ethnic groups. The Standards also aim to ensure that all new teachers know how to equip pupils with the experience and understanding they need to play their part in a socially just society, including through appropriate moral, cultural, social and spiritual development.

GTC Code of Professional Values and Practice for Teachers

The General Teaching Council (GTC) has also developed a Code of Practice, which sets out the beliefs, values and attitudes that make up teacher professionalism. It shows that teachers use high levels of individual judgement and skill to meet the challenges of their profession. It recognises that teachers work within a framework of legislation with many lines of accountability. The complicated and varied roles that teachers need to fulfil make teaching one of the most demanding and rewarding professions. The Code requires teachers to ensure the positive development of individual pupils, and to work within a framework of equal opportunities and other relevant legislation, statutory guidance and school policies. Within this framework, teachers challenge stereotypes and oppose prejudice to safeguard equality of opportunity, respecting individuals regardless of gender, marital status, religion, colour, race, ethnicity, class, sexual orientation, disability and age.

Raising the attainment of ethnic minority pupils (TTA 2000)

This guidance and resource material has been produced by the TTA, in collaboration with the Commission for Racial Equality, representatives of the Advisory Group on Raising the Achievement of Ethnic Minority Pupils, the Runnymede Trust, Ofsted, teacher trainers, LEA advisers, headteachers, teachers and many others with expertise in this field. The main focus of this guidance is on preparing trainee teachers to understand and meet the educational needs of minority ethnic pupils. However, the guidance should be seen in the wider context of a concern for social justice for all, and the principles underlying it as more widely applicable and having implications for promoting the educational inclusion of other groups and for the education of all pupils. Many of the issues and examples outlined can be used and built upon to inform good educational practice for all pupils. This guidance does not specify a course design. It does not purport to offer a comprehensive list of the issues, nor are ITT providers expected to include all the examples in their training. It does not replace the Standards for the Award of QTS, or introduce new requirements for ITT providers. This guidance is intended to help ITT providers in schools and in Higher Education Institutions (HEIs), help their trainees to:

- Understand how inequality operates structurally, institutionally and culturally as well as at a personal level;
- Understand the main issues relating to the differential performance in schooling of some groups of minority ethnic pupils;
- Know some of the ways in which successful teachers and schools work to raise pupil attainment and the quality of their education and prepare all pupils to live in a socially just, democratic, pluralist society;
- Know how to employ in their own practice, strategies that are effective in raising the attainment of minority ethnic pupils and which improve the quality of their education;
- Know where to go to find additional information and support;
- Develop critical attitudes in dealing with information and assumptions about minority ethnic groups.

Much good practice in raising the attainment of minority ethnic pupils requires a whole school commitment. The section on Inclusive schools emphasises that trainee teachers need to understand the important part, which schools can play in contributing to the development of a socially just, inclusive society. They should be alert to the ways in which, intended or not, the structures, procedures, practices and culture of the education system can exclude or disadvantage some groups, including minority ethnic pupils. Every trainee teacher needs to understand the part he or she must play in providing an education which enables all pupils to realise their full potential; and preparing all pupils to play a full part in a culturally diverse, democratic society which values everybody and accords them equal rights.

The New Right and Teacher Education

The development of various Thatcherite think tanks has had considerable influence on Government policy for teacher education. The neo-liberal and neo-conservative strands within the new Right thinking have both been producing a spate of newspaper columns and pamphlets in the last 20 years and have served to undermine confidence in teacher education institutions. The central thrust of their criticism has been that initial teacher training courses place too little emphasis on the learning of subject knowledge and on classroom skills; and too much emphasis is placed on the wrong type of educational theory. They also accuse courses of being obsessed with 'race' and inequality; and of being informed by a spurious neo-Marxist view of culture and that they produce students who have no respect for traditional values. Anthony O'Hear (1988), in making a connection between the academic success of the leading independent schools and their tendency to employ untrained graduates as teachers, implies that teacher-training courses actually diminish the effectiveness of teachers. Sheila Lawler has further claimed that teacher training undermines the subject specialisms of graduates who enter teaching (Lawler 1990).

A recurring theme in the New Right publications is the need to remove from the education system establishments and individuals who are liberal in their thinking and are seen to have been responsible for the 'progressive collapse' of the English educational system. The critics of teacher training institutions who called for the abolition of B.Ed. and PGCE courses in favour of an apprenticeship route for training teachers have failed to notice the illogical assumptions underlying such a suggestion. Today's schoolteachers, who are the products of 'trendy teacher training of the 1960s', are not likely to be best equipped to teach new teachers. This would simply replicate the problem. Furthermore, since HMI reports found the work of experienced teachers no more satisfactory than that of newly trained ones, in practical terms (let alone ideological orientation) schools could hardly be entrusted with the training of teachers. The practical problems are in fact far more significant than the actual shift in policy. School-based training would require significant changes in the structure of the teaching profession and the culture of schooling. Dennis O'Keefe (1990) criticised the theory and practice of 'progressive' teacher education and made a case for revival of 'traditional' education by denouncing the 'cult of school based political equality'. It suggested that 'our society has been partly undermined by the belief that childhood is more important than knowledge, and equality more significant than excellence, in the arrangements we contrive for the education of our citizens' (O'Keefe 1990). Whilst supporting the revival of proper subjects, the emphasis on 'practical' experts and a move from education theory to methods is criticised not because there is anything wrong with the conceptual analysis but because of a fear of so called politicised practitioners and the ideologies underlying the content of methods courses.

It has been suggested that though the central Government has accepted that something is wrong with our teacher education, it has not understood the cause and nature of its downfall, which in O'Keefe's view has to do with the subject matter. He thinks it is due to a collapse of faith in our institutions and faith of life combined with the adoption of what he describes as a 'set of sentimental and strident campaigns about "race", gender and culture'. He accuses the contemporary radical disposition of celebrating the person and his rights but deprecating individual responsibilities and of pursuing flatulent and intellectually lifeless multi-culturalism. He then goes on to attack almost every one concerned with the education including the DES and HMIs, and accusing them of neglecting the maintenance of traditional standards in education and of allowing the education system to become essentially socialist. However his analysis of what is alleged to be wrong with our education system is different from that of other right-wing authors. The unparalleled scale of current legislation for educational change is not likely to necessarily change the system for the better and with that this author can certainly agree. In defining the nature of educational crisis O'Keefe attempts to address the core of the claims made in the DES consultation document of May 1989. The argument put forward by O'Keefe in defining the intellectual crisis is that if wrong notions of what it means to be educated have been transmitted for years, more practice is actually likely to make matters worse. He also suggests that it is much better to concentrate on the transmission of knowledge than on fantasies about training.

He considers facilitating individual learning experiences in the classroom to be as wrong as telling the kids in Brent that the British are a racist lot. In his view the Government has refused to recognise the crisis in teacher education i.e. the belief that the malaise is indeed a practical one and that more assessment, more teachers with recent experience and more practical know-how will solve the crisis. Indeed there are many who will agree with him but not necessarily agree with his analysis of what is wrong with teacher education. His attack on ideological socialism and his call for private examinations, private schools and private institutions of educational evaluation and research are no less ideological than the Marxist theories that he is so critical of. Dennis O'Keefe is apparently so worried about what he describes as the 'hate cults of anti-racism, anti-sexism and multi-culturalism' and the egalitarianism of teacher education courses that it makes one wonder which teacher education institutions he is referring to. If the evidence of various HMI reports and the voices of student teachers is anything to go by, such institutions are rare. However, it is heartening that the minimal pursuit of equality issues has had such an effect on the extreme right that it makes authors like O'Keefe come out with statements like, 'Equality in education is as daft as equality in supermarkets. There is no such thing and there is never going to be'.

It also raises questions about his understanding of the meaning of the term 'equality' and his vociferous but unsubstantiated statements that 'pursuit of equality has forced standards down and that teachers have allowed the pursuit of equality at the expense of efficiency' (The Wayward Elite) are as meaningless as his constant reference to 'race', gender and culture as hateful creeds. Not only does he offer no analysis or reasons for dismissing the issues of 'race' gender and culture as undesirable, but also he acknowledges that they are powerful cults because they have 'managed extraordinarily well to present themselves in a depoliticised form'. He also acknowledges that these campaigns are not evil at root. To quote, 'they are not in themselves evil, that is to say in their inspirational essence.... it is their expansion and their intolerance which are evil'.

One could argue that it is the intolerance of the extreme Right that is evil especially when on the one hand it seeks to affirm 'that prejudice against people on grounds of their race or sex is cruel, unjust and Philistine', but on the other hand objects to any attempts to remove such prejudices even when the attempts are as mild as statements in the DES consultation document of 1989, 'students should learn to guard against preconceptions based on the race, gender or other attributes of pupils' (DES 1989, Section 6 Para iv). This is described as 'indoctrinary litany' on the grounds that teacher education courses cannot possibly recruit students who might have such preconceptions. The DES is accused of complicity with the 'equality-pimps', and the central Conservative Government is blamed for letting the DES officials get away with it. It is O'Keefe's confusion about what is it that he is really unhappy about, that invalidates most of his criticism. Is it the abandonment of theory, or the adoption of child-centred ideology, the egalitarian lobby, or the under-achievement, or perhaps the failure of the education system that is really the root of the problem? He is not in support of the extreme Right's arguments for school-based teacher education either, because in his view more of the same will only make matters worse. However he fails to actually spell out what his brand of traditional education is really about apart from wanting it to be intellectually sound and by that he means it has to be only about *British culture and British intellect and British history* (my emphasis).

Response from the Left to attacks on teacher education

Anthony O'Hear (1988) believes that practical skills of teaching are important but that the theoretical understanding of education is irrelevant. He argues for the expansion of the Articled Teachers' Route, giving more responsibility for training to teachers already in schools. He considers an emphasis on issues of 'race' and equality as unhealthy and suggests that curriculum should not be used to tackle inequalities because according to him 'in practice it usually means watering it down to suit the less than equal' (O'Hear 1988). 'Learning To Teach' (1989) has a similar conception of the nature of teaching. It also argues for the expansion of the apprenticeship route suggesting that competition between different routes to QTS should lead to improvements in PGCE and B.Ed. courses and to a better use of resources. Theory and sociology of education are attacked in this paper as 'irrelevance and bias'. Teachers Mistaught (1990) again attacks the notion that teachers need to study educational theory. The author makes no detailed policy proposals but simply calls for the abolition of teacher education courses and for their replacement by on-the-job training. All the critiques of the extreme Right (except one by O'Keefe) seem to be anti-theory. They have in common a firm anti-egalitarian rhetoric. They see the fundamental job of a teacher as the ability to transmit knowledge as a neutral concept. They all describe the current situation as that of crisis, though they don't necessarily agree on the nature of this crisis.

The view offered by the teacher is one of an individual who should not think beyond a particular subject, if s/he should think at all. Common inter-related themes of the radical Right are that the present college-based system of teacher education should be scrapped, and school-based, on-the-job, skill development should become a major method of teacher training. They argue that college-based teacher education is concerned too much with changing society and/or developing egalitarian perspectives on schooling and society. In particular, they are critical of a model of the multicultural and anti-racist teacher, of the progressive and child-centred-ideology of teacher education and suggest that there is no need for educational theory to be included in the training of teachers. The political and professional response to such attacks has been patchy and very mixed. The call for greater partnership between colleges, schools and LEAs and the call for greater reflectiveness between theory and practice has been echoed within the profession thus leading to more demand for on-the-job training. As far as defending issues of equality and social justice is concerned, there have been few coherent and organised responses. It may be that in the absence of any researched evidence for claims that training colleges are staffed by left-wing extremists, a dignified silence is the best option. Alan Weeks's survey of his colleagues during 15 years in an education department certainly found no such evidence. He concluded that 'It is a joke to imagine education lecturers corrupting teacher training students, most of whom have little interest in educational theory beyond passing the relevant examination in it' (TES Oct 91).

Ian Menter (1992) traced the thinking of the New Right and its impact on recent policy proposals for teacher education. He made reference to the two significant, and closely related, components of the New Right thinking, namely the economic and the ideological, and their influence within the Education Reform Act. On the economic front, proposals for Open Enrolment and Local Management of Schools are a clear example of such influence and on the ideological side the emphasis on

'National' in the National Curriculum and the legislation on Religious Education, together with debates around the content of National Curriculum, and the notable absence of any reference to issues of equality and social justice, witness a distinctly ethnocentric view of what counts as acceptable knowledge and understanding. The Hill-Cole group offers an avowedly leftist critique of the radical right and their policies. The Imaginative Project Group (Hextall et al 1991) described by Dave Hill as being left of the centre, has taken a less polemic and more professional approach. The argument in this publication is that teaching is highly skilled work and that current difficulties can only be overcome by good quality teachers. It takes on board the language of teaching competencies and seeks to reconcile this with a notion of reflective teaching. The writers analyse the radical Right's attack on teacher education and current developments in initial teacher education. Although it is a valuable contribution offering a clear rationalisation of reflective teacher education, it is limited in the sense that it does not develop a critical area of socio-political reflection.

Another left of the centre group convened by Jean Ruddock and David Bridges known as The Future of Teacher Training Writing Group has the support of at least ten Polytechnic and University signatories. The aims of this group are to defend and advance a view of teachers as intelligent thinking practitioners; to value the distinctive contribution schools can make to the training in partnership with HE; to disentangle some of the confusion surrounding the relationship between the quality of initial training and retention of teachers and the mismatch between the nature of training and actual jobs being done by teachers; to challenge and correct the myths about teacher training being dissociated from practical experience propagated by the 'raving right' and to demonstrate their (teacher trainers') capacity to think and work creatively to improve the quality of initial training. Their collaborative intentions are worthwhile, but like the Imaginative Projects Group, they are not explicitly concerned with the development of 'critical, reflective, transformative intellectuals'. They also do not appear to be concerned with developing or maintaining the egalitarian ethos of teacher education courses.

The response from the radical Left is strongly influenced by the anti-racist, anti-sexist and anti-homophobic grassroots activism of the left in 1980s. What is Left in Teacher Education (Hill 1991) goes beyond criticising current Right wing attack on British teacher education, which has taken the form of ferocious, sustained ideological assault at three inter-related levels of discourse. These include the radical Right ideologists, think tanks and academics; the radical Right media (in particular the Daily Mail and Mail on Sunday); and the Conservative education ministerial team (mid-1991 onwards). A specific example was the mid-1991 attack on Culloden Primary School, leading to the controversy on Reading Methods, and to the proposals for de-theorising teacher education and for making it more school-based and school-focused.

Alternative proposals from the Left

'What is Left in Teacher Education' (1991) is not only a response from the radical left to the current assault at both polemical and academic levels, but also an attempt to offer a series of proposals and policies for the Labour Party to take on board. In brief, the Hill-Cole paper recommends policies to widen access; to extend the PGCE course to a two-year course with more school experience (similar to the UDE

Course at Manchester); scrap the Licensed Teacher Scheme but extend the two year B.Ed. courses; and keep the Articled Teacher Scheme with a 65/35 ratio of School/College experience. Many people in the profession will have some sympathy with Hill's argument for more school-based teacher education but without rejecting educational theory and issues of social justice and enabling students to have time and space to become reflective, critical and transformative practitioners. The Hill-Cole authors suggest that teacher education must encourage and facilitate the development of teachers who display civic courage in pursuing social justice and equal opportunities in the classroom, school and society. In their rejection of the total school-based initial teacher training they are not only defending the need for theory and critical reflection in teacher education, but also advocating the inclusion of social justice and egalitarianism in such reflection. Further discussion on the concept of the reflective practitioner can also be found in 'Black Under-Achievement in Initial Teacher Education', and 'The Citizen as Individual and Nationalist or 'Social' and Internationalist?' (both by Clay, Cole and Hill 1990).

According to Hill-Cole's ideological perspective initial teacher education should be aimed at the development of teachers as critical 'transformative intellectuals' and democratic participative professionals and citizens. It should also be about the development of effective classroom skilled teachers able to critically inter-relate theory and practice and should be based on the theory of teaching and learning, both at macro and micro level, in which the socio-political and economic context of schooling and education are made explicit. Finally, resistance to an entirely school-based teacher education is a central theme of their perspective on teacher education. This is not only to preserve the critical theoretical domain, which is justified in its own right, but also to break the inevitable cycle of perpetuating inequalities within the system. Research evidence 'Education For Some' (1986) suggests that many teachers continue to make important decisions about the organisation, orientation and delivery of the formal and informal curriculum on grounds that are racist, sexist and discriminatory. It is suggested that an entirely school-based system of teacher education could well reproduce such discriminatory practices in a systematic way and without giving them the opportunity to articulate reasons for contesting some of the taken-for-granted assumptions about certain groups of pupils.

'Investing in Quality' (1991) also suggested that the Government's proposals for reform of initial teacher education with all its objectives, pedagogy, structuring and citing should be challenged, but that it should be challenged on the basis of research findings and proper consultation with the profession and the providers of such training. Though not radical, these proposals offered an alternative, which was not designed to suppress liberal and egalitarian view on schooling and society. They included:

- National curriculum for initial teacher education to apply to all routes of entry; to integrate and develop equal opportunities for children in schools in such a way that no child suffers from the damaging consequences of labelling, under-expectation, stereotyping and prejudiced attitudes of teachers and peers.
- More school based training than is currently available on initial teacher training courses, but not to the degree proposed by the Government for Secondary PGCE and for Licensed and Articled teachers.
- Closer integration of school based and college based initial teacher training; more meaningful co-operation and partnership between schools and teacher

training institutions over course design and student assessment, but not as suggested by Kenneth Clarke, putting teachers in the lead role. The message from wider consultation was that the schools did not wish to be in the lead. They clearly expressed their wish to reassert their primary objectives to be the teaching of children, not training teachers, and they expressed a concern that a higher profile in partnership will not be accompanied by sufficient resources to enable them to deliver.

- Structured programme of induction which relates both to ITT and subsequent professional development.
- Incorporation of training on equal opportunities *so* that trainee teachers from all routes of entry receive training both in their initial training and subsequent professional development.
- Continuation of CATE to be responsible for supervision of these reforms, and be assisted in that by the Inspectorate organised through Labour's proposed Education Standards Commission.

The response from ARTEN

Anti-Racist Teacher Education Network (ARTEN) was established in 1983 and was initially facilitated by the Commission For Racial Equality. Its origins lie in the concerns that individuals working to implement anti-racist strategies in their own institutions were increasingly isolated. The Network aims to assist in the implementation, monitoring and evaluation of anti-racist strategies at all levels of teacher education and to seek support of people in teacher training institutions and in the wider communities for this purpose. Though teacher-training institutions have themselves been reluctant to support the network, and occasionally there has been direct opposition to its objectives, the membership of 350 individuals (teachers, trainers, educationalists, researchers and administrators in education with a considerable expertise) does indicate a level of direct and indirect support from a range of institutions. In terms of its activities ARTEN network has responded to the attacks on teacher education in various ways and contributed extensively by responding to a range of discussion documents from the Government and by commenting on drafts of policy papers issued by agencies concerned with inspection, validation and accreditation of teacher education courses. In response to Clarke's speech and the Consultation document, ARTEN was concerned that heavily school-based courses may deny the students an opportunity to benefit from an academic and professional expertise and environment of training institutions. It also considered the proposals to use independent schools for purposes of training with considerable scepticism, especially since such schools are not bound by the strictures of National Curriculum, an area in which core competencies of new teachers are likely to be of primary concern. In terms of professional competencies, ARTEN believes that many schools and teachers lack the necessary expertise to equip student teachers with the skills to recognise factors that disadvantage many pupils and do not have a clear understanding of the conditions that generate all forms of oppression and have not been themselves equipped with strategies and skills to counter these oppressions. It is hard to imagine such teachers training student teachers to guard against their prejudices and teach equitably in a multiracial and multi-cultural society.

ARTEN regretted the omission from CATE criteria of any reference to multicultural education and equal opportunities and feared that it could be seen as a

weakening in the Government's resolve to see that education has a crucial part to play in promoting a fairer and just society. The CATE criteria does require that 'all students are prepared to teach the full range of pupils they are likely to encounter in an ordinary school, with their diversity of ability, behaviour, social background and ethnic and cultural origin'. ARTEN has therefore suggested a set of core competencies, which should form a basis of measuring teacher qualities. These include a sound knowledge of the Race Relations Act (1976) and of the Sex Discrimination Act (1975) and their implications for the education of children; ability to deal effectively with incidents of racial and sexual harassment; ability to support the whole language development of bilingual and bidialectal pupils; ability to develop and deliver cross-curricular aspects of the National Curriculum in ways that relate to an understanding of racism and sexism; and the ability to make fair and equal judgments and to promote achievement of all children within diverse classrooms (ARTEN 1993).

School-Based Teacher Education

HMI Report on School-Based Teacher Education (1992) underlined the need for strong and clearly understood links between higher education tutors, their students and the teachers who are helping to train them. The report says that too often in the past schools involved in teacher training have been left unclear about their role. The schools have lacked the resources and teachers have lacked the time to carry out their training tasks effectively. Both have often felt that they were poor relations alongside training institutions. The issues discussed in the report and its findings are therefore firmly in favour of a more equal partnership between school, teachers and tutors in training institutions. The report acknowledges that the concept of school-based training rests on more than just time spent in schools and that its success depends on the quality of the relationship between the training institution and the school, the significant involvement of teachers in the planning, supervision and assessment of the students' training and the active involvement of tutors in supporting the students' work in schools.

The Report also recognises that schools and teachers need to be carefully chosen for more intensive involvement in training and that in the case of primary training there are major constraints to be overcome. The three principles entwined in the proposals argue for more time to be spent by students in schools, an expanded role for the profession in the training of teachers and for financial compensation for schools who carry the burden of students on teaching practice. On the surface of it these are sound principles but they are based on a small sample of Articled Teachers' Scheme, which located 81 percent of course time in schools. However, it has demonstrated that when extra resources are provided, school-based training can be extended effectively. The intensive use of fewer teaching schools is also likely to reduce the profession's contribution to training, not increase it.

On the whole the proposals for school-based training and increased partnership with schools were welcomed by the profession. However, there was also strong support for the HMI view that 'the prime purpose of schools, and the one to which governors and head teachers give priority, is to teach pupils, not train students' and that 'Higher education institutions provide an academic and professional expertise which is crucial in the support both of individual students and of schools' (HMI

1992). There are also a growing number of head teachers refusing to let their schools be used for classroom-based teacher training unless they are paid double the rates currently offered by the training institutions. The reforms introduced by Circular 14/93, such as reduced higher education institution (HEI) teaching time by increasing the time students spend in schools from 20 to 32 weeks on four year B.Ed. courses and from 15 to 18 weeks for PGCE primary courses, required a closer partnership between HEIs and schools in order to manage the new arrangements; introduced competences expected of newly qualified teachers; allowed alternative routes to Qualified Teacher Status (QTS).

The Head of Didsbury School of Education drew attention to the rhetoric that may not resemble the reality. Whilst acknowledging a fairly reassuring pattern of future development which takes on board the continuation of an award for all qualifying teachers, and of the role of CATE in accreditation of courses and the establishment of the principle that schools and HE institutions will need to enter a quasi-contractual relationship, thereby ending the 'grace and favour' element, he drew attention to the unanswered questions such as the reaction of unions to the proposed reforms, the reaction of parents and governors to the intensive use of schools for the purposes of training and the training of 'mentors' in schools. The ways forward suggested included a consideration of financial support for schools selected for the purposes of training, the need for training the trainers (school teachers), strengthening the formal role of schools' responsibilities for teacher training to ensure increased status and active involvement and to provide for the monitoring and inspection of school-based schemes.

Comments and Summary

The proposed changes to initial teacher education are essentially about conformity to right wing ideology and control of what teachers should teach. DFE circular 9/92 for Initial Teacher Training (Secondary Phase) was very much an extension of a competitive, selective, divisive and meritocratic version of schooling which displaces and ignores issues of social justice, which erodes critical pedagogy and views teaching as a craft which can best be picked up by attachment to practitioners. It is not surprising therefore that the Circular is couched in technical-rationalist terms and is set in a completely de-racialised discourse, setting aside all ethical, moral, social and political issues. Anti-racism is simply not in the picture and the tokenist recognition of diversity is merely an acknowledgement. As such Circular 9/92 is one more set piece of reforming legislation, which is intended to further discipline teacher education.

The HMI report on Initial Teacher Training (HMI 1991) only gave a cautious welcome to school focused work but saw a need for the 'essential knowledge and experience from higher education'. The report added that 'the main challenge in initial training is bringing these two kinds of essential expertise together in the most effective way'. What is also crucial for the success of such partnership is a fundamental recognition of the need for transfer of funds, in-service education and reciprocal placements of staff from schools and colleges as equal partners. The concept of equal partnership is endorsed by the Labour Party document, which also proposes a cluster of schools to be used as 'teacher training schools', a suggestion that is not readily acceptable to the profession. The interim report of the Modes of

Teacher Education Project (MOTE) (Barrett 1992) suggests that partnership between higher Education institutions and schools varies according to the different elements of the course, for example, there may be greater involvement in the subject application in the classroom and in school experience aspect of the course than in the subject studies at academic level and in the issues surrounding professional development in a wider societal context.

The report of 'Three Wise Men' (1992) and the ensuing conservative response was an attempt to move hidden curriculum away from child-centred, collaborative, inter-disciplinary group work. The content and methodology of initial teacher education is also being reconstituted along similar lines by attempts to de-professionalise teachers and to turn them into 'technical transmitters of a received national curriculum with its underlying (conservative) values' (Hill 1992). All this is done in the name of improving 'standards'. But this is not really about 'standards' at all. It is more likely about control of children's minds by removing all reference to egalitarianism and emphasising not only 'back to basics' but 'back to chalk and talk' with traditional streaming by ability and 'back to whole class teaching' with virtual doubling of class size. The cross-curricular themes of citizenship, economic and industrial understanding and multi-culturalism have been either completely suppressed or are virtually non-existent in operational terms.

The radical Right's perspective on initial teacher education blames teachers for everything that is wrong with the society, the inner-city riots, lager-louts, disrespect for authority, drugs, permissiveness, cultural relativism, anti-racism, anti-sexism, anti-homophobia. Naturally somebody is to blame for these teachers. The Daily Mail (1982) blames the 'second generation education in the comprehensive over the last two decades, stimulated by "well-meaning but malignant philosophies" of trendy teachers coming out of training colleges with half-baked ideas on mixed ability teaching, egalitarianism, and the abolition of corporal punishment and classroom discipline' (Daily Mail 1982). The excessive phobia amongst the extreme Right about Teacher Education Institutions is absurdly common, as is evident from the following quotations. Teacher Education Institutions are, 'obsessed with inequality, with Racism and other passing political fashions' (O'Hear 1988); 'for preventing and reproduction of nationalism by the constant reform of the curriculum [which] has undermined the attempt to preserve, enhance and pass on the precious heritage of our culture' (Hillgate group 1986); 'too many teacher trainers are more interested in radically changing society than in preparing students for the demanding career ahead of them (Shaw 1990) and 'for propagating the deadly cult of school based political equality' (O'Keefe 1990).

What is really interesting is that the attack on teacher education is so clearly directed at this perceived egalitarianism which is supposedly being practised in such abundance throughout the country, yet it is hard to find any evidence of such practices in HMI reports or in the practices on teacher education courses. In addition to the explicit attack on theory in initial teacher education, attack on the quality of new teachers and an attack on the progressive liberal ideology of the Left, the Right wing model of teacher education argues for an application of competitive market forces by offering a multiplicity of routes into teaching and by semi-privatisation of initial teacher education, whereby schools train their own future teachers.

The school-based models of initial teacher education have not been received very favourably, though there is some agreement within the profession about the need for some increase in the school-based dimension of teacher education programmes and the need for a closer, clearer and more equal partnership not only between schools and teacher training institutions, but also between teacher trainers and student teachers. In this context, the notion of a 'student charter' is certainly a welcome move, whereby rights of students extend from recruitment procedures to learning environment, ethos, curriculum and modes of assessment, so as to allow students to experience teacher education in the broadest context possible to meet their needs as future teachers in a multiracial society. As John Baker said: 'but equality is not an end in itself. It only matters because of its effect on people's lives...and how we relate to each other in "private" either supports or challenges the way power and privileges are structured in society as a whole.... Equality is concerned not just with the structure of whole societies, but also with human relationships in general' (Baker 1987).

There is thus a case to be made for multiple routes in to teaching, especially those that are likely to enhance partnership with schools and improve the quality of teachers. The focus on development of appropriate competencies is certainly a welcome move, especially in view of the growth of multiple routes to QTS. Professor Whitty's (1991) proposals for competency-based approach also recognise the importance of under-pinning knowledge and understanding and generic professional competence as well as specific classroom skills. The notion of exit competencies which can be applied to multiple routes and used as a basis for further professional development makes a lot of sense and is most likely to happen through a training partnership between schools, LEAs and higher education institutions. Professor Whitty, whilst not favouring the notion of teaching schools (these might create elite schools), advocates a consortium approach (similar to the one for the UDE course in Manchester) which can allow one to plan for and support a range of experiences for all trainees and makes a case for few professional development schools which offer facilities for specialist aspects of initial training, further professional development and research. Further discussion of employment based routes and partnership with schools is included in chapter 5.

My last words in this chapter are to remind teachers that they have a responsibility to help achieve the society that the Home Secretary wanted when he was speaking to Black teenagers on 17th March 1999:

Wherever we come from, whatever our roots, or our faith, we have a stake in being British and we can be proud of that. Celebrating diversity and building a fairer, more confident multicultural nation with a fresh, strong sense of national identity is an important and timely project. Having confidence in yourself and holding on to a dream of what you can achieve is so important. Nothing should hold you back in reaching your full potential. I want a society that gives you these chances, a society where each of you, regardless, of colour or race or religion has an equal opportunity to succeed. It is your future and we need to hear from you (Home Secretary 1999).

Chapter 4

Minority Ethnic Participation in Teaching

Introduction

The recruitment and promotion of teachers from minority ethnic groups is not only an aspect of elementary justice in itself, it is also essential to the development of progressive education. One of the factors that hold back minority children is the witting and unwitting low expectations of many White teachers. In the absence of teachers from minority groups such bias cannot be fully overcome. Without positive action and monitoring the crisis will intensify, with fewer and fewer minority ethnic children getting the necessary education to be able to go on and train as teachers, thereby prolonging and recreating the vicious cycle for generations to come. This chapter offers an overview of minority ethnic participation in the teaching profession. It starts with an overview of literature in this respect and includes sections on training and participation of minority ethnic teachers in schools, presence of minority ethnic staff in teacher training institutions; recruitment of minority ethnic students on initial teacher training courses. It also includes a discussion of issues of concern and ends with practical suggestions for improving training and supply of minority ethnic teachers.

Background and Overview of Literature

Up to the mid 1970s 'immigrant' and minority ethnic teachers were assumed to have been trained abroad rather than by qualifying through attendance at teacher training courses in Britain. During the 1960s the teacher shortage in the UK led the Ministry of Labour to issue employment vouchers, letters of 'invitation to seek employment' to overseas teachers (Commonwealth Immigration Act 1962) and the teacher training institutions to set up courses for qualified teachers to improve their English and knowledge of the British education system. However the LEAs were reluctant to employ teachers from minority ethnic groups and even when they did find employment many were subsequently in trouble during their probationary year. On the other hand the need for such teachers had been clearly identified and the Select Committee For Race Relations and Immigration, had hoped that, 'education authorities in all parts of the country will look for more coloured teachers, and that they will be widely employed' (DES 1969 Recommendation xxix).

A CRE survey in 1970 showed that only 3 LEAs believed it was good for the schools to have such teachers, mainly on the grounds that multiracial schools should have multiracial staff. One authority believed this to be a very bad idea on the ground that, 'these teachers usually experience a discipline problem'. One in three authorities believed that children from minority ethnic groups benefit from having teachers of familiar culture or colour either in terms of help with problems of language and culture adaptation or in terms of identification. The majority of LEAs stated that they saw no special reason to employ such staff. The CRE survey also mentioned two institutions (Edgehill and Wolverhampton) that offered full-time in-service courses for practicing teachers and six institutions that were planning to offer courses for qualified teachers from overseas. But it was not possible for teachers from overseas to be considered for these courses unless they had been granted Qualified Teacher Status (QTS) by the DES. In other words, these full-time courses of 15 months duration were not courses of initial teacher education, but refresher courses for teachers from overseas, who were already qualified and may have had many years of teaching experience in Britain or overseas.

A DES survey (1971) reported that there was no accurate estimate of the number of minority ethnic teachers of 'immigrant' origin who had been able to obtain QTS and subsequent employment. However it did mention the development of four-term courses designed to meet the needs of minority ethnic teachers holding QTS. By 1971 there were 15 courses on offer at six different centres, training some 320 students. Though minority ethnic teachers attending these courses were carefully selected to minimize the risk of failure, there were some who failed to stay the course or pass probation satisfactorily. The DES concluded that most minority ethnic teachers attending these courses had been helped to settle to a useful professional life in the UK.

The Association of Teachers in Colleges and Departments of Education (ATCDE) drew attention to the advantages of 'immigrants' as teachers and explained some of the difficulties of their recruitment as students; and the Select Committee on Race Relations and Immigration (1973) had acknowledged that like the DES it did not have any figures for the number of minority ethnic teachers employed. However, in spite of having noted the virtual absence of applicants on teacher education courses (one or two out of 1200 were Asians at Edge Hill College), the Select Committee did not think it fit to make any recommendations for recruiting, training and employing teachers from the minority ethnic groups in the UK. In the same year, Townsend and Brittan reported that a total of 38 out of 132 primary schools had employed teachers who were reported to be from the countries of origin of 'immigrant' pupils. In the secondary schools the figure was higher. A total of 46 schools out of 98 had members of staff who were identified as from the countries of origin of 'immigrant' pupils. The total number of teachers of 'immigrant' origin in these 84 schools in an NFER survey was 142, but only 35 of these were reported to be employed to teach mainly 'immigrant' pupils (Townsend & Brittan 1973). A year later, the policy paper published by the CRC (1974) made a recommendation that Colleges and Departments of Education should make a direct effort to attract as many Black students as have the qualifications and aptitude for teacher training. The educational justifications offered for increasing the number of minority ethnic teachers ranged from their contribution to the education service as role models, helping pupils and colleagues through direct contribution in bridging the gaps in linguistic and cultural understandings to improving relations between minority and majority groups in the school community. The Green Paper (1977a) also made reference to the value, for the schools, of a flow of entrants to teaching who have broad and diverse experiences and interests, in particular those who are from minority ethnic groups and recognized that the education service will need to encourage more young people from the minority ethnic groups to enter teaching and offer special courses of teacher education for mature students.

The recommendations of the CRC/ATCDE report (1974) and of the Select Committee Report (DES 1973) and of the Green Paper (DES 1977a) were further echoed by the Rampton Committee in 1981. Gibbs (1980) reported that minority ethnic teachers, mostly West Indian, experienced difficulties within the school system. They not only had stressful experiences in obtaining and keeping a teaching job but also felt discriminated against in job promotion. The experiences of 27 West Indian teachers in London schools indicated that half of them were on lowest pay scales in spite of several years of classroom experience. Some had made over 20 attempts to obtain promotion. They felt that they had a significant contribution to make in the education of all children but inadequate support from the local authorities and failure to obtain promotion led to low morale and their subsequent departure from the profession. A survey conducted by the Society of Immigrant Teachers (1980) also showed that 60 percent of minority group teachers were on the lowest scale and that they were frequently denied promotion because of their colour. They were also subject to more stringent checks during their probation and had experienced disproportionately higher rate of failure during their training. Little & Willey (1981) indicated that a disproportionately small number of minority ethnic teachers were employed. They were also most likely to be employed in schools with a concentration of minority ethnic pupils. A number of LEAs and schools commented that they wanted to recruit teachers from minority ethnic groups. The Home Affairs Committee (1981) recognised that there were at the time disproportionately few minority ethnic teachers and it was important to increase their number because 'their presence on the staff of multiracial schools is worth a mass of lessons in African or Asian history' (Para 134). The Committee deplored the inability of LEAs to recruit minority ethnic teachers and reported on the introduction of Access courses, the only policy response from the central Government to the widespread recognition of the need for minority ethnic teachers. Subsequent HMI reports and DES Circulars for example, The New Teacher in School (DES 1982c), Teaching in Schools: The Content of Initial Training (DES 1983a), the White Paper on Teaching Quality (DES 1983b) and DES Circular 3/84 for Approval of Courses made little if any reference to the needs of minority ethnic groups in schools or indeed to their presence in schools as teachers or in colleges as students and as teacher trainers. The White Paper (1983) did however suggest that recruitment to teacher training courses should include 'people with broad and diverse backgrounds, experience and interests, including some from the minority ethnic groups' (DES 1983b). Guidelines for Voluntary Colleges (1984) also recommended that 'colleges should positively seek to recruit all staff and students from a wide range of cultural and racial background' and also acknowledged the need to provide appropriate support structures for students, staff development for tutors and to introduce monitoring procedures. Newham Asian Teachers' Association (1985) found that though there were 102 Asian teachers in the Borough (just over 5 percent) out of a total teaching force of 1850, there were no Asian teachers in any senior position in the Borough's schools.

The Swann Report

It was the publication of the Swann Report (1985) that led to a spate of consultation
and discussion documents to address the issue of under-representation of minority
ethnic groups in the teaching profession. The Swann Committee endorsed the view
that some minority ethnic teachers can play a particularly valuable 'pastoral' role
both directly, through supporting and encouraging pupils, and indirectly, through
advising their colleagues on the backgrounds and concerns of minority ethnic
groups. The Report made several recommendations concerned with the employment
of minority ethnic teachers, some of these were directed at the DES for clarifying
the arrangements for granting QTS and to commission research to examine the
experience of former 'Access' students in obtaining teaching qualifications and
subsequent employment. The Swann Committee regarded the under-representation
of minority ethnic groups in the teaching profession as a matter of great concern and
urged both the CRE and those involved within LEAs and the schools in making
appointments to devote far greater efforts to identifying and overcoming racist
obstacles to the employment and advancement of minority ethnic teachers. The
Swann Report also believed the minority ethnic pupils currently in schools to be the
most important potential source of minority ethnic teachers in the future, and
suggested that minority ethnic youngsters should be encouraged to consider
teaching as a career.

The White Paper 'Better Schools' (DES 1985d) was concerned with the findings
of the Swann Committee and expressed an agreement with its recommendation that
a 'larger proportion of the teaching force should be drawn from the minority ethnic
groups and that this increase can and should be secured without any reduction in the
required level of qualifications' (Swann Report, Para 207). The CRE welcomed the
Swann Committee's call for ethnic monitoring to gather statistics on the employment
position of minority group teachers and fully supported the Committee's comments
regarding the development of 'Access' courses. But the CRE did not fully support the
Committee's view that minority ethnic teachers should be employed as 'sources of
cultural expertise' or for pastoral roles. It felt that minority ethnic teachers should be
employed and accorded equal treatment because of their worth as qualified teachers,
and not merely as experts on race-relations. This view was also supported by
National Anti-racist Movement in Education (NAME) which was also critical of the
Swann Committee for not condemning racist practices in recruitment, employment
and remuneration of staff from minority ethnic groups and felt that it could have
made stronger recommendations for action to end racism and racial discrimination.
Black parents too were very critical of the way the Swann Committee outlined the
roles which could be assigned to minority ethnic teachers, for example as role models
for pupils from the same ethnic background, as pastoral support and as a valuable
resource with a knowledge and experience of other religions and cultures and
followed that up with a completely contradictory recommendation that minority
ethnic teachers should never be portrayed simply as token figures within a school
with just a 'curiosity' value or able only to undertake certain specific tasks. In their
view the Swann Report, whilst arguing for more Black teachers, viewed the role of
such teachers as putting the lid on racism, controlling the rebellion of Black
youngsters and making them dysfunctional and not supporting any Black teacher
who dares to challenge the racist practices within institutions.

However, the Government accepted the Swann Committee's findings that many minority ethnic pupils were achieving below their potential and recognized the concern that was felt about this among their parents. Consequently, the DES issued a consultation paper on 'Increasing the Supply of Minority ethnic Teachers' (1985b) with a view to explore, with the education service and the minority ethnic groups, which measures are most likely to increase the supply of qualified and suitable teachers of minority ethnic origin. The questions raised by the DES were about incidence of under-representation of minority ethnic groups in the teaching force, causes of under-representation and possible ways of improving the supply, as well as actions necessary to improve the situation. The rest of this chapter will address each of these questions in the context of available evidence of research and experience.

Incidence of Under-Representation

Minority ethnic teachers

According to CRE (Ranger 1988), of the total number of teachers (20246), only 2 percent (431) were of minority ethnic origin; of which 192 were male and 239 were female. The figures gathered by the DFE over a period of two years (1990-92) suggest that only 3.3 percent of full time teachers come from minority ethnic groups. This compares with estimates that 8 percent of pupils in schools and 5.5 percent of the total populations in Britain are of minority ethnic origin. The CRE survey concentrated on areas with above average minority ethnic populations in the hope that it would give a high number of minority ethnic teachers. A total of 401 teachers (190 minority ethnic groups and 211 white) were interviewed. The survey found that minority ethnic teachers were generally speaking older; 79 percent of white teachers were between the age of 25-44 as against 60 percent of minority ethnic groups, where as 36 percent of minority ethnic teachers were between 45-64, compared with only 19 percent of the white sample in the same age range.

The minority of ethnic teachers were found to be disproportionately on the lower scales, 78 percent of minority ethnic teachers were on scale 1 or 2, compared with 57 percent of White teachers. Conversely, only 5 percent of minority ethnic teachers were in deputy head or head teacher posts, compared with 13 percent of the White teachers. With regard to their presence in certain types of schools, certain phases of education and in certain school subjects, 29 percent of minority ethnic teachers taught mathematics or one of the science subjects, compared with 16 percent of the White teachers. There were roughly equal numbers (39 percent of the White and 40 of the minority ethnic) of teachers who taught in secondary comprehensive schools. Overall a higher number (80 percent of minority ethnic teachers and 74 percent of White teachers) taught in County schools. A much higher number of minority ethnic teachers (92 percent), taught in schools with no religious affiliation than White (79 percent) teachers; a much higher proportion of minority ethnic (15 percent) than White teachers (7 percent) taught in single-sex schools. Only 4 percent of White teachers taught in schools where there were 76 percent or more minority ethnic pupils, compared with 25 percent of minority ethnic teachers. Minority ethnic teachers were represented in higher proportions in schools where there was a governor of their own ethnic origin, for example 41 percent of Indian teachers taught in schools where there was an Indian governor, and 46 percent of Caribbean teachers taught in schools where at least one of the governors was of the same ethnic origin.

The report also found that 78 percent of the minority ethnic teachers were on pay scales 1 and 2 compared with 57 percent of White teachers, and that only 5 percent of minority ethnic teachers were in senior posts compared with 13 percent for White teachers. The findings of the CRE report attracted a great deal of media interest and headlines that were generally seen as expression of concern. However some dissenting voices were also raised, for example: 'we have never had a complaint about racial discrimination from any of our members' (Daily Mail, March 1988).

Minority ethnic staff in teacher training institutions

The need for more teachers drawn from the minority ethnic communities and the presence of minority ethnic staff in teacher training institutions have been frequently discussed in conferences and committees. The expansion of teacher education in the sixties did result in appointing young people in colleges of teacher education, but only a handful of these were from minority ethnic groups and most of them were in posts specifically concerned with addressing issues of multicultural education. The appointments of minority ethnic teachers in schools have also been affected not only by fewer minority ethnic students on teacher education courses but also by the conspicuous absence of minority ethnic staff in teacher training institutions.

ARTEN's survey found that there were only 0.06 percent Black lecturers in teacher training institutions and most of them held posts relating to equal opportunities and multicultural education. It also found that minority ethnic representation on CATE local committees was very limited, and was mostly through community representation and inevitably tokenistic in its effectiveness. The ARTEN submission to the Education, Science and Arts Committee described how minority ethnic teachers could act as role models for Black pupils, articulate their particular needs and suggest appropriate strategies for schools to meet the needs of minority ethnic groups, all of which could help raise levels of achievement by Black pupils. In addition, by helping to challenge stereotypical views held by white colleagues and pupils, minority ethnic staff could reduce the damaging effect of racism on all pupils.

Minority ethnic students on teacher education courses

The questions raised in the consultation document are equally valid in terms of under-representation of minority ethnic students on teacher education courses and teaching staff in teacher education colleges. The ARTEN submission also outlined the present situation with regard to the presence of minority ethnic groups as students on teacher education courses, as teachers in schools and as lecturers in teacher education institutions. It examined the reasons for their under-representation and offered strategies for breaking this cycle of under-representation.

The White Paper (DES 1983b) did suggest that recruitment to teacher education courses should include 'people with broad and diverse backgrounds, experience and interests, including some from the minority ethnic groups'. The Government, having accepted the recommendation of the Swann Committee, that more teachers from minority groups should be recruited, urged the University Departments of Education (UDEs) to give close and sympathetic attention to applications from minority ethnic candidates and involve more minority ethnic teachers in the preparation of students as teachers. UCET NOTE 2 (1986) responded to the Swann Report's call for 'urgent attention and positive action', by advising the UDEs to give close and sympathetic attention to applications from minority ethnic candidates, provide information and opportunities for discussion about careers in education to under-graduate students and to sixth-form students in schools in their area and advertise their courses in the minority ethnic press and through other community agencies. In May 1988, the Universities Central Council on Admissions (UCCA) and the Polytechnics Central Admission Systems (PCAS), agreed to reopen discussions for ethnic monitoring of applicants, as the Committee of Vice-Chancellors and Principals (CVCP) had in the past been reluctant to introduce ethnic monitoring on the grounds that such information could influence the selection process.

The CRE survey (Ranger 1988) was intended to establish a nationally valid reference point against which teacher-training institutions could measure the need for and effectiveness of policy initiatives to ensure equality of opportunity and to improve the accessibility of courses to minority ethnic students. The survey showed that fewer than 300 teachers of Asian or Afro-Caribbean origin, out of a total of some 12000, are likely to emerge from the training system during 1986-87. The CRE chairman at the time commented that the figures suggest we may be facing a decline in the number of Black teachers in school rather than the increase Lord Swann and others have recommended. Overall, the minority ethnic students made up only 2.6 percent of all students in the relevant groups/courses compared with an estimated 5.3 percent in the appropriate age group in the population. The results also showed a significant difference between students of Afro-Caribbean and of Asian origin in respect of the type of course undertaken. Over two thirds (67 percent) of Asian students were in PGCE courses compared with less than half (48 percent) of Afro-Caribbean students. There was also a marked variation of minority ethnic students' representation at an institutional level. About one third of PGCE courses and a little over two fifths of B.Ed. courses had no minority ethnic representation at all. At the other extreme, about one in ten courses had five or more minority ethnic students. The overall picture was that well over half the institutions providing initial education for teachers had either no or only one black student about to emerge as a teacher. Only 5 percent of all institutions had ten or more students of minority ethnic groups on their courses. The figures from the GTTR and CRCH suggested that despite Swann recommendations and DES consultation papers, the number of Black teachers was on the decline. The numbers of final-year students on teacher education courses for 1983 (2.6 percent) also suggested a significant drop-out rate for minority ethnic students.

So the CRE survey concluded that energetic efforts were needed to recruit more minority ethnic students. The CRE was concerned that several institutions, despite reminders, seemed unable or unwilling to respond to a simple questionnaire seeking statistical information about minority ethnic students on teacher education courses. GTTR/CRCH figures for Sept. 1988 indicated that the overall situation for Black applicants was not improving. Though the acceptance figures quoted (3.8 percent for PGCE and 5.1 percent for B.Ed) cannot be relied upon as the ethnic categories used are not consistent ('African' and 'Asian' as used by GTTR for B.Ed. courses and 'Black UK' as used in CRCH figures) and the census question was further modified in 1989, thus introducing three categories of 'Black' candidates instead of one. However, it is clear that PGCE courses only seem to recruit a very small number (0.07 percent) of Afro-Caribbean students as compared with recruitment for B.Ed. courses (ARTEN 1990).

It was also clear that the overall 5.1 percent recruitment of Black applicants was significantly low, when compared with the overall presence of Black pupils in sixth forms in schools. The GTTR figures for minority ethnic students offered places on PGCE courses for 1989 entry was just over 3 percent (Table 16 GTTR Annual Report 1989). The overall figure for 1992 suggests that the acceptance rate of minority ethnic students (24-46 percent) is still lower than the acceptance rate of for White UK candidates (52 percent). The total number of students on teacher education courses in 1992 still added up to only 4.5 percent (GTTR Annual Report 1992 Table ET1 and 2). More recently, the report of the Stephen Lawrence Inquiry pointed out that the need for more balance in the range of school staff applies equally to all White areas as it does to those areas with complex racial mixes. The TTA is committed to increasing the number of teachers from minority ethnic groups. The TTA Corporate Plan (1999-2002) states that:

> Teaching must be more representative of society. We will maintain our effort to increase recruitment from groups currently under-represented in teaching – men (especially in primary); members of minority ethnic groups; and people with disabilities. With our encouragement ITT providers are setting themselves targets for the admission of men and members of minority ethnic groups. At present, minority ethnic groups account for about 6 percent of recruits. We aim to ensure that, by the earliest possible date, this figure matches the proportion of minority ethnic groups in the school population – currently about 9 percent (TTA 1999).

A study commissioned by the TTA (1999) found that the proportion of trainee teachers from minority ethnic groups is low compared with their proportion in Higher Education. It found that only 5 percent of education students (HEI/School Partnership Courses) were from non-white groups, and that 25 college departments had no minority ethnic students registered for their courses. At the same time, nationally, approximately 10.5 percent of higher education students are from minority ethnic communities. The report suggests many complex and often inter-related reasons for the under-representation of trainees from minority ethnic groups. These have already been rehearsed several times over the years.

Causes of Under-Representation

The DES Consultation (DES 1985b) Document sought views on the possible causes suggested by the Swann Committee and others for the minority ethnic groups under-representation in the teaching force. These can be summarized as under-achievement at school and lack of necessary qualifications to enter teacher training by the normal route; minority ethnic teachers with overseas qualifications may be unclear about arrangements for obtaining recognition or upgrading their qualifications; teaching as a career seen to be less attractive and perceived as being of low status compared to other professions; family/cultural reasons inhibiting women from studying away from home; prospects of good quality posts and promotion not seen to be as good as those for white teachers; fear amongst potential students of racial discrimination, marginalization and isolation, especially in 'all white' areas; disenchantment with schooling resulting from their own experiences; inadequate career advice and limited number of 'role models' in the profession and potential students' apprehension about role expectations that may be detrimental to their career development in the 'mainstream' of the profession. All of these possible reasons have an element of truth, though there is not enough evidence to support some of these. There are also some contradictions that need to be examined. First of all, if there is evidence to suggest that many students from minority ethnic are not obtaining the qualifications necessary to enter teacher training by the normal route, they would hardly be in a position to consider other 'higher status' careers and professions as suggested in the second possible cause.

Entry qualifications

BICC survey (1988) of sixth-formers in Bradford schools and students in Further and Higher Education suggests that appropriate entry qualification is not a problem. Teaching as a career is certainly less attractive to minority ethnic students but no more than to White students, and it is certainly not a lot to do with low status, but more to do with stress associated with it and lack of recognition. However social status was marginally more important (64 percent) than job security (52 percent). It is also interesting that of the 31 percent sixth formers who considered teaching as a profession, only 4 percent actually decided to take it up. Ealing's Dilemma (1988) found that Black teachers on the whole were better qualified than their White counterparts (67 percent of Black teachers in Ealing had more than one qualification as compared with only 25 percent of White teachers). The key findings of an exploratory study, commissioned by the Department for Education and Employment (IES Report 309 reported in Research Review 1996), which investigated the employment outcomes and career progress of minority ethnic students, graduating in 1993 suggested that Indians are the largest ethnic group in higher education. The research has shown that differences currently exist in the labour market outcomes of graduates from different minority ethnic groups. Almost one in eight of all UK domiciled students at first-degree level in 1994/95 were from minority ethnic groups, which is more than double their representation in the UK population (5.8 percent).

Career choices and career guidance

The parental influence on the choice of career is also not completely relevant. The students who participated in the BICC survey were very clear about their reasons for not wanting to become teachers and were certainly not influenced directly by their parents. In most cases parents were reported to be encouraging in whatever choices students made and most minority ethnic parents regarded teaching as a respectable and rewarding profession. Though the choice of higher education institution is influenced by cultural attitudes, the incidence of parents not wishing their daughters to study away from home is not substantial enough to be of concern. Ten years later, one of the HEFCE projects reported that the most significant issue in determining whether young people entered teacher training was the availability of accurate advice about routes into teaching. The lack of adequate careers guidance meant that not only did students not see teaching as a potential option but also, in some cases careers advice had actually deterred students from planning a career in teaching. A few students who had decided on a career in teaching at a later stage found their degree choices were not appropriate for teacher training.

Lack of role models

The Swann Committee had accepted that if we are to dismantle racism in our society, both White and Black children need to be offered positive Black role models. They need to be in contact with Black people who have gained professional status and who command respect. HMI (1989) also suggested that Black students act as a catalyst for change in ITE improving awareness of issues of equal opportunities and offering black perspectives. Positive experience at school had led some students to develop an interest in becoming a teacher. In one survey a significant number of student teachers perceived themselves as important role models for minority ethnic pupils. Some students expressed a high level of satisfaction at being given the opportunity to train to teach. The majority of HEFCE projects (1995) reported that the lack of role models had been raised as an issue by the minority ethnic people they had surveyed. One student stated that 'pupils do not see many Black teachers, so they think the job is not for them'. Students themselves stated that seeing more black teachers would encourage them. Those that had had the benefit of working with black teachers during their teaching placements were delighted to be able to talk to someone who could share their experiences.

Racial discrimination

In addition to the lack of clear and consistent career advice, absence of minority ethnic teachers as role models; fear of racial discrimination and racial abuse and fear of being marginalized were certainly echoed by students in this survey. Some students believed that teachers still held stereotypical images that prevented them from understanding the cultural differences and the abilities of children from different backgrounds. A group of Black teachers confirmed the incidence of racial discrimination and marginalization and also gave substantial evidence of the stress caused by their jobs. The CRE survey (1988) also found that 52 percent of minority ethnic teachers experienced racial discrimination in their posts, and career prospects of 75 percent of minority ethnic teachers were adversely affected because of racial discrimination. The incidence of racial discrimination in school was reported by 63 percent White and 81 percent minority ethnic teachers. Ealing's Dilemma (1988) found that assumptions about black teachers' competence and abilities, informed by ideologies of racism, influenced the process of selection, recruitment and deployment of Black teachers. The inquiry reported that despite a specific recruitment drive and clear equal opportunities policy, Ealing only managed to recruit 3 (2.1 percent) Black teachers out of a total of 140 appointed in the summer of 1986 when the total number of minority ethnic applicants was 15.9 percent.

The 150-page report said the inquiry team found it 'extremely striking and depressing' that education managers made gross generalizations about the ability of all black teachers. 'The stereotypes for Asians and Afro-Caribbeans differed but the underlying racism was the same.' The Inquiry team found evidence of racism throughout the system, from unfair references given to Black teachers by prejudiced heads to the composition of panels in the Education Department. The report concluded that black teachers in Ealing were getting a raw deal and, amongst other things, they found it harder to get promoted and that prejudice was apparent in the treatment of Black teachers who worked as supply teachers. There was also evidence that the all White council recruitment team preferred to recruit inexperienced college students to experienced bilingual local Black teachers. This is despite an earlier recognition when Ealing Community Relations Council gave evidence to the 1973 Select Committee, acknowledging that Asian teachers were under-represented, and West-Indian teachers scandalously under-represented in Ealing's teaching force, and recommending that 'No single step which the London Borough of Ealing could take would do more to help the Black teenager than the appointment of Black teachers to the teaching and other professional staff of the Ealing educational service' (Education Volume 12).

A decade after the Swann Report some of the HEFCE projects (Special Initiatives to Encourage Widening Participation of Students from Minority Ethnic Groups in Teacher Training HEFCE Projects July 1995) still found evidence that teaching is viewed as a profession in which some students feel they could be exposed to racism, a view based on students' own experience at school where they sometimes witnessed racism against their own teachers. However, where projects have built positive links with minority ethnic communities, they have succeeded in stimulating a greater demand from minority ethnic groups for teacher training.

Experiences of Minority Ethnic Teachers and Students

The Swann Committee in its visits to schools had noted that minority ethnic teachers were 'stagnating in the system, in posts far below their capabilities and experience', and that in some cases they were regarded as 'token figures' in schools with a 'curiosity value' undertaking only specific tasks in relation to minority ethnic pupils. It is not surprising, therefore, that because of their experiences of racism, marginalization and isolation minority ethnic teachers were leaving the profession and consequently less likely to encourage younger members of their group to take up teaching as a profession.

The cycle of racism

The presence of minority ethnic teachers in schools is thus hindered by a vicious cycle that is perpetuating experiences of racism and racial discrimination. Minority ethnic children's experience of racism in schools, possibly leading to underachievement, thus legitimizing low teacher expectations, further sustained by stereotypical views of their behaviour patterns, resulting in differential placements in sets and streams with a consequent low attainment. This vicious cycle is further extended by their awareness of racism experienced by Black teachers and lecturers, thus discouraging many minority ethnic pupils from considering teaching as a career. It would appear that disproportionately low numbers of minority ethnic teachers in schools and on teacher training courses has not entirely been due to the ambivalence of minority ethnic groups (as suggested by the Best of Both Worlds) but also due to a consistent failure of schools to encourage minority ethnic youngsters, indirectly by their experience of schooling, and directly by visible lack of Black teachers in their schools. Training institutions need to get to grips with the institution itself, and the way in which it prepares all students to teach in a multicultural society. Career conventions and links with schools are important, but a local and national network of community organisations may well serve better in publicising possible options within teaching as a profession.

The training institutions need to take on board the experience of students, their rates of progress and success, and their entry into the profession. Unless these issues are addressed the under-representation of minority ethnic teachers will continue. The gap between idealised commitment and necessary functional systematic response is too large to be ignored. However, I do not wish to end on a pessimistic note. We need to acknowledge the positive achievements of the last two decades and take on board examples of good practice, however rare they may have been. On the whole, though some progress has been made, it is patchy and inconsistent. There are more Black teachers than there were 20 years ago, but their status remains significantly low and they are still in marginal posts, which are mostly race-related. One of the factors that holds back Black children is the witting and unwitting low expectations of many White teachers. The presence of minority ethnic teachers can help to overcome the bias inherent in the witting and unwitting low expectations of many White teachers and encourage Black children to take up teaching as a profession and break the vicious cycle created by the absence of good role models.

'Race'-cast roles

The CRE survey and the Ealing Report demonstrated that we are up against a system in which 'race'-cast roles have been assigned to Black employees for decades and which are legitimized by a system informed by radicalized assumptions and which serve to perpetuate 'white interests, cultural assumptions and the racial status quo of "White" authority and "Black" subordination' (Brandt 1986). The internal policy discussions of Birmingham LEA (Grosvenor 1990) give valuable insight into the genesis of a system of casting Black employees into roles such as 'Immigrant Teachers' for 'Immigrant Schools'. This situation was brought about partly as a cumulative effect of internalizing distorted judgments about Black people and incorporating them into the dynamics of educational and social institutions. The 'race'-cast role syndrome has also resulted in a situation whereby Black pupils have been unable to find Black role models and have also failed to see any real positive valuing of themselves or the racially-defined groups to which they belong. On the contrary what they see is the perpetuation of the stereotype of the Black worker in servicing roles both outside and inside the schools, because when there are a few Black workers in the school setting they tend to be in 'support' jobs and not in senior teaching posts. It was also assumed by Head Teachers in the Ealing survey that the 'expertise of Black teachers' was better suited to those schools with a high level of minority ethnic pupils, and that they were better suited to deal with multicultural issues and to be employed in support services. Even where the Swann Report had emphasised the potential contribution that black staff can make to an all white school, it was in relation to improving 'race' relations.

The NUT was particularly concerned by the roles Black teachers were expected to take. These tended to be in support services, often funded by section 11; expected to deal with contentious issues such as introducing multicultural approaches; tackling racial harassment; expected to have a special relationship with Black pupils and to deal with their discipline and with their parents; to act as interpreters and to take on additional pastoral responsibilities without additional pay or status. These roles inevitably led to low morale and to isolation and insecurity, 'role models' that young people from minority ethnic groups did not (quite rightly so) perceive as viable career options. The appointment of Black teachers to Black schools or Asian teachers only to help with language problems and to speak to parents is not likely to attract younger recruits to the profession. Siraj-Blatchford (1990) also revealed that Black students faced both direct and indirect racism from their peers and their tutors. It found that students on Initial Teacher Training courses experienced this 'Black teachers for Black students' syndrome. HEFCE Projects also found that acting as a role model also faced students with the dilemma of how and why Black teachers were used in the system. In addition, some students were uncomfortable with being identified as carrying responsibility for issues concerning minority ethnic people. However, involving minority ethnic students as a resource for others placed additional pressure on them at a time when they already had to cope with the burden of completing their programmes of study.

Black teachers: white schools

The Swann Committee did acknowledge that Black teachers had a role to play in all-White schools and that the contribution a Black teacher can make to an all-White school can be very dramatic and pronounced, especially as 'role-models'. However, a solitary Black teacher in this situation requires inner strength, 'I know how one becomes an "oddity", seen as having "a chip on the shoulder" and even causing more trouble by raising unwelcome issues. The Black teacher may even come to feel the "token", for that is how the authority often uses them' (Mortimer 1985). The collective wish of everyone in the school to 'assimilate' this stranger may not be very conducive to changing attitudes and the individual concerned may just give in to pressure to conform, not wanting to cause 'problem' or 'rock the boat'. The question of teaching placements has also been identified as clearly difficult for both institutions and students. The isolation experienced by minority ethnic students in higher education becomes much more apparent when alone on a teaching placement and, together with the stresses of teaching practice, causes too great a strain for some students. In some cases there is a lack of choice in placements and getting students appropriate experience is not easy. Some institutions are uncertain whether or not to place Black students in an institution with which they would feel more comfortable.

There seems to be plenty of evidence that minority ethnic groups are under-represented not only in the teaching profession, but also in teacher education institutions, both as lecturers and as trainee teachers. It also seems that there is not sufficient evidence to suggest that it is the lack of necessary qualifications, or the low status of teaching as a career, or indeed the family/cultural reasons which prevent young people from minority ethnic groups to join the teaching profession. But there is sufficient evidence to suggest that the racism experienced by minority ethnic teachers in employment and minority ethnic students on teacher education courses, combined with apprehensions about 'race'-cast roles, and lack of career prospects may be contributing to the alienation of minority ethnic young people from the teaching profession.

Overseas Trained Teachers: The Mystery of QTS

The DES acknowledged that there were a number of first-generation immigrants, who had trained, qualified and taught in their countries of origin but who had not been able to resume their teaching careers in the UK. It also took note of the Swann recommendation that the DES should clarify the arrangements for granting QTS to members of minority ethnic communities who possess overseas qualifications, with a view to encouraging them to enter the teaching profession as long as this involves no diminution of standards. Minority ethnic students often have a diversity of experience prior to higher education. There may also be a mismatch between student's qualifications and experiences and the courses on offer. Therefore, more flexibility is needed in the routes of entry to teacher training to enable student to select an appropriate pathway. This includes recognition by admissions tutors of the prior learning and experience of minority ethnic applicants. Teacher training institutions have also highlighted the difficulties associated with recognition of qualifications gained overseas and the ability to convert these to appropriate teaching qualifications.

The arrangements for obtaining recognition of these qualifications have always been a great mystery to anyone concerned with teacher education. The policies of the DES have been inconsistent, to say the least, and criteria used to determine equivalence have never been made public. It is therefore not surprising that members of the minority ethnic groups with overseas qualifications were unclear about the arrangements. DES Circular 8/83 referred to courses of training and special qualifications obtained overseas which are regarded as comparable, but went on to say; 'It is not practicable to reproduce a complete list of these. Authorities should consult the dept. about qualifications obtained overseas before making any appointments'. An extract from a letter written by Sir Keith Joseph in Nov. 1984, tells a different story:

> The acceptability of such qualifications is a matter for the admitting institution, drawing on any advice which the British Council can offer, and this department would not normally expect to be able to offer guidance... judgments are made on the basis of an assessment of course content in terms of its comparability with provision at teacher training institutions in this country. In some individual cases the DES might be prepared to grant exceptional recognition as teachers to instructors, lacking the normal qualifications, but the initiatives must come from employing LEAs (Joseph 1984).

As for the upgrading qualifications, the situation was similarly vague. If there is no indication from the DES about the value or equivalence granted to existing qualifications and consequently about the gap between the qualifications people hold and those that are required for them to become teachers, it is extremely unlikely that people would know how to upgrade them. Furthermore the inconsistency, with which similar qualifications from the same universities (but in different years) are treated, leaves the people concerned more confused than ever before.

Though the analysis offered in the Consultative Paper was very good in terms of difficulties and anomalies experienced by teachers with overseas qualifications, the suggested measures for improvement were not so simple and straightforward. The proposals for part-time PGCE courses, shortened B.Ed. courses and the introduction of new routes to QTS such as the Licensed Teachers and the Articled Teachers were all subject to the requirement of an adequate standard in Mathematics and English and Science (GCE 'O' level or equivalent). In practice not all institutions were able or willing to make the necessary arrangements for recognition of existing qualifications or for enabling candidates to obtain these at the point of entry. There are also difficulties of bringing together a group of students whose backgrounds are sufficiently similar to allow remission for the first two years of a particular B.Ed. course.

The Education Teachers Regulations Circular (13/91) introduced a new route to QTS intended for graduates who have undertaken their training outside England and Wales and who have at least one year's teaching experience. This route is separate from the Licensed Teachers route. The Circular also includes guidance on the training of Overseas Trained Teachers comprising of a detailed list of knowledge and competencies required. The proposals for new arrangements for granting QTS were designed to produce 'a simpler and more effective system'. The proposed reforms of the non-standard routes are mainly in replacing them by a single non-standard route whereby an employer rather than an individual would apply for a Licence to Teach in a specific school. The Licensed Teacher would then be eligible for QTS, upon the recommendation of the employer, after two years. However, Circular 13/91 did not reflect the comments made by the CRE and other organisations. The suggested route for Licensed Teachers was also seen to be problematic and not likely to improve the position of minority ethnic applicants with overseas qualifications. Under the new regulations self-advocacy has been ruled out, applicants have to be employed by a school or an LEA to register as a Licensed Teacher. Since the national record for the employment of minority ethnic teachers is not very encouraging, it is going to be even more difficult for applicants with overseas qualifications to even get entry into the system. Furthermore the system of scrutinizing the overseas qualifications still remains a complex mystery. The arrangements were also seen to be discriminatory and unfair in that the applicants with qualifications from Scotland, Northern Ireland and the EEC can be awarded QTS on the basis of 3 years Higher Education, whereas applicants from other parts of the world will need much higher level of qualifications and training. The National Union of Teachers strongly opposed the introduction of The Licensed Teachers' route to QTS on the grounds that the entry requirements were inconsistent with those laid out in circular 3/84 and that the training required did not have to meet with CATE criteria for approval of courses. The guidance offered in the Appendix 2 of Circular 13/91 described in detail the knowledge and skills required of an overseas trained teacher before being recommended for QTS. The content of training required was not stipulated, except to say that they should be assessed on their suitability for QTS in the light of competencies listed.

Possible Ways of Improving Recruitment and Retention

Ethnic monitoring

Following on from the recommendation of the Swann Report (1985), ethnic monitoring of teachers was required by the DES from January 1990 (DES Circular 8/1989). However, the Statistical Bulletins (23/93 & 24/93) issued by the DFE had not published any ethnically based statistics concerned with teachers on the grounds that the limited information they have received was not viable for statistical analysis. The majority of HEFCE projects (1995) raised the lack of data on minority ethnic students within institutions as an issue. Whilst data was generally collected for monitoring admissions, institutions' own equal opportunities policies made it impossible to utilise it for any other purposes. It was a large barrier to monitoring student retention and progression. If real progress is to be made in improving support and retention of minority ethnic students then institutions will need to be able to access appropriate data. This is clearly a sensitive area that requires careful consideration and negotiation with minority ethnic groups in order to agree a code of practice whereby institutions can access the relevant data without students feeling threatened or vulnerable. Initial teacher Training Performance Profiles (1999) did include ethnically based statistics for recruitment from year 1997. As the introduction of the RRAA (2000) requires all public sector institutions to produce and publish an analysis of monitoring figures from May 2002, it is hoped that ethnic monitoring of teachers will now be forthcoming and that institutions will produce analysis of ethnic monitoring with detailed information such as the ratio of minority ethnic applicants to places offered to them, the reasons for refusal, retention on ITT courses and the success rate of those accepted on the courses and first destinations by all ITT providers.

Career guidance

The Swann Committee was also of the view that the most important potential source of minority ethnic teachers in the future is the minority ethnic pupils in schools, and that career teachers should encourage minority ethnic youngsters to consider teaching as a possible career. The DES consultation document took note of recommendations made by the Swann Committee, and suggested that central government could use its promotional materials to illustrate the presence of minority ethnic students and teachers in the training institutions and in schools. It also suggested that LEAs should ensure that their recruitment and promotion procedures are fair and that they do not discriminate on the grounds of 'race' or sex; that career advisors should encourage young people from minority ethnic groups to consider teaching as a profession and seek to involve minority ethnic teachers in schools for that purpose; and that Teachers' Associations could consider ways of encouraging minority ethnic pupils to contemplate teaching as a career.

Recruitment procedures

There are barriers in recruitment process such as inconsistent recognition of overseas qualifications and/or of previous teaching experience, cultural bias in admission interviews, lack of institutional commitment to equal opportunities, reluctance to recognize and challenge incidence of racism, and inability to change practices that have proved to be also discriminatory and thus damaging to the profession. Institutions offering Initial Teacher Training courses have been advised to make greater efforts to advertise their courses in the minority ethnic press; promote and develop links with multiethnic schools; involve minority ethnic teachers as occasional lecturers on their courses; examine their recruitment and selection procedures with a view to remove any bias on racial, cultural or religious grounds and emphasise in their courses the importance of preparing all teachers to teach in a multiethnic society. There is a need to acknowledge that bilingual teachers may have a particular contribution to make and institutions could consider proposals for courses that could train graduates with a knowledge of community languages to be classroom teachers.

A range of short term and long term strategies to involve minority ethnic staff in teacher education include use of experienced minority ethnic professionals in education as a resource to consult and teach on the basis of part-time contracts; teacher fellowships to encourage minority ethnic teachers to participate in teacher education courses; better promotional/career prospects for minority ethnic teachers; greater collaboration between trainers from various professions such as education, social work and youth work with a view to benefit from positive developments in each field; and better and fairer recruitment and selection procedures in colleges of education. Further suggestions to improve the recruitment of minority ethnic students on to teacher education courses have included the need to acknowledge that qualifications in non-European languages can be, and are, recognised as equivalent for University entrance requirements; the need for criteria applied to exceptional entry candidates to be formally stated and available for public scrutiny; and the need for teacher education institutions to make personal contact with schools and FE institutions for the recruitment of potential minority ethnic students for their courses and make their publicity material available at career conventions in schools and FE institutions. This last point was further echoed by an HMI, when he suggested that 'individual training institutions need direct links with schools that have minority ethnic children in the same way that Oxford and Cambridge have always had direct links with some of the schools their students are drawn from' (Singh 1988).

The ARTEN paper raised further questions about the balance between fairness and justice to the pupils and fairness and justice for the students. It asked the UDEs to consider the role of admission interviews in establishing the suitability of students for teacher education courses, and to consider what sorts of procedures and evidence are required for making judgments about temperamental unsuitability to teach. It raises important questions about the role of school teachers (as teaching practice supervisors) in forming judgments about professional suitability.

Access courses

The induction courses and/or Access courses set up to enable members of minority ethnic groups to obtain the necessary qualifications for qualified teacher status or for entrance to a teacher education course have succeeded to a varying degree. However, the lack of financial support for these courses has deterred potential Black teachers, especially mature students with family responsibilities. The recruitment practices of certain institutions are still blocking a large number of potential teachers from getting onto teacher education courses. Even where minority ethnic students have the appropriate entry qualifications, the admissions procedures and tutors have acted as gatekeepers, thus contributing to disenchantment and alienation of members of minority ethnic groups who had considered teaching as an option.

The general success of Access courses in public sector Higher Education has prompted UDEs to become more involved in collaborative arrangements with other teacher-training institutions by getting involved in validation or research activities related to such courses and/or by offering a range of conversion courses for students with overseas qualifications. However, the CRE has offered a word of caution to institutions of Higher Education by asking them not to marginalize minority ethnic students in 'special Access courses' and by alerting them to the danger of seeing short-term benefits of access courses as a substitute for examining their recruitment procedures in general. Access courses may be a necessary strategy to redress the imbalance within the teaching profession; it is still only an interim response and as such not a substitute for total reassessment of structures and procedures in the system which have caused minority ethnic groups to be alienated from the profession in the first place.

The general success of Access courses is not only due to a positive attitude of tutors, but also due to a closer collaboration between students and tutors, and important lessons need to be learnt from this by teacher training institutions. Though teacher-training institutions have become more interested in offering a range of conversion courses for students with overseas qualification, such as two-year PGCE courses and shortened Bed. programmes, the CRE has offered a word of caution that they may lead to marginalization of minority ethnic students. The short-term benefits of Access Courses should not be seen as a substitute for examining recruitment procedures. Access courses may be an important strategy to reduce the imbalance within the teaching profession, it is still only an interim response, and, as such, not a substitute for total reassessment of structures and procedures in the system which have caused minority ethnic groups to be alienated from the profession in the first place.

Challenging racist practices

There is evidence that minority ethnic students on teacher training courses receive little support in institutions and face hostility during teaching practice. There is also evidence that Black students' experience alarmingly high level of racism in initial teacher training (Siraj-Blatchford 1990). There is also evidence (Clay, Ghadia & Wilkins 1991; Siraj-Blatchford 1991; Clay, Cole & Hill 1990) of insufficient support for students who experience racism during school experience. Examples of such experiences included total indifference to White students' expression of racist attitudes, marginal attention to issues concerned with equal opportunities and challenging racism. Siraj-Blatchford's study of Black students' experiences in Initial Teacher Education also revealed practices that contravene the 1976 Race Relations Act. Her research suggested that factors as diverse as accommodation, course content and school placements influence the perception of students on initial teacher training courses. It is especially notable that only five of the seventy respondents in this survey felt that they had not experienced any racism during their training, which clearly suggests that the rest of the respondents experienced racism at one level or another. This has clear implications for review of course content to ensure that it is inclusive and covers racial awareness/equal opportunities issues; for support on course for trainees with specific needs, e.g. English as an additional language; for support for trainees experiencing racism on the course, including on school-based aspects of courses; and for training for school-based tutors to include appropriate cultural elements.

Ten of the HEFCE projects raised racism as one of the main issues encountered. Several incidents were quoted and many students had encountered overt or covert racism in schools and higher education institutions. Teachers commented that they felt they were not valued as a professional and put down by fellow staff. Others had experienced abusive language from parents. Student teachers had experienced isolation and intimidation from white teachers. Although there were no specific examples of overt racism within higher education institutions, students had felt uncomfortable at jokes made by staff about Black students. One student commented that it was difficult to complain because it was difficult to define exactly what racism was. Students felt that staff should be more ready to challenge racism in schools and institutions. Evidence from HEFCE projects also indicated that there was a lack of support for students on placements and some inappropriate placements were arranged. Sensitive and more effective support systems are needed to cope with this. Some institutions were actively involved in producing guidelines for both staff and students on how to handle these problems. Students and institutions expressed concern at the difficulties of challenging the racism encountered in schools. These issues raised further concern about the planned increase in placement time in the new curriculum and the need for support structures to aid retention of minority ethnic trainees. Equally important is the evidence of Black teachers experience of working in schools. Most of them speak of the mechanisms operating against their promotion and their isolation in mainstream schooling. Minority ethnic teachers are often either in 'race-cast roles', or employed to support services. Expected to deal only with Black pupils, to act as interpreters but never really seen as part of a school's mainstream staff. Isolation and insecurity resulting from such a situation inevitably leads to low morale and disenchantment from the profession. They were also particularly critical of the pressure to become the 'multi-cultural teacher' in their school (Mac an Ghaill 1988).

Summary

This chapter has explored the position of minority ethnic groups in the teaching profession. It has considered the incidence of their under-representation, possible causes of such under-representation, and looked at ways of improving the situation. On the whole there is evidence that some progress has been made, though it is patchy and inconsistent. There are more black student teachers than there were 20 years ago, and that democratic discourse and egalitarian principles of justice and equality are not dead. The available evidence suggests that the presence of minority ethnic groups in the teaching profession is hindered by a vicious cycle that is perpetuating experiences of racism and racial discrimination, thus hindering any progress. The incidence of racism at various levels is well documented. Many minority ethnic children experience racism verbally and physically (Learning in Terror 1988); possibly leading to underachievement of minority ethnic pupils (Swann Report and numerous LEA surveys); legitimising low teacher expectations of certain minority ethnic groups, further sustained by stereotypical views of their behaviour patterns (Wright 1986), and resulting in differential placement in sets and streams with a consequent low attainment.

This vicious cycle is further extended by high level of awareness of the racism experienced by Black teachers and lecturers in educational institutions, thus discouraging many minority ethnic pupils from choosing teaching as a career. Ealing's Dilemma (1988) has a lesson for all LEAs, a lesson that a lack of political will coupled with ad-hoc recruitment practices is a recipe for disaster. In Ealing's case, it was not the lack of policy, but word-of-mouth recruitment, and a system of personal patronage, which excluded minority ethnic teachers from entering the pool in the first place and the discriminatory practices in the actual process of short-listing and interviewing (for example, references on the phone, short-listing without reference to job specification and verification of overseas qualifications etc.) served to further exclude the ones that did apply.

Furthermore there are barriers operating in recruitment on to teacher education courses and these include, inconsistent recognition of overseas qualifications and/or of previous experience of teaching; cultural bias in interviewing; lack of institutional commitment to equal opportunities; reluctance to recognize and challenge incidence of racism and inability to change practices that have proved to be discriminatory and thus damaging to the profession. The Black Teachers' Annual Conference (1990) expressed concern that minority ethnic students on teacher education courses received little support as potential Black teachers and faced hostility during their teaching practice. They were also concerned about the roles minority ethnic teachers were expected to take, often employed in support services, expected to deal with only Black pupils, to act as interpreters and to deal with parents and yet not seen as part of school's mainstream staff. Isolation and insecurity resulting from such a situation inevitably leads to low morale and disenchantment with the profession. HEFCE's 'Special Initiatives to Encourage Widening Participation Of Students From Minority Ethnic Groups In Teacher Training' (1995) was aimed to address the problem of serious shortfall in the number of entrants from minority ethnic groups into teacher training. The wide ranging projects concentrated on a number of issues such as student support, routes of entry, development of recruitment procedures and improvements in course delivery. Not surprisingly the key issues identified through these projects included barriers to participation, student experience of higher education and institutional issues.

To sum up, it would appear that the disproportionately low number of minority ethnic teachers in schools and minority ethnic students on teacher education courses has not been entirely due to the ambivalence on the part of minority ethnic groups and within the institutional structures of the educational system, but also due to a consistent failure to encourage minority ethnic youngsters to enter the teaching profession. It may be suggested that the very experience of schooling and the visible lack of teachers from their own ethnic groups may discourage young people from seriously considering teaching as a profession. Teacher Education institutions need to get to grips with the institution itself, into which Black students would want to come, and the way it prepares all students to teach in a multicultural society. The key may also be not to rely entirely on career conventions, LEAs and school links. A local and national network of community organizations may well serve better in publicizing routes to higher education and to increase awareness of the possible options within the teaching profession. Once the students are recruited, the institutions need to take on board the experience of students, the rates of progress and success, acquisition of appropriate skills and competencies and entry into professional employment. The gap between idealised commitment and necessary functional systematic responses is too large to be ignored.

Chapter 5

Initial Teacher Training Partnership

Introduction

To achieve his ambitious target of finding new ways of increasing the supply of teachers, the Secretary of State for Education (1989) outlined the need to attract more mature students to teacher education and to improve opportunities for women and for students from the minority ethnic groups. To attract former teachers back into the profession and to devise new and flexible routes into teaching, his proposals were aimed at not only combating the teacher shortage in some subjects, but also at the reform of the non-standard routes to Qualified Teacher Status (QTS). He promised to 'cut away the jungle that engulfs people trained overseas' and acknowledged that 'many good teachers from overseas have been refused QTS simply because of technicalities in the rules, which have nothing whatever to do with their competence as teachers' (DES 1989d). The main points of the Government's plan included, amongst other things, proposals for CATE to play a key role in determining the nature of school-based work; schools and training institutions to have equal partnership; training to become the responsibility of the 'best' teachers, who will act as 'mentors'; and the introduction of a new accreditation criteria, in the form of competencies, setting out what employers may expect of a newly qualified teacher. However, it omitted all reference to race and sex equality. Teachers' Unions gave a general welcome to the proposed increase in the level of school-based training. But they expressed reservations on the amount of funding announced, decline in academic rigour and the extra burden the proposals will place on already overloaded teachers. AMMA dismissed the proposals as 'ill thought out and under-funded against no background in detailed research of how it will work'. The NUT and the NASUWT also saw the proposals as politically motivated. As for the non-standard routes, it was thought by the teachers' unions and the leading figures from HMI that QTS should not be granted too early, and it was suggested by NASUWT that the probationary year should be regarded as the last year of training and QTS should only be granted after a successful year of probation.

The proposals for the reform of the non-standard routes were based on the belief that because of the difficulties arising from the present arrangements, it was important to have the new regulations in place by the time schools were operating with delegated budgets and associated increase in responsibilities for staffing matters. The proposals for the reform of non-standard routes were aimed at enhancing quality by ensuring a minimum appropriate level of training; at linking the non-standard routes to QTS, and to the staffing needs of employers; and at a reduction in the administrative complexity, with corresponding gains in the speed of processing applications. This chapter is an exploration of these non-standard routes introduced to obtain QTS and their implications for the recruitment and training for minority ethnic teachers. The discussion in this chapter will be informed by evidence from direct and practical experience of working with schools and teacher training institutions. It will also consider the contribution Training Schools can make in training teachers for the future. Some examples of new modes of training courses specially introduced to increase collaboration with schools and to recruit minority ethnic students will be included along with any reports of evaluation of such schemes as may be available.

Non-Standard Routes to QTS

The Licensed Teachers Scheme

DES Circular 18/89 replaced the existing non-standard routes to QTS with the Licensed Teacher Route, also available for overseas trained teachers not covered by the EC directive. The Licensed Teachers' Route was proposed as a single non-standard route to QTS and the new status of Licensed Teachers was described as that of a third category of teacher, between the 'unqualified' and the 'qualified'. Applications for Licence can only be made by the LEAs for maintained schools without delegated budgets; with the consent of the LEA, by governing bodies of maintained schools with delegated budgets; and by the governing bodies of grant-maintained schools and non-maintained special schools. To qualify the individual candidates must have obtained grade C (GCSE) in English and Mathematics, or the equivalent; completed an aggregate of two years' full-time HE and be at least 26 years old (later reduced to 24), except in the case of overseas-trained teachers. In general, the Licence is for six terms; largely in the classroom under the guidance of a 'mentor' teacher before an application for QTS can be made. Exception can be made for granting early QTS (schedule 5, paragraph 2) for a candidate who has at least two years' teaching experience in independent schools or in further and higher education institutions and has completed successfully at least one year's service as a Licensed Teacher; or has at least two years' teaching experience as an Armed Services Education Officer or Instructor and has completed successfully at least one year's service as a Licensed Teacher; or is an overseas-trained teacher who has at least three years' teacher education and at least one year's teaching experience in England or in Wales or elsewhere, and who has completed successfully at least one term's service as a Licensed Teacher (DES Circular18/89 Para 35).

As for the training it was up to the respective LEA or the governing body to assess an individual's training needs, considered by some (NATFHE 1992) a 'recipe for potential disaster'. However, Appendix 2 of Circular 18/89 does include guidance for the training of Licensed Teachers. This included a list of knowledge and competencies required to take charge of full classes. These may have been acquired before or during the period of license. With the exception of experienced teachers, all Licensed Teachers were expected to be allocated an appropriate 'mentor' teacher; spend one month on observation of classes in at least two schools in the age group in which they hope to teach; be assessed at the end of the month to identify further training needs; and be released to undertake such training as deemed necessary by the LEA, but for the equivalent of not less than one day a week. They were also expected to be supervised for an agreed number of lessons and have the opportunity to discuss these with whoever is responsible for training and be assessed towards the end of the licensing period to determine their suitability for QTS.

Licensed Teachers were to be paid on qualified or unqualified rates, as the LEA or the governing bodies see fit.

The essence of the Licensed Teachers route to QTS was that it was individually tailored, and employment-based, not course-based. It was expected to attract a great variety of people, with a great range of backgrounds and experience. Decisions about whom to employ as Licensed Teachers, the nature and method of the training to be provided, and the arrangements for the support of Licensed Teachers were deemed to be matters for the employing LEAs and schools, and were to be tailored to their own circumstances and those of the individual Licensed Teachers. Despite the Select Committee's recommendation that 'the Licensed Teacher's education should lead to the award of a PGCE equivalent qualification, under arrangements accredited by CATE'; the Government did not wish to see standard Licensed Teacher Training courses which could be accredited, but looked to employers to demand the same high performance standards from Licensed Teachers as they expect from other teachers.

The CNAA suggested that Licensed Teachers should be able to qualify for its own Certificate in Education, as this would not only give the teachers concerned a nationally recognised award but would also encourage LEAs, schools and colleges to provide them with training and study opportunities which reach national standards. It would also ensure that the training of the Licensed Teachers was not too narrowly focused on the career structure of one school. Those who followed this route were required to be able to demonstrate that they had the necessary personal qualities, subject knowledge, classroom and other professional competence before QTS is awarded. A licence is issued for two years in the first instance and is normally specific to employment in a named school, and with the LEA that recommended them for Licensed Teacher Status. It was suggested that the proposed new arrangements would not only remove much of the administrative complexity of the current arrangements but would also provide an enhanced role in these matters for LEA staff and school head teachers, best equipped to make a judgement on the professional qualities of the person concerned in order to recommend that they receive QTS. The proposals were condemned by most of the teachers' unions. It is what they feared, that this was an attempt to get round the problem of shortage by dilution instead of responding to market forces by increasing pay to attract better teachers (NASUWT). The NUT considered the proposals as outrageous, 'In the same week that the Government declined to give licences to unqualified people to drive black taxi-cabs, they also decided to issue licences to unqualified people to teach children' (McAvoy 1989).

Both the NUT and the NASUWT concentrated on persuading local authorities and governing bodies not to take on Licensed Teachers, persuading parents not to allow their children to be taught by unqualified people; and to shun any mentoring scheme that did not include non-contact time and training for the mentors. The scheme was criticised on the grounds that it represented an unacceptable lowering of standards of teacher education and training. Evidence from HMI report of Hertfordshire Action on Teacher Supply (HATS), and from comparison of the performance of trained and untrained graduate teachers suggested that such extreme forms of 'on-the-job' training were not very effective. The scheme was also criticised on the grounds of inadequate supervision and support for trainee teachers; denial of parents' rights to have their children taught by properly qualified and trained teachers; location of trainee teachers in schools with greatest difficulties of recruitment and high staff turnover and, most importantly, for the scheme to be outside the Government's own system for accreditation through CATE. The Government refuted the claims of some of the Teacher Unions that the scheme will reduce quality, but said that it will help enhance quality by ensuring that candidates get the training they need and demonstrate their competence in the classroom before they are granted QTS. Though LEAs gave their support to the Licensed Teacher Scheme, they were not too happy about the proposals for differential salaries to ease shortages.

Another concern expressed was at the revelation of a loophole whereby students who failed to qualify as teachers during their initial teacher education could then become Licensed Teachers, because 'LEAs are entitled to offer a Licensed Teacher job to any applicant who has completed the equivalent of two years of higher education and is of 26 years of age' (DES Circular 18/89). Mr. Kane, of Manchester Polytechnic, who raised the issue with the DES, had this to say:

> The Government has told us that one of our problems is that we allow unsuitable people to gain entry to the teaching profession by not applying sufficiently rigorous standards. It would seem, however, that when we harden our hearts and take the necessary action, those who we failed might enter the profession as Licensed Teachers (Kane 1989).

He was also concerned that the DES was doing nothing to help 'women returners' who had been out of teaching for years while raising a family. Unlike the Articled Teachers and the Licensed Teachers, they had to pay their own way to get back into the system. A spokeswoman for Warwickshire regarded the Licensed Teacher scheme as a disaster. She said it was frustrating for foreign teachers wanting to teach in this country. Qualified teachers from overseas can no longer get QTS before they can be employed as Licensed Teachers and in some cases they are employed as instructors. Teaching as a Career Unit (TASC) saw the introduction of the Licensed Teacher route as a golden opportunity for LEAs, teacher trainers and teachers themselves to develop schemes of training targeted at local requirements, thus allowing the profession to control the quality of training. (TASC Bulletin 1990). It did seem that if the scheme was adequately promoted, then it could increase teacher supply, but whether it could promote or even mention teacher quality was unclear because that was likely to be determined by the quality and character of the training to be provided.

O'Hear (1988) argued that theories of learning play no part in the apprenticeship of students and education courses are 'obsessed with passing fashions such as questions of "race" and inequality and "anti-educational" issues to do with social engineering'. In his view, employers should be free to appoint people to their teaching staff who have good knowledge of the relevant subjects, and then induct them and guide them into teaching within the school. After two years as a Licensed Teacher, the school should, in consultation with those who have guided the Licensee, be able to recommend that a satisfactory candidate be granted QTS. O'Hear sees any involvement of professionals from outside the school as dangerous, as theoretical and ideological issues might creep in. His suggestion, that the practical concerns of the particular school are all that matters, and that teacher supply and quality would be ensured by opening up the Licensed route for everyone needs further examination. There seems to be no evidence that the current demands of professional training are deterring any potential teachers. The one-year PGCE course (36 weeks duration) for graduates qualifies for mandatory grants and is almost exclusively used for intending secondary school teachers. Though the four-year B.Ed. programme (now almost entirely focused on primary sector) may seem to be a deterrent for those who may not wish to make a career decision at the outset, they do have the choice to do a PGCE, and delay making a career decision after obtaining a degree. So opening up the Licensed Teacher route will do very little to increase the supply.

As for improving the quality, by placing students entirely in the hands of schools alone they are likely to miss out on the essential inter-face between theory and practice. The reflective practice, which is the hallmark of current teacher education courses, can in no way be replaced by pure apprenticeship with practising teachers. There is also the issue of training the practitioners to be 'tutors' or 'mentors'. My experience of working with practising teachers suggests that they are not always confident about taking on the responsibility of supervising student teachers, let alone be completely responsible for their training. The Licensed Teacher Scheme was also seen, by some, as a cure for shortage of modern language teachers, especially since the national curriculum requirements for modern languages presented schools with a problem of finding suitably qualified modern language graduates. The scheme also gave hope to the National Council for Punjabi Teaching, even though it was unhappy about the Government's guidelines which divide modern languages into two groups – European languages (which the school must offer); and 'other' languages (minority community languages), which could be offered, only as long as a school offered at least one European language.

Evaluation of the Licensed Teacher Scheme
Though the Government had made available to 54 LEAs enough money (£2.1 million in 1989 through LEATGS) to train more than 750 teachers under the Licensed scheme, only 50 potential teachers had embarked on the training in the first year. In April 1991 a total of 439 teachers were recruited under this scheme. In the second year, a total of 617 people were being trained in 50 authorities. One of the problems has been a wide disparity in allocation of funds; for example, London Borough of Bromley received £900 per Licensed Teacher, while Ealing received nearly £5,000 for each Licensed Teacher. The DES commissioned the NFER, to evaluate the scheme over a period of two years. This evaluation involved a national study of LEAs participating in the scheme, a further national study of licensees, and case study work in schools and institutions of higher education. The evaluation was aimed at obtaining detailed information of the operation of the first two years of the scheme, monitoring effects and implications of the scheme at school, training establishment and LEA level; and analysing the impact of the scheme in encouraging and expanding recruitment to the teaching profession while ensuring maintenance of professional standards. The HMI inspected the work of 161 Licensed Teachers in 20 LEAs, between September 1990 – July 1992, and saw them teaching 257 lessons. The final Ofsted report was on the whole complimentary. The main findings indicated that a high proportion of the Licensed Teachers seen by HMI were satisfactory or better; that a major factor in the overall success of the Licensed Teachers scheme was the rigorous nature of the selection process; that more than half of Licensed Teachers were qualified as teachers overseas and many of the others had had some teaching experience; that few schools provided well-

structured training for Licensed Teachers and that the training, of mentors was very limited at first though it did improve in quantity and quality over the two years of the survey.

By July 1992, over 1500 licences had been granted, of these more than 50 percent were to overseas trained teachers, but there is no further information about the countries in which these teachers were trained. Of the 161 Licensed Teachers whose work was inspected, 79 were overseas-trained, 60 of whom taught in primary and 19 in secondary schools. Some LEA recruited overseas teachers in their country of origin while others recruited those who were already resident in England. Three of the LEAs inspected by HMI, which had newly arrived overseas-trained teachers, provided short courses (one to two weeks) designed to introduce them to the English system. The teachers generally found these courses to be relevant and helpful. The HMIs thought it was essential that such courses should be available to deal with the likely culture shock that overseas trained teachers might experience. One other LEA also provided a longer (eight-week) course for overseas-trained Licensed Teachers, which included aspects such as classroom control, National Curriculum core subject content and teaching styles and also provided a four-week block of school experience. The HMI also found that overseas-trained teachers were on the whole significantly less well supported, and were more likely to be given full teaching loads than those changing careers.

In terms of the quality of work of the Licensed Teachers, the HMI found that the new entrants taught slightly more satisfactory or better lessons than did overseas-trained teachers, partly because they had needed time to adjust to British system. On the whole schools where Licensed Teachers were employed found little overall difference in competence between overseas-trained teachers and those changing careers. They were well pleased with the personal qualities displayed by Licensed Teachers and considered them to be academically competent for their tasks. By November 1992, a total of 443 teachers had received QTS through this route. LEAs say that teachers' and schools' hostility seems to be fading. For some like Julian Debnam from Dartford in Kent and Barry Thompson from Bedford, who took a considerable drop in salary to enter the teaching profession, it has been a fulfilling experience. 'I love it. My only regret is that I didn't do it 10 years earlier.' Barry Thompson found it hard work but says that teachers in his school were very supportive. However there are things that he would like to change about the scheme. He thinks that 'licensee teachers should not have to teach solo for the first three weeks. That time would be much better spent observing how other teachers manage their classes or teaching with the support of another teacher'. He also felt that there should be time off in the school day for licensee teachers from different schools to get together to offer each other support. The Head Teacher of Barry's school viewed the scheme as 'something at the margins of recruitment' and considered the possibility of lighter teaching loads for the licensee and for the mentor as a major difficulty (Education Guardian 24 Nov. 1992).

For others, like Brigitte Peyrac, with a degree in French and experience of teaching adults, becoming a Licensed member of school staff was unrewarding and frustrating. Though she welcomed the opportunity for mature graduates to enter the teaching profession by a simpler route, she felt that there needs to be substantial support and guidance, as set out in the Government Circular for Licensed Teachers. 'If it is a device for filling vacancies as conveniently as possible then it is a retrograde step' (TES 7 Feb. 1992). She resigned because she said, 'I can think of less stressful and more constructive ways to earn a few pounds'. The Licensees in Kent seemed to be getting the best deal since the LEA had decided that they should be supernumerary members of staff for the first year of the scheme. But there is no doubt that the scheme is expensive and extremely demanding for everyone concerned, teachers, LEA, trainers and not least the Licensed Teachers themselves. But if the choice is between a Licensed Teacher and no teacher, schools and local authorities are biting the bullet, at least for graduates in shortage subjects.

Articled Teachers Scheme

The pilot schemes for this route were set up in September 1990, to be run jointly by LEAs and teacher education institutions. The proposal was that students would enrol as PGCE students at an institution, follow a two-year course leading to the PGCE award, but that they would be trained as far as possible in schools, and would be paid a bursary (£5000 in the first year, and £6000 in the second year, which has since been increased to £12,000 from September 1992) for their teaching contribution to the schools. The amount of time to be spent in schools was not initially specified, but has since been determined to be 80 percent, with a progressive increase in the teaching load. LEAs and teacher unions reacted cautiously to 'earn-as-you-learn' proposals for school-based teacher education. One of their concerns was that if schools were short of cash they would offer employment to 'earn-as-you-learn' trainee teachers rather than to already- trained ones because the former would be cheaper. It was clear to everyone concerned that what the government was looking for was a 'quick-fix strategy', and a fast low-cost solution to teacher shortages, rather than a thought-out coherent strategy for teacher education. The other concern was that this could lead to the collapse of other traditional PGCE courses, as all students would want to earn as they learn. There was also the usual concern about standards, echoed both by the NUT and the NASUWT. No one wanted to see dilution of standards in a rush to get more teachers into schools. The Articled Teachers Scheme was seen as the Government innovation almost everyone liked. It was advertised as providing quality training over two years, with good planned support from both the experienced mentor in schools, and teacher trainers from outside. Initially 12 pilot schemes offering 500 graduates, 'on-the-job' training were approved.

On the whole, despite some problems in finding supply cover for mentor teachers, under-recruitment in some schemes and under-estimated costs in others, the actual nature of the scheme especially the school-focused element has been met with great enthusiasm. A year after the introduction of the Articled Teachers Scheme, the DES admitted that it might have to rethink its funding arrangements for the scheme in which it pays two-thirds, and local authorities one-third of students' bursaries. The low take-up (of the 600 places made available at the cost of £3 million, only 400 were taken up in 1991) meant that the scheme was in danger of failing. However, from April 1993 the DFE has agreed to pay the full cost of Articled Teachers' bursaries. The unpublished report from the NFER found that the LEAs were the 'weakest link' in the schemes run by consortia of colleges, schools and LEAs. Though some authorities had pulled out because they found the scheme too expensive, others felt that they could not find enough trainees to fill places. Even where the scheme had been somewhat disruptive for schools, like in Havering, it was still seen as a great opportunity for professional development –

There is no doubt that this course has been a god-send... the Articled Teachers Scheme has given me the opportunity to be a full time teacher, but, with the benefit of strong caring leadership, it has also given me the time to explore beyond my subject and to become part of the whole school (Pugh, TASC Bulletin 1993).

As for an improvement in quality, the OFSTED report has shown that the new Articled Teacher Scheme, with 80 percent of time in schools, did not reach a higher level of competence than those trained on the less expensive one year PGCE, with 50 percent time spent in schools. The Articled Teachers Scheme costs more than £10,000 over two years without counting fees, while the PGCE costs less than £4,000. However, it did show that 10 percent of the trainees performed better than the best conventional full-time PGCE students and as well as experienced teachers. The quality of training within any one consortium running the scheme was found to be inconsistent. The two other problems highlighted by the inspectors were superficial knowledge of the foundation subjects among primary Articled Teachers coming to the end of their training and for some secondary Articled Teachers, their original degrees did not provide the knowledge and skills they needed to teach the national curriculum effectively, and the schools in which they were trained were not equipped to help them. The NFER report found that the trainees wanted more theory to underpin their teaching practice and more opportunity to spend time in college reflecting on their early experiences in the classroom. In one of the schemes (West Sussex Institute of HE) it was found that mentors too needed more theory in order to teach the students effectively.

The judgements on the effectiveness of the schemes cannot be made properly until there has been the opportunity for evaluation of experiences of teachers qualifying by this route. However, increasing the college-based element and enhancing the theoretical knowledge are not likely to be favoured by the government which believed that learner centred pedagogy picked up at teacher education colleges has largely caused the decline in basic skills in primary schools. The 'sitting next to Nellie' approach to teacher education favoured by the government has only been marginally successful. Its apparent strengths are that it incorporates greater classroom experience than established routes of teacher education and training; facilitates close interaction between the experience and college-based studies, and enables graduates to complete their initial education and training over two years rather than one and with a bursary (£5000 in year 1 and £6000 in year 2) set at much more realistic level than the conventional PGCE grant of £2845. Its possible weaknesses are that trainees may have too little time to develop their subject knowledge. They may also be unduly influenced by the culture and practices of one particular school. The NFER report found that there was a narrowness of classroom experience and the trainees did not get a wide enough view of different social settings or ethnic groups. There were also conflicting messages from the college-based tutors and the school-based mentors, and considerable ambiguity surrounding the status of Articled Teachers. The scheme makes considerable demands on the schools within which trainees are placed, at a time when schools are already suffering from innovation overload and it is relatively expensive.

The Graduate and Registered Teacher Training Programmes

The Graduate and Registered Teacher Programmes are new employment-based routes to Qualified Teacher Status (QTS). The Graduate Teacher Programme and Registered Teacher Programme replace the Licensed Teacher, Overseas Trained Teacher and Registered Teacher Schemes from 1 December 1997, except for candidates who have already embarked on those schemes. Under the Graduate Teacher Programme, graduates who do not have QTS may be authorised by the Teacher Training Agency (TTA) to work as teachers while following an approved training programme designed to enable them to attain QTS. The programme will normally last for one year. Exceptionally, trainees with suitable experience may train in a shorter time; the minimum is three months. The same standards are required for the award of QTS whether trainees follow an employment-based route or any other course of initial teacher training The programmes will be particularly suitable for those who have trained as teachers overseas, or have teaching experience in, for example, further education or independent schools. They may also be suitable for people seeking to enter teaching after experience in other kinds of employment.

Teachers from overseas

The Overseas Trained Teachers route to QTS was aimed at teachers trained outside the European Union. They were to be initially employed under an authorisation to teach, issued by the Secretary of State and were to be given QTS only after the successful completion of appropriate training, generally, but not exclusively, after one term (DES 1991). They were required to have a degree in education or one year post-graduate qualification in education, and must have reached a standard equivalent to the GCSE grade C in English and Mathematics, and have at least one year's teaching experience. They could be paid as qualified teachers or as unqualified teachers, depending on the LEAs or the governors concerned, and the same applied for considerations concerned with acceptance of qualifications, and to the amount and nature of training required. If the overseas teachers had the academic qualifications, but not the teaching experience, they were then considered eligible to be employed under the Licensed Teacher route. It is interesting to note that overseas teachers were being recruited to the profession through the very route that is at present least effectively regulated in terms of the standards required.

But those recognised as teachers in the EC Member States or in Scotland or Northern Ireland were able to gain QTS by writing to the DES (now DfES). However, the teacher unions warned that once other EC countries implemented the same directive, 'the traffic across the channel is likely to be one way with better pay, conditions of service, status and support elsewhere in Europe' (The Independent 12 May 1989). Whilst there are some success stories of projects designed to encourage exchange, induction and employment of EC teachers in England & Wales, for example, the collaboration between Charlotte Mason College and Baden Wurttemberg in West Germany and the European Language Teachers Project at the University of York Language Teaching Centre (TASC Bulletin 1990), there are also several reports of disappointing and indeed very discouraging experiences. For example, an East German teacher found 'British bureaucracy tougher to crack than the Berlin Wall'. Applications for jobs in state and private schools from the 30 year-old who left Germany after the Wall came down were rejected, despite her qualifications being recognised by the DES. Head Teachers in East and West Sussex told her: 'We always have problems with foreigners'; 'Your accent will cause difficulties;' and 'You have never taught in an English school before'.

This was really frustrating for this teacher who was unable to find a teaching job, despite her teaching experience of seven years in East Germany and her ability to teach German and Russian, and at a time when Britain needs nearly 1750 (estimated in 1991) teachers of modern European languages to implement the language requirements of the national curriculum (TES 2 August 1991). In the same month TES also reported the case of a Science teacher from Mauritius, who faced deportation despite the fact that he had a work permit and a job. He was granted a work experience and training permit by the Department of Employment, but it was never stamped in his passport. Another case of a 28 year-old teacher from Tasmania highlights the bureaucratic minefield that has to be crossed by non-European Community teachers who are willing and qualified but end up feeling unwanted and frustrated. Equally frustrated are hundreds of Overseas qualified teachers resident in the UK who have been ignored, discriminated against and put through the bureaucratic hoops for years only to be told at the end that they are either too old, over-qualified to receive any grants or that they have to, start from a scratch because their previous qualifications and experience are not recognised.

Partnership with Schools or Schools Based Training

School-based PGCE courses have attracted considerable interest as possible models of training which incorporate and value greater experience in school than many other PGCE courses, but also recognising the contribution that the higher education institutions have to make. The key characteristics of such courses are that they involve partnership, and equal esteem between teachers in school and college staff. However, teacher trainers have been very critical of the Government's plans to transfer the major part of post-graduate training into schools, as they believe 'that this could lead to substantial reductions in the numbers being trained' (TES Jan. 1992). Chris Pascal, Professor of Early Childhood Education at Worcester College of HE said that the irony was that while other professions such as nursing were moving towards a more theoretical and academic content with time for reflection and studies based predominantly in higher education, the reverse was happening to teaching.

Two year PGCE courses

Radical proposals to extend the PGCE to two years, were first put forward (Preen & Collier 1987) when a UDE was already participating in a pioneering joint initiative by offering a two-year part-time PCCE to train bilingual instructors from LEAs in the North-West (for details see Arora 1994). They argued that both CATE and the White Paper, Teaching Quality, had not taken sufficient account of key factors that motivated against training quality. Their proposal to grant QTS at the end of two years and to combine initial training and probationary year, and the experience of part-time PGCE at the UDE, seem to have formed the basis of Articled Teachers' Training. They also argued that these proposals would not only not require extra funding, but would be a major advantage by involving the schools in a very real and close partnership with teacher education institutions. The authors suggested that the inductee posts could only be established in particular schools, deemed to be suitable both by LEAs and training institutions, but that they should also be available in pairs, with a junior and senior inductee sharing teaching responsibilities. University of East Anglia PGCE Project, despite its numerous advantages for the students, the course tutors and for the staff of participating school and its pupils, was abandoned after a year as it was found to be unworkable. The reasons for its failure included ambivalence on the parts of trainees in terms of their roles; the strain of providing cover for school staff involved in the training of students and from the pressure tutors felt by working so closely with the school.

McLennan & Seadon (1988) challenged the central assertion (Furlong et.al 1988) that schools are necessarily the best place to develop 'reflection-in-action', essentially an intellectual application, of insights acquired through practice and experience, backed up by a knowledge of principles and pedagogy. They also suggested that if school-based work was to fulfil its potential, it was important to take account of the 'personal' as well as financial costs and that even with the appropriate contractual allowance and adequate funding, the main beneficiaries of such a scheme may well be the school and not the trainee teachers. In the Oxford scheme (Secondary PGCE) the participating schools had the advantage of 10 supernumerary helpers, available to undertake projects of value to the school, the stimulus of their questioning, and the enhanced professional skills of the mentors and professional tutor. The key principles of this scheme, partnership between school and college; joint organisation and assessment; and classroom experience, are all equally applicable to primary PGCE and B.Ed. courses. The strengths of the Oxford scheme were the amount of classroom experience, the level of advice and support provided, the close integration of school and college-based learning, and interaction with other student teachers. A significant weakness was a lack of experience of more than one school and a great demand on students in terms of work at the university and in the school.

Hertfordshire Action on Teacher Supply (HATS) was launched in 1987 to meet a shortage of Mathematics and Physics teachers. Beginning with a one-week 'taster' course, this mainly on-the-job course caught the imagination of many LEAs, and has been regarded as a blueprint for the Government's Licensed Teacher Scheme. Herts County was also the first to apply for licence when the scheme was announced in 1989. For Hertfordshire, the scheme has proved to be an outstanding success, with some 127 trainees recruited in the three years. In this 'action-reflection' model, emphasis was placed on the practical aspects of teaching at the beginning, encouraging students to try new techniques and then to reflect and analyse the outcomes. Until recently the HATS trainees received QTS on the completion of their course. Under the Licensed Teachers' regulations, they now receive QTS at the end of their first year of training and complete a further probationary year in school.

Though the HMIs (1990) regarded the scheme as well conceived and reported that the majority of trainees seemed to have the potential to develop into satisfactory teachers, they also found that the HATS scheme had turned out many poor teachers and commented that 'the filling of a vacancy seemed more important than the placing of trainee teachers in schools where they can be well supervised and observe good practice' (TES Dec. 1990). DfEE news bulletin 67/93 announced the First Wholly School-Based Teacher Training Project in March 1993. The new scheme, to cover both primary and secondary training, was intended to give schools real power to decide how new members of the teaching profession should be trained. The schools and CTCs were to be responsible for designing the courses, recruiting the students and training them, using outside expertise only where they consider it to be necessary. The message was clear: 'We know from the Articled and Licensed teachers' schemes that the school-based approach can be very effective in training both primary and secondary teachers.... I want schools who are willing and able to take the lead in teacher education to be given the opportunity to do so' (Patten 1993).

The Initial Training of Primary School Teachers (Draft Circular 1993) proposed tough new criteria for all training courses, including a greater role for schools; a continuing need for study in higher education institutions; and a greater diversity of courses, including a new one-year course for those with experience of working with children, preparing them to teach nursery and infant pupils. The Government claimed that it was to improve the quality and relevance of ITT as a whole, so that all newly qualified teachers can contribute to raising standards in schools. The NUT questioned the wisdom of introducing more specialist subject teaching and warned that the proposed two and three-year B.Ed. courses could be regarded as 'second class' qualifications. The UCET criticised the amount of training time allocated to the new proposed schemes, as it was at odds with the general trends towards individual study in higher education. Tutors of Advanced Courses for Teachers of Young Children (TACTYC) was surprised that at a time when the Government had itself commented on the over-supply of primary teachers and cut the number of would-be teachers entering initial teacher education, that could justify the need for different '*low-level*' routes into the profession (TES 30 July 1993a).

Proposals for mum's army

'A policeman's wife with several children of her own and strong maternal instincts' was to be the new model infant school teacher of the future. Baroness Blatch's proposals for Mum's army, to allow nursery nurses to teach in primary classes, were rejected by CATE, which published an unprecedented statement distancing itself from the Government. CATE claimed that it had not drawn up any plans for accrediting child-care workers and had not endorsed a two-tier system (generalist B.Ed. and specialist PGCE) of entry into the profession, through proposals for school-based training in the primary sector. Professor Gammage (TACTYC) protested that the one-year course for mums would have an adverse effect on children's education both in primary schools and later on, and that the line must be held for an all-graduate teaching profession (Education, June 1993). The training institutions and the unions also saw the proposals for 'Mum's army' of non-graduate primary teachers as divisive, discriminatory and insulting (NUT July 93). Key people in education such as Ted Wragg of Exeter University and Chris Woodhead, Chief Executive of the NCC, and others claimed that it will demean the status of teaching and that moving funds for training to schools may mean that some education departments will close. Professor Jennifer Latto, Chair of the Polytechnic Council for the Education of Teachers, said: 'It will fuel a discussion going on in some universities about whether they want to continue to be involved in teacher training.' Professor Richard Pring of Oxford University said some departments would 'wither on the vine' and others would give up PGCE courses (Anthony Dore on Patten's Mum's Army recruitment plan (TES June 18 1993). The Education Guardian reported in September 1993, that despite bitter opposition from the education unions, John Patten was unlikely to back down on his proposals for the Mum's Army, but by November 1993, the government had stepped back from its widely disliked proposals for non-graduate infant teachers (TES 26 Nov. 93).

In contrast, the Government's revised plans to introduce a certificated course for classroom assistants have been widely welcomed. The course is supposed to provide 'a rigorous period of study of successful approaches to the teaching of reading, writing and mathematics and of the ways in which classroom assistants can contribute to the teaching and learning of basic skills in support of qualified teachers' (DfEE Circular 67/93). These plans fit in well with the recent findings of a research project on 'The innovative uses of non-teaching staff in primary and secondary schools', commissioned by the DFE and based at the University of London's Institute of Education. Professor Mortimer and his team found that there was inadequate pre-service and in-service training of non-teaching staff and that they needed better job descriptions and to be involved more in the school.

Training Schools Project

The Green Paper – 'Teachers: Meeting the Challenge of Change' (2000) proposed a network of high quality Training Schools that will demonstrate good practice in ITT, train subject mentors and professional Mentors and undertake research. A Training School was described as:

> A School, that in partnership with HEI or SCITT and others, will demonstrate and develop excellent practice in initial teacher training, explore and try out new approaches to training teachers and carry out and use teaching research. It will build up and share good and developing initial teacher training practice with other schools and teacher training providers, both within their existing partnership networks and beyond.

Each Training School was expected to set itself targets for developments and improvements to initial teacher training and propose innovative plans for achieving them, including the imaginative use of ICT. Funding for Training Schools was made available through the Standards Fund (Activity B5), with an upper limit of £100,000 per application per year. The process of making application for Standards Fund was clearly described in the DfEE information booklet entitled 'Better Training – How to become a Training School'. The booklet invited suitable schools to submit an application for Training School Status. The guidance included the priorities of the Training Schools Initiative and explained what schools and their partners have to demonstrate and show how progress will be achieved each year of the duration of the project. Schools were not expected to meet all the targets, but these were only included as a guidance for priorities for the Training Schools Project. The targets did offer opportunities for schools to train teachers to teach children with Special Educational Needs, and to teach children from disadvantaged groups. There was also an opportunity for working with outside agencies and community partners (out of school experience for trainees) and make innovative use of employment-based routes in to teaching, and programmes for teaching assistants working towards QTS. Though a third of all schools (33 percent) offered training to teach SEN children (Target 11) and 25 percent offered training for trainees to maximize the use of classroom assistants and other non-teaching staff (Target 12), only 7 percent of all schools offered training to teach children from disadvantaged groups (Target 13). In terms of wide ranging targets, experience of other teacher training routes (Target (16) was also addressed by 20 percent of all schools. Working with outside agencies and community partners (Target 17) was addressed by another 50 percent of al schools.

The Training Schools Evaluation Report (Arora 2002 for the DfES) found a lot of good practice in schools across the country with regard to successful teaching of children with special educational needs and of children from disadvantaged groups. This good practice needs to be harnessed for training future teachers, who don't always get sufficient training or opportunities to address these issues. The report also found that Training Schools have a tremendous potential for filling this gap and making issues of equality an integral part in the process of ITT courses as well as for those who are newly qualified. These schools have opportunities to collaborate and learn from schools with examples of good practice. Though the information booklet sent to schools did not make any reference to equal opportunities, the schools were asked to consider two specific targets related to the training to teach children with Special Educational Needs (target 11) and training to teach children from disadvantaged groups (target 13). It is encouraging to note that 33 percent of the schools had addressed the issues related to the training of teachers to teach SEN children and another 7 percent have addressed some of the issues related to teaching children from disadvantaged groups. There were some good examples of the ways in which these issues were addressed. These included issues of gender, special educational needs and social inclusion. One school identified its key strengths as training of minority ethnic teachers and another school considered implications of teaching in a school with a multicultural community for subject mentors. Exploring and supporting employment-based routes into teaching was another example of one school's interest in promoting issues of equality.

The important message from this evaluation was the consideration of what additional support schools can offer in training teachers. They can certainly help adapt to the changing requirements of the school curriculum more speedily and effectively. As practicing teachers they have more control on the skills that need to be developed in the trainees. It was clear from the evaluation that more evidence of visible partnership with HEIs would be helpful. This could be in the form of joint course planning meetings, an ongoing joint course review group to monitor the progress of trainees and make speedy adjustments wherever appropriate.

Courses for Teachers from Minority Ethnic Groups

Two-year B.Ed. at Derbyshire College of HE (validated by Nottingham University)

In the light of Swann (1985) recommendations, Derbyshire College decided to redesign its programme, to enable candidates with a degree from overseas, who were not able to gain entry to the PGCE, but still met the specified entry requirements for B.Ed. The overseas degree qualifications of potential candidates were to be considered in order to gain exemption from the first two years of the four-year B.Ed. degree, provided their first degree was in a subject offered in the four-year programme. The candidates were also required to complete a Bridging Course (two terms), with a specific aim to re-orientate themselves to academic study commensurate with an Honours degree and to gain experience in a primary school related to their chosen age phase. The programme was planned in line with the CATE criteria (Circular 3/84) and was designed to prepare students for two complementary roles, principally that of a 'generalist' class teacher and to a lesser extent, that of 'specialist', preparing for potential curriculum leadership. The students were to be taught, for part of their programme, jointly with students training for other professions and also with those on a four-year B.Ed. programme. The teachers emerging from this course were seen to be as 'normal' teachers in primary schools, able to teach across a full range of the primary school curriculum. It was recognised that the 'value of their ethnic background will be their ability to communicate with children from a similar ethnic background, and/or enable a faster degree of permeation of the knowledge of minority cultures by being members of a school staff' (Derbyshire Submission document, 1987).

Polytechnic of North London: Two-year B.Ed. for minority ethnic teachers (early years 3-8)

As with Derbyshire College of HE, this course offered a combination of academic study and practical work with children in schools. The course, like its four-year counterpart, was designed to train students to teach in the inner-city schools, and for much of the course students were to be taught alongside students on the four-year B.Ed. course. But unlike the four-year programme, this course offered an additional dimension of 'Communications in Education' and was designed to train students with bilingual skills to become early years' teachers, not community language teachers. The communications in education component sets out to orientate the students to the English education system and enables them to examine issues relating to the use of students' cultural and linguistic skills within that system.

As for entry qualifications these included the usual requirement of a qualification in a subject relevant to the primary school curriculum and that along with other relevant experience, was credited as the equivalent of one year's study of a B.Ed. degree. With regard to the requirement of GCE 'O' level or equivalent in English and Mathematics the Polytechnic had devised its own written tests to determine equivalence and also offered help to candidates who did not feel competent to sit the exceptional entry procedure tests, by supplying the requisite syllabus for these tests.

Two-year B.Ed. (The Primary Language Studies Course) at Bristol Polytechnic

This was designed specifically for mature students with graduate or equivalent qualifications from overseas (not recognised by the DES for entry into PGCE), and who had the experience and personal characteristics suitable for developing into the qualities required of graduate primary school teachers in the 1990s. The experience of bilingualism, bi-dialectalism and minority ethnic group membership was considered significant. The entry requirements for the course included evidence of competence in both Mathematics and English language. As for graduate status, there was considerable flexibility to acknowledge qualifications that may be equivalent. In addition to a BA, BTEC, & Dip. HE, consideration was given to successful completion of the first year of undergraduate study from a UK institution, or such other equivalent entry qualifications as approved by the course management committee in consultation with the admissions officer. What was not clear from the documentation was whether this criteria and the two interviews applied to all candidates for initial teacher education, and not just to those of minority ethnic origin. However, like all other courses for initial teacher education, this course was subject to CATE approval and the usual monitoring and evaluation procedures of the institution.

The overall aim of the course was to provide an opportunity for advanced study of language and a sound preparation for a beginning teacher. It was planned on the basis that students' own linguistic and cultural background will provide a rich resource for reflecting on the processes by which language is learnt and is used in learning. Similarly the students' work in schools, alongside personal reflection was to provide the basis for considering how children learn. The thematic structure of the course was meant to ensure an integrative approach to learning and teaching. The need to provide practical experience as a basis for reflective learning and teaching led to the decision to provide serial school experience throughout the course, with two substantial block periods of teaching practice. Both the pattern of assessment and the teaching and learning methodology were underpinned by the concept of reflective pedagogy and the integrative philosophy of the course. A significant dimension of this course was its concern to address the issues of equal opportunities, with particular reference to 'race' and gender; issues of multiracial education and of special educational needs. A central focus of the course was the understanding of the opportunities offered by linguistic diversity, both by the study of linguistically and culturally diverse populations and by drawing on students' life experiences of living in and with different cultures and languages. In addition to the general philosophy of permeation in all aspects of initial training courses, specific focus on multicultural and multiracial education was evident in certain themes that run through the curriculum. The study of language and society, through topics such as attitudes to accent and dialect, the nature of bilingualism and the question of non-standard languages and dialects ensured that the students gave careful consideration to the relationship of various communities to schools.

The Sheffield United Multicultural Education Service (SUMES)

SUMES along with Sheffield LEA and the Polytechnic (now Sheffield Hallam University) also devised a pioneering shortened B.Ed. course for instructors from minority ethnic groups. A group of 15 women who had been on one of the SUMES' Access courses (12 were instructors with SUMES) were recruited for this shortened B.Ed. programme. They were all juggling family and domestic commitments with work and study. Many had degrees; some had teaching qualifications from overseas. All were bilingual and all found their qualifications were not accepted by the DES, so SUMES's first job was to train them to meet the entrance qualifications for the B.Ed. with a main component of language studies. Unfortunately, unlike some other institutions (Bristol Poly), HND and BTEC diplomas did not count. Nisha, one of the trainees summed up the benefits of this pioneering course in two short sentences. 'At the moment, I am just doing a job. After this, I will have a career.'

The Polytechnic of North London two year PGCE (part-time)

The rationale for this course was rather different from that of the East Anglia scheme (described earlier), in that it aimed to develop in the students an appreciation of the role of the bilingual teacher in an urban primary school. The course therefore focused on the diversity of cultural, social and language backgrounds of the children, and also aimed to develop in students an understanding of the social and community context of urban primary schools and to examine issues of 'race', gender and class and their implications for learners and teachers. The whole course was designed in such a way that students spent two-thirds of their time in schools and only a third in the polytechnic.

Leeds Metropolitan University two year PGCE (part-time)

This was designed for the training of graduates whose overseas qualifications were not recognised by the DES for entry into the teaching profession. The course (validated by the CNAA) was open to mature students (over 22) of minority ethnic origin who were either graduates or had followed a broadly based higher education course for 3 years. The course was designated as providing training under positive action (Section 37 of the Race Relations Act 1976). The purpose of the course was to increase representation from minority groups within the teaching profession, and to attract teachers whose cultural and linguistic experience will enable them to support the learning and personal development of young children from minority groups in West Yorkshire. The course was organised on the basis of two days a week for two years plus two periods of full-time teaching practice, four weeks in year one and six weeks in year two. Though five LEAs in West Yorkshire supported the course, only eight of the fifteen course members were employed, in one of the LEAs, as home/school liaison workers, mother-tongue teachers or as nursery nurses, but all without full professional status. Since the course was designated as eligible for mandatory awards (DES Mandatory Awards Regulations, Section 10 (d) iii) all applicants accepted on the course, but not in employment, were entitled to receive grants to pay the fees and a small subsistence.

This part-time course seemed to demand a great deal more from the students as there was an expectation that teachers trained through this route will have to demonstrate competence both in the specialist bilingual/biadialectic role as well as the generalist role of a class teacher. In addition, it was presumed that given the nature of the student group (minority ethnic students with bilingual skills) 'the issues of 'race', racism, equality and pluralism will be of concern, as will the implications of such issues for the students' own personal and professional development' (Foundation Studies, page 3). However, though there was a specific unit of study (Curriculum Studies) for 'Language and Learning in the Multi-Lingual School' which supported the development of the aspect of teachers' role which was concerned with bilingualism and education, there did not seem to be any such visible focus in the Foundation Studies on issues of 'race', racism and equal opportunities to underpin the practice of students. Though the course document suggested that it contained all the elements of a full-time PGCE course, it was not clear whether it was taught as a separate course or in conjunction with the full-time course.

Kirklees Trainee Teachers Scheme (KTTS)

The KTTS was introduced with a view to attract trainee teachers from Black and Asian communities. The objective was to give the trainee teachers practical experience of working in a school, while they were attending an initial teacher education course leading to QTS. The institutions offering the initial teacher education course (BICC and Leeds Metropolitan University) had the responsibility for providing the training including arrangements and supervision of school experience and teaching practice. The Head Teacher or a senior teacher in each participating school had the responsibility for the trainee's work experience in school. An LEA personnel officer was responsible for the smooth running of the scheme. The trainees received a bursary in addition to their college fees paid by the LEA and each of the participating schools received financial support for providing 'on the job' training. The entry requirements were the same as those for full-time PGCE, e.g., a degree or equivalent from British institutions, or MA/Msc from most of the Indian and Pakistani Universities plus GCE 'O' level or equivalent in English and Mathematics. The posts were advertised with a very clear intention to implement positive action as per section 38 (1 & 2) of the Race Relations Act. Whilst it may appear to resemble closely the Licensed Teachers Scheme and the Articled Teachers Scheme, the KTTS was significantly different in two respects. Firstly, it was an LEA initiative designed to enable local trainees to take a part-time course, whilst being employed as non-teaching assistants in the first year, and taking greater responsibility for teaching in the second year. Secondly, it had the confidence and the support of professional associations and of the head teachers within the authority, and it was important to have the support of key people in monitoring the progress of the trainees.

Evidence from Case Studies

It is clear from the brief descriptions of courses designed specially to recruit minority ethnic teachers, that it is possible for institutions to be more flexible and imaginative, and that with appropriate support from schools, such courses can indeed be successful. The evidence from two case studies further supports this argument.

Part-time PGCE: a pilot course at Manchester University

The QTS course (Part-time PGCE) was much appreciated when it was first set up. It was a pilot scheme and aware of the dangers of 'Black teachers for Black pupils', it strived to promote equality in all its senses. This part-time course at the UDE provided a course of training for overseas graduates and recruited a total of 31 students who intended to be primary teachers. The first three cohorts demonstrated 90 percent success rate, that is a total of 19 teachers out of 21 recruited are now in posts in LEAs in the Northwest. The course demonstrated that there is merit in the part-time PGCE mode that combines work experience in schools with training at the University. The evaluation conducted by the UDE also concluded that the course served a useful purpose and was well received by the students. It provided the LEAs with much needed minority ethnic teachers, who are bilingual and are ideally placed not only to facilitate the home to school transition of minority ethnic children, but also to act as role models for minority ethnic young people who may consider teaching as a career.

It was also evident from the range of qualifications and experiences brought to the course, that students with higher qualifications, such as an M.A., did not necessarily make better teachers. What seems to be important was the kind of work experience they came with and how well they could transfer the skills they had already acquired. It was also evident that older male students with qualifications and experience from overseas didn't necessarily find it easy to work with younger children. The first-hand knowledge of bringing up children seems to have been a great asset for some of the female students, but experience of working with young children had also had tremendous benefits in equipping them for the classroom. However, the UDE evaluation, the HMI report and the fieldwork indicate that there is need for reconsideration of some aspects of the training and the infrastructures that support it. Most new developments and initiatives undergo a period of adjustment and take time in establishing new ways of working and this part-time PGCE course was no exception. But what does cause concern are the issues that remained unresolved, despite early signals by LEA advisors, and constant attempts by successive course tutors to seek improvement. These included inadequate staffing arrangements, ill-equipped primary resource base, unwillingness of the UDE staff to fully integrate the part-time students in tutorial provision, and little, if any, progress in recruiting minority ethnic students on the full-time PGCE course.

Similarly, the intention to integrate part-time students with the full-time course, and to improve contact and co-operation between staff teaching on the full-time course and the course-tutor for the part-time mode never really materialised. Three years after the course started, the HMI report still found that, 'Line management and communication links between the director of the full-time PGCE primary course and the part-time course tutor at this stage were weak' (HMI 1991, Para 46). Though the UDE evaluation suggested that these links had been improved, and that other weak aspects of the course had also been strengthened, the course was closed in spite of its success in meeting a very real need for training minority ethnic teachers. The real reasons for its demise are still unclear. The UDE put it down to the changes in Section 11 funding, and to the critical report published by the HMI. There was no suggestion in the HMI (1991) report that the course should close, only that it should make certain changes and address the areas of weaknesses. My attempts to seek clarification about the real reasons for its closures confirmed that the HMI report had influenced the UDE to close the course. What is of real concern is that small-scale initiatives, like these, get scrutinised to a point of distraction from the real issue, which is the inability of teacher training institutions to handle new developments and meet new needs.

DTECC case study

The purpose of this case study of a department of education in a Higher Education Institution (DTECC) was to consider how initial teacher education responded to inevitable changes of political ideology and economics, both at a national level and at a local institutional level. The study focused on how courses of initial teacher education prepare all teachers to teach in a multicultural society and on the recruitment and employment of minority ethnic students and staff in the institution. It also included a description of the positive action initiatives taken to increase the number of minority ethnic teachers in schools. On the one hand the institution demonstrated its responsiveness very effectively, by maintaining its commitment to equal opportunities, in the face of considerable external imperatives. On the other hand, there were clear indications of a level of student dissatisfaction, which need further exploration. Though the picture on the whole is one of great achievement, as despite the numerous institutional mergers, constant external imperatives and changing criteria for validation of courses, the teacher education programmes at the DTECC succeeded in maintaining their primary focus. The HMI reports and the reports of external examiners suggest that the teacher education courses at DTECC are preparing teachers adequately to meet the challenges of teaching in a multicultural society. They clearly meet the official criteria for Validation and Accreditation, and are popular, as is evident from the healthy recruitment figures. However, there is also substantial evidence, and not just comments from individuals with high ideals, that Black students in particular do not feel that the courses prepare them adequately for their role in multicultural schools, and that they do not address the issues of 'race' and racism in sufficient depth. Further work needs to be done to identify the reasons for student dissatisfaction with the initial teacher education courses.

It seems that DTECC has succeeded in running courses that satisfy conventional assumptions about initial teacher education for a multicultural society, but interviews with black students on the courses, comments from minority ethnic teachers employed in schools and available research evidence suggests that the courses are not always sensitive to the needs of Black students and do not address the needs of minority ethnic children in schools. It could be argued that the courses in question have a reputation built on skilful impression management during inspections and validations, and that they do meet the official criteria, because that in itself does not require a very explicit commitment to the issues of equal opportunities. DTECC recognizes that we need and deserve teachers with high levels of bilingual and intercultural skills. It has therefore, offered additional opportunities for minority ethnic students to qualify as teachers. But these courses have had some problems. The ones that have been reasonably successful (Part-time PGCE & The Articled Teachers Scheme) were only on offer for one year. More work needs to be done to identify why some of these courses have worked better than the others. The DTECC also needs to incorporate the lessons learnt from running these courses in its mainstream provision. Despite significant opportunities for redressing the imbalance (due to early retirement of staff), the staffing of the DTECC itself remains exclusively white. The monitoring of its recruitment process suggests that there have been a number of minority ethnic applications for teaching posts in the DTECC and that with one exception, lack of qualifications was not listed as a reason for their rejection. It does suggest that there may be hidden bias in the process, which ends up rejecting suitably qualified people from minority ethnic groups because they don't have sufficient experience, even though they do meet the specified essential criteria (qualifications and experience) to be short-listed.

Finally, the requirements of National Curriculum and of the Circular 3/84 may have led to a more balanced programme for curriculum areas, but they also may have led to the reduction in focus on multicultural issues. The arguments for a model of 'permeation' whereby all courses address the issues of multicultural and anti-racist education are strong, but they can only be sustained if the process of validation of courses and assessment of students and evaluation of outcomes clearly includes criteria, which not only directly addresses these issues, but requires evidence of successful 'permeation'. Equally necessary is the provision of opportunities for students to undertake distinct modules to develop their expertise in areas such as multicultural education, anti-racist strategies and bilingual Education. The message that needs to be taken on board in this context is that in a 'permeation' model it should be possible to provide for, both an integration of a multicultural perspective across a whole range of curriculum areas, and an opportunity to develop specialist expertise.

To Practice the Theory or to Theorise the Practice

It does seem that Government policy on initial teacher education and training has been developed in isolation from the continuing professional development of teachers, as no coherent relationship has been established between initial training, the induction or probationary year, and subsequent in-service training. It also seems that the Secretary of State for Education may not have been as fully informed about the current state of teacher education as he might be. Most institutions already spend 50-60 percent of their time working in partnership with local schools, and what he sees as the 'lefty liberal teaching of sociology and philosophy of education ceased to exist 7-8 years ago' (Chambers, Yorkshire Post 1992). In Ted Wragg's words: 'The Education Secretary's speech shows an ignorance of and utter contempt for the expertise of teacher trainers' (Yorkshire Post 1992). Furthermore, the proposals for the reform of teacher education and the introduction of new routes to QTS are introduced without any reference to research evidence on the effectiveness of different methods of training and success or otherwise of different routes into QTS. Such evidence as does exist is provided by the reports of HMIs which show that whilst particular areas need improvement, the initial education of teachers is on the whole good (Standards in Education, 1987-88). The report recognised that most teacher education institutions had worked hard to create effective working partnerships with LEAs and schools, and acknowledged that the success of such partnerships depended largely on the goodwill of teachers and the relationship between schools, LEAs and colleges. It also noted that courses in ITT, especially the one year PGCE, faced a serious 'quarts-into-pint-pots' dilemma, and made reference to some of the persistent serious weaknesses that had initially emerged from the New Teacher in School (HMI 1988).

In 1988-89 too, the HMIs found that almost half of the 20 primary courses inspected were reported to be good in all respects, three were weak overall and the remainder had a number of particular strengths and weaknesses. At the same time as much as 25 percent of the lessons taken by newly-qualified teachers were judged less than satisfactory (HMI 1988). The problems identified by the HMIs in Standards of Education (1988-89) included a challenge to adapt the courses to take full account of the requirements of the National Curriculum; to take account of a range of national reports such as Kingman (1988); Cockcroft (1982); and the EOC reports of 1989; and to have a closer partnership between schools and training institutions (DES 1990). The report also stressed the importance of all routes into QTS to be of high, comparable quality, regardless of differences in duration and mode. The 1989-90 HMI Report found the initial training of primary and secondary teachers to be satisfactory or better in most institutions. Despite the general satisfaction, the report was critical of initial teacher education courses for not providing sufficient training to equip students to be effective subject coordinators. They also recognised, yet again, the 'quarts-into-pint-pots' *pressure* on one-year PGCE courses. The treatment of special needs, of teaching for the most able, and of other issues relating to equal opportunities was found to vary in extent and quality and the message was that unless 'it was consciously and explicitly planned for, organised and overseen. It will not simply happen' (DES 1991). However, the need to prepare new teachers for the National Curriculum (NCC 1991) has helped to clarify thinking about what is reasonable to expect of an ITT course.

The HMIs also found induction of new teachers to be the weakest link in teacher education, but recognised that there was increasing co-operation between training institutions and schools. The HMI Report 'The New Teacher in School' (HMI 1988) revealed that only 37 percent of primary and middle schools and 66 percent of secondary schools claimed to provide a structured induction programme for probationers. The report also revealed considerable criticism by probationers and heads of schools with regard to lack of support from LEAS, inadequate level of visits by advisers and inspectors and lack of supply cover for training meetings. It is this lack of support during the crucial period of induction and the absence of any structured link with the initial education and training of teachers that contributes to both the unacceptably high proportion of unsatisfactory lessons (25 percent in 1988) identified by HMI, and the equally unacceptable rate of newly- qualified teachers leaving the profession (18 percent leaving within 2 years).

The HMI also acknowledged that the Articled Teachers Scheme and school-based work make heavy demands on schools and on individual teachers, and that making time for suitable brief and training for the school-based mentors was a challenge. It was recognised that a broad range of teachers were being recruited under the Licensed Teachers Scheme, including overseas-trained teachers, instructors and recruits from industry and commerce, recruited directly by schools to fill specific vacancies, and that there is likely to be limited scope for LEAs to run common training programmes for their wide ranging training needs. Historically schools have been blaming colleges for not preparing teachers for the real world of the classroom and colleges have been blaming schools for not supporting the newly trained teachers in trying out new ideas and new methods. However, despite this continuous cycle of blame and counter blame, schools and ITE institutions have built alliances over many aspects of the Education Reform Act and have also defended the child-centred liberal democratic ethos of the post-Plowden era and some of the equal opportunities developments such as anti-racism and anti-sexism.

During the last decade, the imposition of the National Curriculum and more school- based involvement in teacher education courses both as planners as well as trainers and the need for college tutors to have 'recent, relevant and substantial teaching experience' in schools has led to a new combined role for schools and colleges and a greater willingness to examine strengths and weaknesses to the mutual benefit of both institutions and the students. It is worth mentioning that a number of USA studies (1990) highlighted considerable deficiencies in school-based teacher education. These included unsatisfactory mentoring of student teachers, inadequate theoretical input and inadequate supervision of teaching practice. The implications for the two recently introduced school-based innovations are clearly visible, especially where such schemes, as in the case of Licensed Teachers, are likely to lack theoretical inputs. The two-year Articled Teachers

Scheme can indeed have an effective mentoring system with the collaborative effort on the part of schools and training institutions, but they do need adequate time for reflective discussions and the mentors need to be adequately resourced and rewarded for their time and effort. The HMI publication 'New Teacher In School' (1988) highlighted areas in which 297 teachers felt inadequately prepared by their ITT courses. Although the survey was carried out on students unaffected by 1984 CATE requirements, it did itemise in valuable detail a number of competencies and areas of awareness identified by probationary teachers. An unpublished study by Waddop and Hill looked at some of the needs voiced by teachers, advisory teachers and head teachers. Of the fourteen statements recorded as the most common responses gleaned from unprompted verbal interviews and written questionnaires, at least 50 percent related to the content of ITT courses and a similar number to the relationship between schools and colleges and another 50 percent to the debates concerning the model of the teacher.

It appeared from this study that schools wanted teachers not merely to have appropriate knowledge, skills and attitudes, but to be active, critical and reflective practitioners, who understand how children's 'race', gender and social background affect their learning and also affects how they are treated by teachers. Professor Whitty (1991) offers a common framework for teacher education, as an alternative to the one prescribed by the New Right, a framework which recognises that there is a lot of good practice and innovation going on within conventional routes but also takes on board the justifiable criticisms. His framework aims to ensure some commonality of standards and a diversity of routes into teaching without making them into a hierarchy (e.g. Licensed Teacher route will be as valid as the Articled Teacher route). What is missing from this framework is a reference to equal opportunity issues as central in preparation of all teachers and to the need for recruitment, training and retention of minority ethnic teachers and the participation of minority ethnic groups in the bodies that are responsible for validation, accreditation and assessment.

Though there have been many well-publicised and successful initiatives undertaken by Initial teacher education Institutions, whereby students have been trained largely or wholly in partnership with schools, there have not been many comparative studies of different training approaches or studies of the longer-term impact of school-based schemes on teacher effectiveness. One such study (MacLennan & Seadon 1988), found the school-based PGCE at East Anglia to be extremely expensive, not only in terms of financial resources and contractual arrangements, but also in terms of the 'personal costs' of time, energy and commitment of all those involved in it. Another DES commissioned study (Furlong and Hirst et al 1988), a long-term review of four school-based training programmes, communicated the need for clarity about various levels of training. It guarded against the dangers of simple slogans for and against the school-based schemes. Blake & Blake (1990) also identified the attitudes and responses of professional teachers as the key aspects of school-based training as subject of investigation. The findings of this investigation have important implications for the planning of teacher education courses embracing more practitioner involvement, and for courses for the practitioners themselves. The teachers in this sample were very critical, even contemptuous about the effectiveness of trainers and their institutions. With regard to the attitudes of teachers to school-based training the findings reveal certain ambiguities. On the one hand there was apparent certainty on the part of teachers that recent classroom experience and the personality of the teacher are most important attributes of the training process, on the other hand teachers revealed an uncertainty about their own ability to do the job of training. The study also found that a large number of teachers had an ambivalent attitude towards their profession. It may well have implications for students in that this ambivalence might affect their attitude to the training they receive and indeed to the profession on the whole. On balance the evidence from this study suggested that, much of the political debate on teacher education and training has missed the crucial importance of the quality of partnership between institutions of teacher education and training, schools and local education authorities. The focus seems to be mainly on where teacher education is undertaken, rather than on how the different essential elements of subject knowledge and understanding, pedagogy, classroom training and induction can best be combined in a coherent whole.

Equally, on the vexed question of the role of 'theory' in teacher education, much of the public debate has overlooked the extent to which the application of the CATE criteria and the introduction of the national curriculum have already displaced formal theory from the content of courses of teacher education and training. Lawler (1990) accused teacher trainers of teaching students to think and of giving them the opportunity to put theory into practice. She seemed to sneer at all the things CATE had prescribed through its criteria. Cox (1989) considered philosophy of education and sociology of education to be totally irrelevant and regards the success of some independent schools as a proof that teaching qualifications are not necessary for good teaching. Her facile conclusions about independent schools are in fact more dubious than the research studies in Sociology of Education that she dismisses as dubious (TES 6 January 1989). The important question is not whether there should be any theory or not, but whether it is taught rigorously, and relates properly to the knowledge, understanding and skills which an effective teacher needs to acquire. The impact Training Schools can have on initial teacher training is much more than the visible impact on newly qualified teachers and professional development of school staff in partners schools. Good schools could further enrich the experiences of trainees and their subject knowledge and can have a visible impact on the course planning for ITT in partnership with higher education institutions. Equally, Training Schools can provide sufficient experience and training to address issues of equality and diversity in schools.

Comments

This chapter has described some of the recent developments introduced by the Government to improve teacher supply and to remove barriers for intending teachers of minority ethnic origin. It has also drawn attention to the anomalies faced by schools, which, on the one hand have been criticised for failing the children and on the other hand asked to train future teachers. The critical dilemmas faced by the teaching profession and the teacher education institutions have also been highlighted. It is important that trainee teachers have a solid grounding in the concepts, principles, knowledge and purposes underlying good practices in education. They must be able to reflect constructively upon it in order to develop professionally and be better equipped as teachers. A coherent programme of continued professional development along with a programme of teacher induction should be not only a requirement, but also an entitlement for each individual teacher and this needs to be part of CATE criteria for accreditation of training programmes. Such a programme should also include training geared to the wider responsibilities of teachers, for example in relation to the Childrens' Act, the Race Relations (Amendments) Act, the Sex Discrimination Act and the Disability Discrimination Act.

As far as theory is concerned, it doesn't really matter whether student teachers learn to apply theory, taught initially in the colleges, or learn to theorise from practice in the classroom. The important thing is to get the balance right, to ensure an effective partnership and to train teachers to be 'reflective practitioners'. For once I find myself in agreement with one of the foremost critics of 'progressive educational ideology' who said that, 'the answer to bad theory might be no theory; but good theory would be better....'. (O'Keefe 1990). Whilst it is true that students benefit from working closely with teachers and receive the context-specific knowledge they need to relate to particular children in particular schools, it is wrong to assume that a well-structured school experience is all that students need. They do need a broad perspective, offered by staff in higher education, that comes from involvement in a large number of schools, through their familiarity with current literature in the field, through their access to libraries and specialist facilities and through their active involvement in research. Even if schools had all the necessary resources, education of teachers will never be a first priority for schools. They are primarily there to teach children, not to educate teachers. The history of teacher education and training in Britain demonstrates that 'on the job' training in schools alone was unsatisfactory. Nor can the preparation of the teacher take place solely in institutions of higher education and teacher education. It has to take place in both, in partnership. It is time to get that careful balance right.

Chapter 6

Equality Assurance: A Framework for Permeation

Introduction

This focus in this chapter is on how teachers can ensure that their teaching is in accordance with equal opportunities in all its dimensions and how they can address the issues of ethnic diversity in their classrooms and educate all children in such a way that it not only encourages and promotes inter-cultural understanding, but also teaches them to recognise and challenge bullying, harassment and racist practices. Naturally teachers can only do that if they themselves have a clear understanding of what equal opportunities are about and are adequately equipped to deal with sensitive issues of religion, culture and race. They need to gain a substantial knowledge of the positively diverse nature of British Society and view the presence of minority ethnic children in British schools as an asset rather than as a liability. National legislation on education (ERA 1988) has the potential to reduce inequality in schools and provides valuable opportunities to do so. Reference to the 'development of pupils and of society' in the ERA 1988 was further supported by the requirement that there is a need for balanced and broadly based curriculum which promotes the spiritual, moral, cultural, mental and physical development of pupils at the school and of society; and prepares such pupils for the opportunities, responsibilities and experiences of adult life.

The DES Circular 5/89 then adds: 'It is intended that the curriculum should reflect the culturally diverse society to which pupils belong and of which they will become adult members'. The DES also gives guidance to head teachers and governors on the production of school development plans to help implement the new legal requirements, and emphasises the concept of entitlement. 'In effect', it says, 'the Act entitles every pupil to a curriculum which is broad and balanced', and it adds: 'The principle that each pupil should have a broad and balanced curriculum which is also relevant to his or her particular needs is now established in law' (DES Circular 5/89). It seems apparent from all the guidance from DES and the National Curriculum Council in the 1990s that the role of teachers in this context should be to foster respect for fellow human beings; to question the stereotypes which limit children's behaviour and achievements, and to challenge, when necessary, instances of sexism and racism. The message seemed clear enough that schools are communities of children who are culturally diverse and that schools should address these issues in a positive way by embracing the opportunities offered by diversity. However, despite a clear guidance and plethora of government circulars, 'Her Majesty's Inspectorate Annual Report on Education in England' (1992) refers to difficulties faced by primary schools 'serving areas of marked social and economic disadvantage' (paragraph 33), and notes that:

Progress on equal opportunities is best described as patchy. In some schools and colleges, awareness of the take-up of educational opportunities as between the sexes and among ethnic minority groups is high; in others it is totally inadequate. Most institutions have policies for promoting equality of opportunity but too often the gap between policy and practice is unacceptably wide (HMI 1992, Paragraph 28).

This is hardly surprising as in the same year the message from one of our political leaders was 'Discipline and self-respect.... Let us return to basic subject teaching, not courses in the theory of education. Primary teachers should.... not waste their time on policies of race, class and gender' (Major 1992). The primary purpose of teaching should be about ensuring high Quality Education for all children, to support the Development of Cultural Identities of all children and to prepare them for Full Participation in Society. What follows is a brief discussion of each of these themes with references to official documents from which they have been extracted.

Quality Education For All

There is substantial research evidence that schools can and do make a significant difference to pupils' life chances. There is also evidence of the differences in average attainment connected with class, gender and ethnicity. Inspecting Schools for Race Equality documented Ofsted's failure to concern itself sufficiently with ethnic variables in achievement. A subsequent document 'A Synthesis of Research Evidence' (2000) reveals more evidence of the glaring and persistent inequalities between the main ethnic populations in English schools. This evidence has been really slow in forthcoming, 'Slowly and almost grudgingly, like old toothpaste squeezed from a tube' (Eggleston 2000) the most striking feature of this work is the evidence that these inequalities are unnecessary. As the report further emphasises, all ethnic categories can achieve, 'Although at the national level Pakistani youth are less likely to attain five higher grade GCSEs than their white peers, this pattern is reversed in some areas. In four out of ten LEAs that monitor by ethnic origin, Pakistan; pupils are more likely to attain this benchmark than white pupils locally' (Osler & Morrison 2000). However, there is still a picture of marked inequality elsewhere: there are almost four times as many LEAs where the picture is reversed and White pupils outperform each of the Black groups. But the important point to note are that overall the EMAG returns demonstrate that no ethnic group is inherently less capable of academic success. Nevertheless, the average attainment of children from certain minority ethnic communities and backgrounds is still lower than that of the rest of the population. If the implicit conclusions of the reports are indeed valid – that children of all races start school with a similar spread of ability and are made unequal during the school years, we do need to have a really good look at what happens during the school years.

These differences in attainment do seem to influence teacher expectations of any one particular child. This is because schools seem to accept (wrongly in my view) that inequalities of outcomes of schooling merely reflect inequalities of wider society and that teachers can't really do anything about it. There is evidence, both from research and from practical experience, that schools can take specific measures not only to avoid perpetuating inequalities, but also intervene to help redress and reduce inequalities. In my view, there can be no Quality education without Equality. By that

I mean not just Equality of Access, Opportunity and Treatment, but also Equality of Outcomes, results and benefits. Quality and Equality strengthen and support each other. The Ofsted reports and the NCC documents indicate that every school should be concerned with providing equality as well as excellence. The TTA clearly states that teachers need to be knowledgeable about, and sensitive to the children as individuals, and as affected by characteristics such as their cultural, religious, linguistic backgrounds, their gender, mental and physical levels of development etc.

> Effective teachers have high expectations of their pupils, and ensure appropriate pace and challenge. Teacher expectation is the key to pupil performance. Any social, cultural, and economic disadvantage which pupils experience can be compounded, if with well-intentioned but misguided motives, teachers are unwilling to add further pressures in the shape of academic demands. Education must not be another aspect of disadvantage but a means of providing escape. Nor is under-expectation confided to schools in disadvantaged areas (TTA 1996).

Another area of great concern to teachers and many minority ethnic communities is the number of minority ethnic children being excluded, in proportion to their overall numbers. The 1996 Ofsted report included frightening evidence of this, particularly in relation to Black boys. Teachers may wish to research assessment/achievement and if so they would need to fully understand what are possible frameworks that could be applied, for example, children and teachers' stereotypes, the effect of second language on perceived level of performance and so on. Another issue, which has been highlighted by schools, related to the achievement of boys. Within gender equality the performance of girls, and their take up in many subjects such as maths and science has been a matter of policy makers concern since the 1970s. The current concern deals with the lagging behind of boys in classroom and examination performance. For many secondary schools there are related aspects, which have to be tackled, for instance, are the boys affected by the content of the teaching, or is it related to perceived job prospects and job satisfaction.

Development of Cultural Identities

Thus when the TTA documents are examined carefully, it is clear that the task of teachers and thus teacher educators would be to ensure that the professionalism of the teachers acknowledged the above-mentioned tasks. What the documents do not do is to indicate the extent to which these points must encompass the implications of cultural and sexual diversity. Every individual child needs to develop a sense of identify which is: 'Confident, strong and self affirming; open to change, growth and development; and curious and generous towards other identities and prepared to learn from them' (Runnymede Trust 1993). Since not all cultures and communities have equal power and status, the development of personal identities takes place in very uneven access to power and influence. Schools and teachers can help with this development by including in their teaching schemes knowledge, skills and attitudes which form part of a wide range of cultures and communities and which help develop a positive view of all cultures and communities. Following is a summary of objectives (extracted from Equality Assurance in Schools) for developing such knowledge, understanding, skills and attitudes.

Knowledge and understanding

This includes knowledge of the history and development of one's own cultural traditions, and of the ways in which these both foster and constrain one's own personal identity; knowledge of the history of different cultural traditions within Britain, Europe and the wider world; knowledge of the physical, social and psychological needs which human beings have in common, including nutrition and shelter, and values relating to freedom, self-respect, belonging, and a sense of meaning and purpose and knowledge of the various ways in which different cultures, communities and societies respond to these fundamental needs and moral concerns.

Skills

This includes ability to contribute to one's own cultural traditions, including the traditions of mainstream public, cultural and political life; ability to learn from different cultural experiences, norms and perspectives, and to empathise with people with different traditions; ability to analyse and criticise features of cultural traditions, and to identify instances of prejudice, intolerance and discrimination and ability to engage in discussion, argument and negotiation with people with traditions other than one's own.

Attitudes

This includes willingness to sustain the positive aspects of one's own traditions, and therefore willingness to be constructively critical when appropriate; willingness to learn from different traditions, cultures and identities; willingness to challenge instances of prejudice, intolerance and discrimination and willingness to accept reasonable and equitable procedures for resolving conflicts.

Full Participation in Society

Over the years a range of concepts have been used in primary and secondary education, which make a reference to this aspect of education. These include concepts such as moral education (Education Reform Act 1988), education for Citizenship (National Curriculum Council & The Council of Europe), political education and education for democracy (The Swann Report 1985). National Curriculum Council Curriculum Guidance on Education for Citizenship (1990) proposed several areas of study under the general heading of 'A Pluralist Society'. These include the interdependence of individuals, groups and communities; similarities and differences between individuals, groups and communities and their effects; the existence of differences of perception and the ways in which these may be reconciled; Britain as a society made up of many cultures, ethnic groups, faiths and languages; the diversity of cultures in other societies; a study of human development and culture from different perspectives; international and global issues and the origins and effects of racial prejudice in British and other societies. In response to one of the recommendations from the Stephen Lawrence Inquiry report that, 'consideration be given to the amendment of the national Curriculum aimed at valuing cultural diversity and preventing racism, in order to better reflect the needs of a diverse society', the DfES has introduced Education for Citizenship. Within the new national framework for personal, social and health education pupils will be taught to respect differences between people, to appreciate others' feelings and points of view and recognise the effects of stereotyping, prejudice, discrimination and racism.

Education for Citizenship has become a statutory subject in Secondary schools from September 2002. It includes three interrelated areas of study, namely social and moral responsibility; community involvement and political literacy. This will ensure that, for the first time, all pupils will be taught about the diversity of national, religious and ethnic identities in the United Kingdom and the need for mutual respect and understanding. It will provide distinct opportunities for pupils to develop an understanding of fairness and social justice, raise awareness of the nature of prejudice and teach pupils how to recognise stereotypes and highlight the consequences of anti-social and aggressive behaviours like racism and bullying and develop skills to challenge them assertively. The concept of personal, social and health education provides a valuable framework for teaching about prejudice and discrimination and for supporting the development of cultural identities of all pupils. The Council of Europe's Statement (1985) on Human Rights in the School Curriculum considers Human Rights as an important dimension of the social and political education of all pupils. It also identifies particular skills associated with an understanding and experience of Human Rights in an intercultural and international context. The Council of Europe places considerable emphasis on studying various forms of injustice, inequality and discrimination, including racism and sexism. Further discussion of key concepts such as Moral Education, Education for Citizenship, Political Education and Personal, Social and Health Education can be found in the Equality Assurance in Schools document.

Dr. Sean Stitt (1997) exposes a paradox permeating teaching, which is euphemistically known as a 'caring profession' and a preparatory system for living in a democracy. He suggests that the key obstacle to this democratisation continues to be the nervous reluctance of the educational system supported by traditional school governance and educational professionals. The educational status quo, it seems, is not just agnostic about issues of human rights and the various charters associated with it and unaware of the legal system's interpretation of Human Rights declaration, it is also uninterested in the ethical considerations influencing the interactions between children/students and their human rights environment. The outcome is that while children are legally compelled to attend school, their democratic rights and freedoms are greatly endangered and uncatered for in the school. Children who are different because of their class, race, gender, religion, ability, sexuality are more vulnerable to damage by the education system, manifesting in higher non-completion rates, low attainment standards, fewer opportunities at higher education level and abuse. However, there is an expectation and a common agreement, even in the corridors of power that: 'A society needs responsible citizens who can understand the purpose of law and respect the rights of others. Such attitude of respect may be nurtured and encouraged by all those with whom young people come into contact. Schools can play an invaluable part in the promotion of social and moral responsibility' (Howard 1994).

Equality Assurance and Anti-Racism

One advantage of our decentralised system is the power and autonomy it gives to individual schools and teachers who shape the present and future of individual pupils. The issues of 'race' and education confronted by schools today are different from those identified by ethnic, cultural and religious differences of the migrant groups of the 1970s and the 1980s. Concentration on meeting 'special needs' had led multicultural education to be identified as something that was relevant only for certain minority groups, and consequently as something which could only be provided through special courses. The emphasis on its cultural dimension and language issues meant that multi-culturalism either completely ignored 'racism' or relegated it to cultural misunderstanding. The shift in emphasis from the 'adding on' approach to the notion of 'permeation' of the whole curriculum, which occurred in the 1980s, is an indication that teacher education courses are recognising the importance of consistent experiences of multicultural perspectives across the curriculum. The Race Relations (Amendment) Act 2000 places a duty on all educational institutions to not only provide equality of opportunity for all, but also to ensure that their policies and provisions do not directly or indirectly result in racism. A good example of how this can be addressed is to be found in the Multi-Cultural Anti-Racist Education Guidance from General Teaching Council for Scotland. It believes that multi-cultural and anti-racist education should be included in all courses of initial teacher education and that all institutions should have in place monitoring systems to ensure that coverage is effective.

The focus in dialogue has to change as the significant factors have also changed. For more people in Britain today, cultural diversity is visible and a part of life. It is no longer possible to talk about immigrants and there is a slight increase in the visibility of women and minority ethnic people in positions of power. The debates thus need to take into account the needs of different groups and how they can live in harmony, rather than only giving racism the platform. A more rigorous analysis of equality issues as an academic discipline will provide a more solid basis for equality is action in Britain today. Located in an international context, it should enable greater understanding about the impingement of different factors on the diverse approaches seen in different countries today. This does not exclude, but supplements the dialogue that is generated by the real life consequences of inequalities. Trainee teachers need to understand the important part which schools can play in contributing to the development of a socially just, inclusive society. They should be alert to the ways in which, intended or not, the structures, procedures, practices and culture of the education system can exclude or disadvantage some groups, including minority ethnic pupils. Every trainee teacher needs to understand the part he or she must play in providing an education which enables all pupils to realise their full potential; and preparing all pupils to play a full part in a culturally diverse, democratic society which values everybody and accords them equal rights. As an integral part of an overall concern for social justice, racial equality is an issue for all trainee and new teachers, whatever their ethnicity. It is also a concern for all schools, including those with an all or mainly White population. Schools, therefore, have an important part to play in helping all pupils to become informed, concerned citizens, and in increasing mutual understanding, respect and appreciation of cultural diversity.

Those involved in training teachers have a responsibility to equip every trainee to foster an inclusive education system that meets the needs of all pupils. Ofsted evidence shows the considerable impact that effective teachers and effective schools can make on raising pupils' attainment and improving the quality of their education. It also highlights that schools and teachers are most effective if they systematically monitor and evaluate performance in order to identify and target groups of pupils that underachieve. Teachers need a number of strategies and organisational policies that can ensure a just balance in the curriculum. Permeation as a strategy can be effective especially if teachers take on board the need for a range of activities, which are inter-linked. These could include a checklist of practical contributions that each subject can make and consistent experiences of anti-racist perspectives across the curriculum content and the process of teaching and learning. It could also include organisational issues such as a culture policy across the curriculum whereby pupils will constantly, and throughout their school career come across ideas and images that relate to their families and cultures in a whole variety of contexts.

However, there is relatively little discussion about what is actually meant by 'permeation' and how it can be achieved effectively and comprehensively. For 'permeation' to be effective the curriculum content should include aspects of different cultures from which children derive their meaning. Such a curriculum, in which all cultures are equally valued, considered different but not deficient, and should be equally available to all children. The realities of contemporary cultural diversity, the social, political and economic conditions surrounding all learners, their families and communities must also be reflected in all the learning arrangements that an institution makes. A graphic illustration of some of the key features, and these are not exclusive, that determine the ways in which a 'permeation' policy across an institution can be implemented is shown in Figure 6.1.

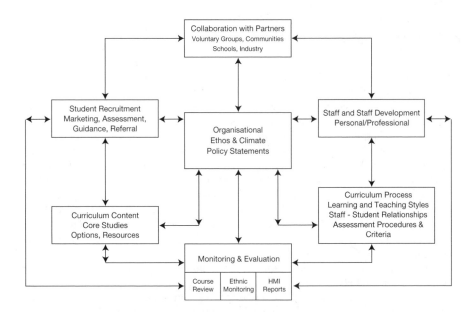

Figure 6.1   Anti-Racist Teacher Education: A Framework for 'Permeation'

One of the key messages that I wish to convey through this graphic illustration is the inter-relationship between various aspects of curriculum delivery and their relationship with institutional and organisational procedures. Some of these features are described later on in the chapter. Clearly, if we want professionally and socially aware teachers who are enthusiastic, well qualified and with adequate teaching skills, we need to strike a balance between legal and political constraints of Government circulars, and the wider education needs of the real world. We need to reconcile policy with educational philosophy and gauge the degree of interpretations, which the language of official documents makes possible. The Teacher Training Agency has made some attempt to address the two main areas of recruitment and professional education of the intending teachers. In relation to recruitment the TTA is very much concerned about diversity, as illustrated by the section on Recruitment (TTA 1996). The commitment to diversity is clear, although the Licensed Teachers Programme relates more to economy than to furthering diversity in the teaching profession. It is important to note that the standards set by the TTA for raising the profile of teaching, and emphasising professionalism included an expectation for closer links between institutions providing initial teacher training, and professional associations as well as those who could assist in widening access to teaching to students from the ethnic minorities and other disadvantaged groups. Equality Assurance in Schools (Runnymede Trust 1993) offered one example of the ways in which requirements and expectations of official documents can be translated to ensure high quality education for all pupils.

The task facing the teachers is to continue to construct a growing web of connections at school, local and national levels, between what happens in the classroom and the wider political struggles outside it. These connections are perhaps not so difficult in respect of theoretical agreement for a comprehensive programme for anti-racist education in schools, but may appear to be unrealistic when it comes to organising campaigns to implement or defend specific reforms, or to unite the social forces capable of implementing such programmes. The task therefore is two-fold. Firstly, the teachers need to recognise the educational inequalities within Britain, and understand the myriad ways in which institutional racism serves to perpetuate them. Secondly, they need to educate and support all pupils to tackle the issues of 'race' effectively, thereby reducing the effects, on all children, of educational inequalities and racist practices. NATFHE (1982), in its evidence to the Committee of Inquiry into the Education of Children from Minority Ethnic Groups, described very explicitly the qualities required of teachers and suggested that they will largely depend on their ability, professionally and personally, to cope with the accelerated pace of social change. This presupposed a capacity to relate to a diverse range of human beings, to be able to confront their own prejudices and to recognise their need as educators and as individuals, and to take effective steps to fulfil them. The skills required of a teacher included an understanding of all children as individuals and of the environmental, relational and personal factors, which affect their growth. These correspond to the three themes identified earlier on in this chapter, namely quality education for all, development of cultural identities and full participation in society.

What follows is a framework for 'permeation' and an agenda for action, which includes strategies for the effective implementation of policies concerned with 'race' and education. The development of anti-racist education as a response to the ideology of cultural pluralism and equal opportunities also entails a consideration of a 'black perspective' as an essential component. The other essential components of education for racial equality and anti racist education should include social, political and moral education of all children (as necessary for Full Participation in Society) positive action to provide equal opportunities and quality education for all, and awareness training to include the development of Cultural Identities and an analysis of how racist practices operate at a personal and institutional level. At this point, it is important to describe my understanding of 'Black perspective'.

Black perspective

By this I mean a perspective on education that emphasises equality of opportunity, not just in the sense of equal treatment and/or equal access, but also by ensuring equal share and equal outcomes. My understanding also includes a perspective that acknowledges the central and pervasive influence of racism in education and emphasises in their teaching of all pupils, knowledge, skills and attitudes necessary for combating racism. It is also a perspective that should ensure that courses committed to combating racism and fostering equal opportunities are informed and influenced by the experiences of the people who bear the brunt of racism. This means developing new kinds of consultation and liaison, consultations that are intended for full participation by Black people and in which contributions from a Black perspective lead to a real change in course organisation and content. Another dimension of this perspective is to enable all pupils to become competent in matters related to social, moral and political education in a context, which is worldwide. Finally, such a perspective should foster recognition and understanding of the ways in which institutional procedures and practices discriminate against minority ethnic pupils and children and of the damage such discrimination causes to all children.

Key Features of 'Permeation'

The key features illustrated in the Framework For Permeation have been chosen not because they are any more important than the others, but because they are more directly related to the work of teachers in the classroom.

Curriculum content

Curriculum is the sum of all learning experiences provided for the children in a school. A whole curriculum is much more than maths plus reading plus science plus art. It is about the totality and the quality of learning experiences. Whole curriculum decisions are moral decisions, entailing value judgements about how children and adults ought to live. The permeation of anti-racism in curriculum terms therefore transcends all areas of learning and is very much a decision about the whole curriculum. During the 1970s and early 1980s, optional courses dealing with issues of 'race' were the order of the day in teacher training courses. But options without a core element in the training course were not adequate as they were only taken by a small number of students and also did not indicate a serious commitment to 'race' issues on the part of training institutions. It is important for crucial issues of 'race' and culture to be progressively incorporated and adequately spaced out to enable the practical application of ideas to different teaching situations. Teachers need to recognise that academic studies within each society are designed, naturally enough, within the prevailing dominant socio-cultural framework and reinforce and confirm that cultural reference. It is likely that most of the teachers themselves part of that dominant socio-cultural framework, and therefore unable to acknowledge that such a framework generally tends to distort perceptions of other cultural frameworks. The application of different frameworks of reference and new concepts are never easily accepted, especially when they seriously challenge existing well-established traditions. But an anti-racist perspective on education requires teachers and academics to do just that, both through a programme of staff development and through recruitment of staff with a range of different socio-cultural frameworks.

It is also important to recognise that the selection of subject content, of particular theories, models, examples, and textbooks offers significant opportunities to include or omit what a teacher considers relevant and appropriate or irrelevant and inappropriate. The significant question that needs to be addressed is, how far these selections are informed by a concept of relevance, which takes account of the values of people of all cultures and colours; or by use of stereotypes in examples and misrepresentations of cultures; and by an understanding of cross-cultural perspectives. Stereotypical beliefs, racist and sexist assumptions and attitudes need to be analysed and challenged across the whole range of the curriculum. Another question that needs to be considered is, when teachers, through a process of selection and omission, legitimate one form of cultural/educational experience and denigrate another, they are not likely to take on board and reflect the experiences of all children in their classrooms. When teachers are not prepared to treat knowledge of and about Black children from minority ethnic groups with equality of respect and consideration, how can they treat Black children from minority ethnic groups with equality of respect and consideration?

Curriculum process

Equally important, but more problematic, are the processes by which the curriculum is delivered and the learning is assessed. Focus on process is less attractive than innovation in curriculum content because it calls into question our assumptions and expectations and the messages we convey in the process of teaching. It exposes a hidden curriculum of power, class and racial inequality, not only in the traditional forms and content of education, but in much that is thought of as progressive. Messages delivered through these processes can, however unwittingly, support institutional racism. In any learning situation there are several layers of power structures, such as teacher-student, young-old, male-female, black-white, that get in the way of learning. In addition, traditional teaching styles perpetuate established power structures in the same way as traditional curriculum content does. The process of shared learning as equals and not as teacher and taught, which is largely reinforced in formal teaching situations, may help reduce inequalities that create barriers in learning for all children, but more so for children from minority ethnic groups. This can sometimes be achieved by more work in pairs and in small groups. Individual styles of curriculum delivery are therefore crucial.

It is important that before issues of 'race' and cultures are introduced, children are put at ease to prepare a basis for rational discussion. Experience of a wide range of activities such as experiential learning, learning by doing and group learning may also help break some of these barriers and make learning more meaningful. Teachers need to give children adequate time and space to express and discuss their views in a safe environment and identify their individual needs. They need to be able to challenge myths and misconceptions, and dismantle their prejudices and stereotypical attitudes in a non-threatening environment. Teachers also need to be aware that in order to be credible with children who are apprehensive about anti-racism and issues of 'race' and culture, the children need to be provided with an opportunity to voice their concerns and get some rational answers. It is possible that some teachers may themselves feel inadequate to handle such issues constructively, especially if they themselves are only paying lip service to the issues of 'race' and culture. There are several other issues related to curriculum processes, which can help or hinder learning. Presentation of materials, use of language to explain the content or issue instructions, staff-student relationships and assessment procedures are just some of the examples. In any teaching situation a key component of curriculum process is the interaction between staff and children. This is also the one that, to some extent, determines the success and failure of learning and teaching strategies. All members of staff need to be aware of the ways in which it is possible to collude with racist institutional practices. They also need to be aware of factors that underpin children's confidence in the institution, and in their teachers. Staff expectations and their knowledge of children need to be free of any false notions of inherent ability based on ethnic, racial or cultural distinctions. This is as important as an awareness of significant cultural strengths and perspectives of children.

Organisational ethos and climate

The security well-being, confidence and identity of all pupils is enhanced by the schools' attitude and respect for differences plus a conscious effort to avoid procedures which may make children uncomfortable. For example, simply providing a choice of meals to accommodate vegetarians is far more inconspicuous than singling out children who do not eat meat. The schools need to create a climate where it is easier to discuss issues such as race, prejudice and stereotyping in a constructive and educational way. Such a climate would encourage a critical examination of the values inherent in the materials presented to pupils and more importantly an examination of teachers' attitudes which in spite of their virtues of decency, tolerance and some degree of respect for those different from them, find it difficult to raise themselves to the level of others, thus falling back into the habit of reducing others to the limited proportions of their own linguistic habits and conventions. This is evident in classrooms where teachers don't wish their pupils to speak languages other than English. By ignoring a child's linguistic resource, or worse still by punishing them for it, the schools can and often do reinforce stereotypes by implicitly emphasising the superiority of the dominant culture, rejecting any notion of parity of esteem between English and other linguistic systems. Any school suppressing the pupil's language but taking an interest in his cultural background is bound to be confusing, to say the least, for children who speak languages other than English. Teachers need to consider, amongst other things, situations where children for whom English is a second language might be unduly criticised or marked down for grammatical accuracy or expression and where minority ethnic children might be unfairly penalised for not using recommended or accepted literature which may in fact ignore the reality of multiracial Britain. They also need to make sure that 'white' Teachers and assessors do acknowledge the different experience, knowledge and analytical base of minority ethnic children and do not expect them to 'write as if they were white'. They need more frequent and active contact with parents and communities, and recognise them for what they are, the powerhouse of richly diverse capital cultural capital. It is not enough to tolerate and respect minority groups. To quote Professor Parekh:

> Unless we can enter into the spirit of other societies and cultures without reducing them to the limited proportions of our own linguistic habits and conventions, we cannot appreciate their strength; and by failing to appreciate their strength, we fail to appreciate our own weaknesses and limitations (Parekh 1981).

It is also vital that schools employ more minority ethnic teachers who can work towards providing a just balance in the curriculum – a balance of images and a balance of lifestyles and values that derive from models other than that of the dominant culture. However the presence of minority ethnic teachers in itself is not enough. Several studies have demonstrated that no matter how unjustified it may seen, the minority ethnic teachers will always have to prove themselves to be 'twice as good' to be accepted as 'less than at par' with their white counterparts. Equally important are staff relationships with pupils and their attitudes and expectations, an awareness of factors, which promote or undermine pupils' confidence in the school, their experiences outside the school and their expectations of school. Some examples of the ways in which staff can undermine the confidence that minority ethnic children may have in their teachers and the institution include ignoring local racist incidents and the effects that these may have on our children; avoiding talking about and confronting colleagues with racist attitudes and maintaining a divide between classroom learning and the use of such learning in real life and not supporting children when they come up against racist teachers and/or parents in teaching practice schools.

Staff and staff development

An important aspect of a 'permeation' strategy is the employment of staff with a commitment to implement issues of 'race' and culture and a willingness to acquire appropriate knowledge and skills to make such a commitment meaningful. Some institutions have adopted a range of practices in this regard. These range from an appointment of an individual as a co-ordinator for equal opportunities, and/or the setting up of a working party of interested members of staff, to the establishment of a committee structure to oversee the implementation of policies concerned with equal opportunities. In an ideal world, a combination of all three strategies is likely to be more effective in making sure that the onus of implementation of 'race' policies rests with all staff and not just with one individual or a committee. The knowledge and experience of minority ethnic staff in terms of 'race' issues needs to be recognised and validated, but typecasting of minority ethnic staff (race related roles) is as damaging as stereotyping of minority ethnic children. This also has implications for the career progression of minority ethnic staff, causing further isolation from mainstream posts and colleagues. The appointment of a co-ordinator can also lead to abdication of responsibility by other members of staff.

I am not suggesting that the appointment of minority ethnic staff in itself would lead to adequate treatment of the issues, but that their presence, especially in mainstream posts, is likely to act as a catalyst for change in various ways. Firstly, it would inspire confidence, amongst minority ethnic children, in the institution and its commitment to take minority ethnic people seriously. Secondly, they would act as role models for minority ethnic children and would encourage them to consider teaching as a profession. Thirdly, it would also encourage staff to consider the issues of 'race' and culture seriously and would help create a climate in which issues of 'race' and culture can be discussed constructively and can benefit from a Black perspective, without it appearing to be tokenistic. However, a single Black appointment can still be construed as tokenistic, especially if stereotypical role expectations, such as stronger community links and community involvement, are associated with the post and the individual. Such role expectations are not justified where they are different from that of the role expectations of white colleagues in similar posts.

In terms of staff development, it needs to be initiated by staff and needs to be ongoing and focused, based on the needs identified by individual members of staff. Though members of staff who happen to be black can help in this process, but individual members of staff need to take responsibility for their own development, which should be assisted by the institution. Similarly, the training needs of minority ethnic members of staff also need to be met and supported by the institution. Other issues that need attention in this context include institutional procedures to deal with discrimination and personal harassment; unspoken and informal surveillance of minority ethnic staff by white colleagues, and how that informs judgements about black staff; lack of recognition and marginalisation of Black staff by White colleagues who invoke 'professionalism' to hide their prejudice.

Monitoring and evaluation

Institutions that claim to have effective 'race' policies and a strategy of 'permeation' need to be able to support such claims with evidence of not only how, when and where the issues of 'race' and culture are addressed, but also how children respond to the treatment of these issues. Many institutions have a process of ethnic monitoring and course reviews, but don't necessarily believe in seeking children's views, on the assumption that if a subject matter or an issue has been dealt with, children must have learnt it. They are also under a misapprehension that if you don't ask, there can be no problems, and fail to recognise that 'passive' learning of this kind can lead to internalisation of misconceptions and misinformation. If unchallenged, these misconceptions can only serve to confirm racist attitudes and beliefs. What is required is an ongoing evaluation, aimed at both staff and children. This can be done through questionnaires and other means, and it would help not only in assessing the effectiveness of teaching strategies, but also in reviewing and adapting programmes planned for each year. The usual process for evaluation and monitoring on the basis of regular inspections and also needs to include evidence of how written assignments and teaching practice documentation incorporate issues of 'race' and culture. The key function of monitoring and evaluation has to be one of addressing the gaps and weaknesses that are identified through this process and of informing future planning in a constructive way.

Agenda For Action

It is quite clear that to be effective in terms of permeating anti-racism, what teachers can do needs to be as complex and pervasive as the racism they are challenging. They need to take account of the tension experienced by minority ethnic children and also need to be informed by an analysis of contemporary, regional and political issues, which directly affect Black children. They need to use strategies, which are subtle and covert and permeate the whole institutional structures. The arguments for a model of 'permeation' whereby all courses address the issues of multicultural and anti-racist education are strong, but they can only be sustained if the process of validation of courses and assessment of students and evaluation of outcomes clearly includes criteria, which not only directly addresses these issues, but requires evidence of successful 'permeation'. Equally necessary is the provision of opportunities for students to undertake distinct modules to develop their expertise in areas such as multicultural education, anti-racist strategies and bilingual Education. The message that needs to be taken on board in this context is that in a 'permeation' model it should be possible to provide for, both an integration of a multicultural perspective across a whole range of curriculum areas, and an opportunity to develop specialist expertise. Schools in Devon, Cornwall and Somerset need anti-racist approaches at the heart of their curriculum as much as schools in London, Birmingham and Bradford. What I have outlined may appear to be idealistic at best and Utopian at worst. But I do believe it is a viable proposition. No doubt it will require more than a serious commitment to anti-racism and a great deal of soul searching on the part of teachers. It will also require strategic planning to collaborate and construct a growing web of connections, between what happens in educational institutions and the wider social and political struggles outside them. The strategies for intervention at various levels of policy making and policy implementation are explored in chapter seven along with the role teachers and teacher trainers have in making the ideal of anti-racism a reality. The gaps identified in this framework can only be filled if both schools and teacher training institutions (as partners in the training process) create a climate in which it is easier to discuss issues of 'race', racism, prejudice and stereotyping in a constructive and educational way. Institutions, which are symptomatic of the 'virtues of decency, tolerance and some degree of respect for others' (Parekh 1981) need to move beyond that and learn to appreciate and enjoy people from other societies, and their religions, cultures and languages.

Chapter 7

Positively Diverse: An Agenda for Action

This chapter includes a discussion of key issues and implications for policy and practice. It also identifies some key agents and a context for change and ends with some practical suggestions for what teachers can do to acquire appropriate knowledge and an understanding of the principles and practices concerned with the delivery of education that is multicultural.

Introduction

The precise nature of the relationship of policies with the literature that seeks to evaluate them, and in some cases contributes to the analysis that underpins the policies, is not straightforward. The growing discrepancy between official rhetoric on racial equality, and the way educational policies are supporting a kind of educational nationalism, is sustained by the myth that minorities have full and equal access to opportunities to assimilate into British society and that barriers to equal participation are created by the minorities themselves. However, it is difficult to sustain such a myth in the face of contradictory evidence, such as the provision under the Education Reform Act, which allows White parents to keep their children away from schools with large numbers of Black pupils (according to a poll by London Weekend Television in 1987, 40 percent of white parents in the Southeast favoured 'race' segregation in schools). Furthermore, the Education Reform Act has been given precedence over the Race Relations Act, whereby 'Parental Choice' was granted to White parents to remove their child from a school attended by a large proportion of minority ethnic children, thus not taking account of the implicit motive of racial segregation. The High Court ruling established that Cleveland Education Authority was correct to allow a five-year old child to change schools, even though it suspected that the mother was motivated on racial grounds (TES 1991). But the same right was denied to Bangladeshi parents in Bradford who wanted to choose a school near their homes (The Education Guardian 1993). Thus 'Parental Choice' has, in some instances, come to mean schools choosing parents, and not parents choosing the schools. Added to that, several studies concerning racial inequality in education (Wright 1987, Tomlinson 1987, Gilborn 1990, CRE 1988) have demonstrated a differential in acceptance rates of White, Asian and Black applicants, even when their qualifications were of equal value. Such evidence of differential treatment clearly does not support the myth that barriers to equal participation are created by minorities themselves.

A literature review of Teacher Education (Chapter Three) has revealed that on the whole, policies and practice over the last 20 years or so have helped to highlight a perceived mismatch between need and provision, and between policy and practice. Teacher Education has experienced, through three major thrusts in Government policy since 1989, a trinity of chaos that could reverse the progress made in teacher education in the last two decades. These have been the increased regulation of the curriculum of teacher education courses, virtually the introduction of a national curriculum, (Circular 24/89); Circular 13/91 to introduce two new Apprenticeship Routes for Teaching (DES 1991); and Circular 9/92 for all initial teacher education to be largely school-based and school-focused. The impact of extreme Right and the development of government quangoes is nowhere more clearly visible than in the recent changes, disguised as the 'Reform' of Teacher Education. The review of teacher education has also shown that there is a visible lack of minority ethnic people in the profession at all levels. It is also clear that the reasons for people from minority ethnic groups not taking up teaching as a profession included the lack of clear and consistent career advice, the absence of minority ethnic teachers as role models; fear of racial discrimination and racial abuse and the fear of being marginalized. These were certainly echoed by minority ethnic students and groups of minority ethnic teachers, who further confirmed the incidence of racial discrimination and marginalisation and also gave substantial evidence of the stress caused by their jobs.

Some of the recent and current developments (Chapter Five) in initial teacher education include those designed to attract more minority ethnic students onto teacher education courses and employment initiatives such as the Licensed Teacher Schemes and the Articled Teacher Schemes. It is strange that the critics of teacher education institutions, who continue to call for the abolition of B.Ed. and PGCE courses in favour of an apprenticeship route for training teachers, have failed to notice the illogical assumptions underlying such a suggestion. Since HMI reports found the work of experienced teachers no more satisfactory than that of newly trained ones, in practical terms (let alone in terms of ideological orientation) schools could hardly be entrusted with the education of teachers. There is also some concern that minority ethnic student teachers and mature women will be attracted into the profession through these low-status dead-end positions and school-centred routes. They will inevitably find themselves restricted to schools in areas of high minority ethnic population. They will receive minimal preparation for recognising and handling racism and sexism in classrooms and staff rooms and for making strategic use of the limited potential of the National Curriculum.

The part-time PGCE course at Manchester (UDE) is just one example, and a relatively successful one, of the new initiatives described in Chapter Five. As a pilot scheme, it was by all accounts, found to be tackling the issue of minority ethnic teacher recruitment, albeit in a limited way. In the words of an LEA Director of Education 'We are not talking about teachers for minority ethnic children; we are talking about good teachers for all children' (TES 1988). The process of recruitment of bilingual assistants for this course highlighted the situation of many graduates from overseas, some with teacher training qualifications and higher degrees, whose qualifications had not been recognised by the DES, but who were very interested in and well suited for the teaching profession. In the face of an acute shortage of minority ethnic teachers and widespread concern about lack of potential recruits, it was crucial to channel these candidates in appropriate directions. The performance of students on this course was beyond the expectation of some of the head teachers involved, as is evident from many comments like: 'What I didn't realise was that we don't quite appreciate how well educated some of these students are, because their qualifications are not really publicised' (Arora /UDE 1989).

There are clearly important lessons to be learnt from this pilot. The different emphasis in terms of their role as that of 'helping the children or helping the school and the staff' did create anomalies for the post-holders. In particular, the students on the UDE course felt that they were very unsure of what was expected of them in their role as bilingual assistants and/or instructors. They needed to work with the children as part of their training, but were also expected to act as experts and consultants for issues of bilingualism and multicultural education, a role that they did not always feel confident about. The central purpose of their employment, that is to promote, encourage and maintain bilingual skills of young bilingual children, and to use their bilingualism as an aid to learn English, seemed to have a very low priority in the minds of their white colleagues, head teachers and LEA advisers.

Another Case Study of a Department of Education in a Community College (DTECC), exemplifies one institution's attempt to get the emphasis right in its teacher education programmes. This is done through an analysis of the developments in that institution, partly in response to the changing national, political and educational scene and partly in response to the changing local communities and the wider context of the changing nature of the institution on the whole. The DTECC Case Study provided a very different, but a complementary perspective on teacher education and minority ethnic groups. To some extent the students in this case study confirmed the experiences of minority ethnic students in the UDE study, especially those on newly introduced apprenticeship routes, such as the Licensed Teachers Scheme and the Articled Teachers Scheme. But it also offered a very positive example of the way in which a DTE can adapt to the numerous internal changes and external challenges and still maintain its commitment to equal opportunities. However, there was also some evidence that some tutors in the DTECC case study assumed that they all start from the 'same starting point of entry'; that they undergo and experience the same opportunity and learning process (initiation into academic standards) and realize their achievements and outcomes solely by virtue of their ability and effort. The problem with this assumption was that it ignored the highly differentiated and unequal chances to benefit from and exploit the 'learning process', a process which represents a spurious notion of standards to which an undifferentiated student mass should perform and conform.

Nevertheless, the two Case Studies have demonstrated that teacher education institutions can and do respond flexibly to the changing needs of their student population. It is also clear from these accounts that where there is a will, it is possible to find a way to overcome what may seem like insurmountable obstacles to equality of opportunity. Both Case Studies, despite their positive achievements, have left a number of key questions, which are further explored in this chapter.

Key Issues and Implications for Policy and Practice

The policy and practice of permeation

There is evidence (Fuller 1992) that where the racial and ethnic background of pre-service teachers differed from those of the diverse school communities in which they will teach upon graduation, and where pre-service teachers, coming from largely White, middle-class backgrounds were receiving teacher education programmes that did not broaden their racial and ethnic experiences and had limited exposure to racial and ethnic diversity during the course, they were not prepared for understanding and appreciating their students with different cultural and ethnic backgrounds. The study also found that the absence of minority ethnic teachers in schools and in teacher education colleges gives non-white children a demeaning message that power in contemporary society rests with White middle class people like their teachers and is generally unavailable to persons from backgrounds similar to theirs. Cohen's (1989) study of student teachers' perceptions of minority ethnic groups in Britain also indicated that only a small proportion of the students had any contact with visible minority ethnic people and generally exhibited considerable ignorance about minority ethnic groups. The study concluded that such ignorance was likely to produce teachers who were more likely to exhibit higher levels of prejudice, than those with some knowledge and experience of minority ethnic groups.

The question addressed here is concerned with institutions that claim to practice a policy of permeation, and in some cases are known as national leaders in their provision for the preparation of teachers for a multicultural society. Despite the glowing reports from external examiners and inspectors, some of these institutions still fall short of preparing all teachers adequately for teaching in a multicultural society, and also seem to fail in meeting the needs of their minority ethnic students. There is evidence that some institutions have succeeded in a number of ways in equal opportunity terms, and consequently, larger numbers of minority ethnic students have gained access to initial teacher education. But there is also evidence (East 1992; Siraj-Blatchford 1990) that in ant-racist terms nothing really has changed. Individual students still experience racism in all its subtle variations, in role expectation, in assessment, in the unavailability of support and understanding; and there is still institutional racism that blames the students for failure rather than the system.

Though the primary purpose of the UDE course was to increase the number of minority ethnic teachers in British schools and enable overseas-qualified graduates to enter the teaching profession, there was, however, an undeclared and implicit agenda to cross-fertilize the conventional full time PGCE course, which recruited mainly white British graduates. It was also intended to incorporate, in their course programme and staffing structure, increased awareness of education for a multicultural society and issues of 'race' and education. Consequently, over the two years, the full-time PGCE course programme was slightly modified, to include a module for multicultural education, for the students on a full time primary PGCE course. The recruitment of full-time students also showed a small but significant shift in terms of ethnic composition. However, there was no change in the staff composition to reflect this commitment and the course, as described in the course booklet, did not include any consideration of the needs of children from minority ethnic groups, nor was there any reference to preparing teachers for working in a society that is multicultural, multiracial and multi-religious. It was therefore hardly surprising that the head teachers interviewed for this study commented on the lack of knowledge newly qualified teachers exhibit in the field of multicultural and anti-racist education. The attitudes of the University tutors, who regarded the issues of 'race' and multicultural education as peripheral, certainly had a bearing on students' practice in the schools and subsequently in their teaching, especially where it was not likely to be challenged by the school. It further strengthened the prevalent notion of 'Black teachers for Black children' syndrome, and made the part-time students feel isolated and marginalised. One of the ways in which such alienation might have been avoided was to have mixed tutorial groups for part-time and full-time students. But this was perceived to be problematic, because it would have required the tutors on the full-time course to develop a greater understanding of and involvement in the part-time course.

It seems that in the case of DTECC, in spite of the 'permeation' approach gradually replacing the mono-cultural curriculum with added extras, many teachers in schools and tutors of initial teacher education were unwilling or perhaps unable to address the question of racism inherent in their knowledge base. Those who claimed not to discriminate, and treat every one equally, had not yet faced the crucial question, 'How can you treat all individuals with equality of respect and consideration if you are not prepared to treat knowledge of and about them with equality of respect and consideration?'. The assessment process within initial teacher education, as was the case in both case studies, did not always take account of students' level of awareness of racism and their readiness and ability to adopt anti-racist approaches in teaching; nor did it always ensure that minority ethnic students did not suffer discrimination in their assessment on initial teacher education courses. It seems that unless teacher education courses are validated and assessed in the context of an anti-racist perspective, the gap between perceived success and actual success would continue to grow.

Participation of people from minority ethnic groups in teacher education

a)   Recruitment of minority ethnic students
Despite central Government's professed support for training and employing minority ethnic teachers, minority ethnic participation in teacher education has only increased marginally in terms of student numbers. The UCCA (1993) Report shows that 1992 applications to University undergraduate teacher education courses included only two percent from Asian students and one percent from Black students. In contrast 24 percent of applications for Medicine and seven percent for Law courses were from Asian and Black students. Some higher education institutions with positive action programmes have made a significant impact on under-representation of minority ethnic students entering teacher education courses and have also begun to address the wider issues (East 1992). But it is a fragmentary and contradictory picture. Though many institutions have equal opportunities policies and a lot of politically expedient rhetoric, very few have gone beyond the question of access and addressed problems of retention, performance and success of minority ethnic students on teacher education courses.

Analysis of this problem has been theoretically confused and politically naive. It seems that there is insufficient evidence to suggest that it is the lack of necessary qualifications, or the low status of teaching as a career, or indeed family and cultural reasons, which prevent young people from minority ethnic groups to join the teaching profession. But there is sufficient evidence to suggest that the racism experienced by minority ethnic teachers in employment and minority ethnic students on teacher education courses, combined with apprehensions about 'race'-cast roles, and lack of career prospects may be contributing to the alienation of minority ethnic young people from the teaching profession.

b)   Experiences of minority ethnic students

The experience of many minority ethnic students on teacher education courses indicated that their background and experiences were not validated, and that the focus on the needs of White students created an environment which not only excluded the sharing of different kinds of knowledge but also blocked the skill development of some participants. In the case of UDE case study, it was clear that how their roles were interpreted determined how much help children received in their learning and how much help teachers in the school received to facilitate their teaching. Since the students were employed by the LEAs, with Section 11 funds, as bilingual assistants and/or instructors, the schools sometimes treated them as employees and not as students. However, on certain occasions they were not really prepared to treat them as part of the staff and saw them as outsiders.

Clearly the ethos of the schools is important and if they don't have adequate support systems for introducing minority ethnic teachers and developing them, it is not just the minority ethnic teachers who will lose out but it will be a greater loss for the children and the schools. The student teachers in the UDE case study found themselves in a situation where the decision to use them as a 'support person for the children' or as a 'support person for the teachers' rested with the head teacher. The guidance from the advisers seemed to vary from a clear instruction to vague suggestions. Such vagueness, coupled with duality of their roles, clearly made a number of students very nervous and very diffident. Similar situation exists in social work placements where minority ethnic students are seen as 'Race' Experts. There is also evidence that minority ethnic students experience alarmingly high level of racism in initial teacher education (Siraj-Blatchford 1990).

c)   Minority ethnic staff in teacher education

However, even when training institutions have succeeded in recruiting minority ethnic students, they have not been able to adequately recruit minority ethnic staff. Though there is not sufficient empirical evidence to identify the reasons for under-representation of minority ethnic staff in teacher education institutions, it is quite clear that minority ethnic teachers and tutors with some experience of working in teacher education institutions have not found them to be very welcoming. ARTEN's (1989) head count survey revealed a figure of 0.6 percent for minority ethnic staff in teacher education, with many of these in 'race'-cast roles rather than in mainstream posts. There is no evidence of any increase in terms of staff in teacher education institutions. On the contrary there may have been a slight decline. The involvement of minority ethnic staff in the education of teachers is not only desirable on the grounds of equity, but it is also necessary for setting the issues of Anti-Racism in a context in which political and ideological constraints and values are made visible, and examined openly. It is also important to employ minority ethnic staff to provide an authentic perspective of student 'need' and learning 'experience', and a first hand familiarity with the issues of 'race' and racism.

d)   Minority ethnic teachers in employment

It seems strange that despite a national under-representation of minority ethnic teachers, a substantial number of well qualified teachers from minority ethnic groups are unable to find a decent job. The responses of head teachers in Ealing (1988), when asked why there were so few minority ethnic teachers, were varied. Those who thought, 'There was no problem' also said that they thought 'the authority bends over backwards for them'. The myth of 'no minority ethnic applicants' was also accompanied by comments such as, 'minority ethnic groups want money; teaching is seen as a poor profession'. The myth was challenged by the fact that 61 out of 382 applicants for the 140 jobs were from minority ethnic groups. Some head teachers clearly regarded minority ethnic teachers as a problem, problematising the victim rather than looking at procedures and practices.

The Swann Committee did call for more minority ethnic teachers, but banned positive steps from achieving this, because it will lower standards. Its stance implied that minority ethnic people are 'rightly' (in their view) not employed as teachers at the moment, not because of racism, but because they are no good. Insistence on 'professional standards' (whatever that may mean) is widely acknowledged to be one of the most common forms of institutional racism found in education and employment. It is really important to dismantle this mythical notion of 'professional standards', or at least to unpack it to determine the precise nature of these barriers. A notion of 'professional' behaviour is usually defined as working through consensus, not rocking the boat, supporting professional colleagues, and is antipathetic to the need to challenge institutional racism. The power of professions in propagating official, and often racist, views about minority ethnic people, and of educational issues through the media and establishment reports threatens to marginalise and discredit the anti-racist movement. Furthermore, the notion of the 'professional' as an expert undermines the legitimacy of Black perspectives, because it is based on and determined by the existing, traditional and exclusive assumptions about 'professional' attitudes (Menter & Braunholtz 1991, Gurnah 1991).

Minority ethnic teachers' experience in schools suggests that White colleagues expect them to have a greater workload, but without due recognition. They are expected to act as interpreters, carry out menial jobs and responsibilities, but are given low status, have a sense of isolation and experience sexism and racism. They also feel the pressure from minority ethnic parents to take greater care of their children, but white parents have low expectations of them and do not really take them seriously. White children also see minority ethnic teachers as inferior, and minority ethnic children see them as a novelty. They are expected to promote multiculturalism in schools, but are not really trained for it. There is also evidence of situations, similar to that of social work placements (de-Souza 1991), where a solitary minority ethnic teacher is seen as the 'honorary White', and where the White colleagues do not recognise that the minority ethnic teacher might bring specific life and work experiences, that are both valid and relevant. Other evidence of minority ethnic teachers' experience of working in schools indicates that in addition to the pressure to become the multicultural teacher in their school (Mac an Ghaill 1988), there are mechanisms operating against their promotion and for increasing their isolation in mainstream schooling (Ranger 1988, BICC 1988).

On the whole, though there is some evidence of positive achievements of minority ethnic teachers and head teachers, for example, 'Asian head who dares and wins' (TES 1991) and 'A long Journey to Contentment: Teaching Dynasties' (TES 1992). This, however, is heavily outweighed by the evidence of discrimination leading to industrial tribunals and by the evidence of white backlash, for example, 'Asian Biased head suspended' (TES 1985) and 'Head in Grievance row over parents in staff room' (TES 1985), both of which are of serious concern. The issues that need further exploration are not just about recruitment, but also about the content of training offered to all students, and the opportunities for subsequent employment for minority ethnic teachers. Student experiences and their perceptions of what they experience in the name of training are extremely important to identify the gaps between rhetoric and practice. Further work needs to be done to look at the experience of minority ethnic student teachers, both in training institutions and in schools. Particular attention needs to be paid to the ways in which the staff can undermine the confidence that minority ethnic students may have in their tutors and training institutions.

Key Agents and Context for Change

The tension between anti-racist ideology and the politics of education arises, inter alia, from the assertion by anti-racism's protagonists that racism is mediated through state institutions. On the other hand, in terms of actual political practice, contact with the state at certain levels is not only inevitable but may even facilitate the successful outcome of anti-racist activities. This is particularly true in the case of teacher education institutions, whose job it is to prepare all teachers to deal with and eliminate racist practices. Such tension is in fact very necessary as it helps to clarify the nature of our task. It is important to recognise that conflict is an inevitable and productive part of 'permeation'. It is an essential element in achieving innovation and change in any field. Anti-racist teacher education, too, must recognise the reality of conflict or dissonance in our society. Too heavy an emphasis on consensus can ignore the fact that consensus is usually achieved through suppression of struggles based on 'race' class and gender. It is only by questioning their own racism, which will inevitably arouse conflicting and often painful feelings, that student teachers and teacher trainers will understand its nature and clear the ground for changing their practices.

It also has to be acknowledged that complete elimination of racism is only possible when it no longer serves the interests of those who are the custodians of allegedly racist state institutions. Anti-racist initiatives by anti-racist individuals in teacher education institutions cannot, by themselves, provide the legislative framework, or create a non-oppressive culture, which effectively reduces discriminatory practices. They can, however, contribute to promoting a non-oppressive culture, by helping to defend and protect the rights of individuals against discrimination. These initiatives might all seem to be token gestures, for example, the successful outcome of an individual case of discrimination, or the making of one special provision for a particular minority group, or the provision of one day of anti-racist teaching, or the appointment of one Black member of staff. But all these initiatives are part of a process necessary to change long established practices that continue to perpetuate inequalities in education. This process has to be as complex and pervasive as the racism that it seeks to challenge and eradicate. But these initiatives also have to be seen in the context of the contradictions that govern the Tory policies on 'race' and education. These can be partly explained by the Government's repressive attempts to avoid unacceptable social conflict in the streets and the loss of Tory seats in the cities, as the excessive and counter-productive expression of White racism constitutes a threat to the role of law. On the other hand, there are a range of integrationist measures such as the Race Relations Legislation, the Commission for Racial Equality, the Race Equality Councils and limited funds for Urban Programme for projects run for and by Black people.

However, it is difficult to accept the contradictions that operate between the professed ideology of a teacher education institution facilitating equality of opportunity, and its actual practice in failing to recruit minority ethnic staff over a long period. It is also difficult to accept the contradiction in terms of the schools' professed commitment to cultural pluralism and their actual subordination of minority ethnic cultures. They wish to re-establish cultural monolithism, 'not to celebrate cultural diversity but to integrate them (the blacks) in a direct political way into the Tory ethos for Britain' (Hatcher & Shallice 1983).

The biggest indictment of all the Government's education policies is that it has been criticised by the very people it appointed as custodians of these policies, and who were responsible for ensuring their implementation. For example, Eric Bolton (ex Senior Chief HMI), regards the English education system's greatest success throughout its history 'has been to fail most children. Our system is better than any other in the developed world, at failing people and turning them out from the education service with a sense that they have achieved nothing of any value'. and that 'There is a risk in education that the Government is heading in the direction of a closed darkened room. It listens so selectively and has so firmly closed the windows and curtains that it does not seem to hear or see, the education scene as most people out in the world experience it' (Bolton 1992).

In terms of 'race' and education, the Tory Government argues for social cohesion not through cultural pluralism, but social cohesion despite cultural pluralism. This does not entail the exclusion of ethnic cultures, but their incorporation and de-radicalisation, as subordinate and peripheral elements. Michael Howard (1994) outlined a vision of 'a society which is comfortable with its differences, and a society which sees nothing particular to comment about the ethnic background of any of its members, because people of all races are to be found in all walks of life doing as well as their individual talents and efforts merit' (Howard 1994). This was indeed a welcome speech in which good race relations were regarded as something at the centre of any business or society which believes in fairness and giving every one the chance to fulfil their potential, and not as some sort of extra; an additional burden; a temporary fashion or a matter of positive discrimination. No one could argue with the message that 'Promotion of good race relations and equal opportunities is the most effective way of ensuring that all of our citizens have the same opportunities, and can achieve and contribute all that they can to the fulfilment of their own potential and the wider aspirations of our society' (Howard 1994).

But there is no room for naive complacency or paralysing pessimism. It must be recognised that progress has been made and equality is still, though only just, on the agenda. Despite the fact that the LEAs with policies for equal opportunities have either been abolished, rate-capped or dis-empowered in many different ways, and even though the market forces have disenfranchised issues of equality to some extent, there is no doubt that the quest for equality will remain there until the deeply embedded inequalities resulting from discrimination and racism can be removed. While the use of legislation has indeed changed the rhetoric in some places, deeply entrenched assumptions and philosophies of inequality remain in place. These cannot be counteracted by goodwill alone. It needs systematic reconstruction of attitudes, behaviour and procedures within the framework of a dynamic discourse. However debatable the effectiveness of law in combating discrimination may be, legislation can be a valid and necessary tool, though not the only effective weapon for change.

Working within the law, while accepting that it needs extending to increase its effectiveness, is not a bad thing. Advocates of a more radical approach perceive the law's limited powers as a diversionary smoke screen, syphoning off energy and resources in few individual cases, whilst sustaining the status quo and maintaining an unequal and fundamentally racist society. What is even more important than a strong legal framework is sustained political commitment because without that political will even strong legislative measures are ineffective. But it is only when such sustained political commitment is translated into a set of cohesive and linked strategies for intervention at all levels of operation that we may begin to see some results. This may sound like a pious hope, but we need this feeling of hope and urgent action to counter the tide of racism that could be very destructive for the future of all our children. At the moment it is difficult to predict whether a change of Government alone would ensure a brighter and more equitable future for education in this country. It seems that centralisation and managerialism in education are here to stay, so the hope for future lies in a set of linked strategies to ensure that we do go back to basics, the basic principles of equity and justice. The following strategies are offered with that principle in mind. Figure 7.1 illustrates the fluid inter-relationship between various key agents responsible for the organisation and delivery of teacher education courses, and those who are, directly and indirectly, at the receiving end of such training. The circular configuration implies a kind of interdependency of these key agents, who can create and influence the context of change for teacher education, and make anti-racist teacher education a reality.

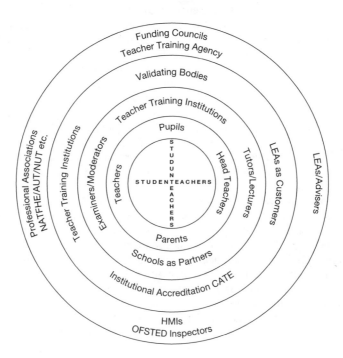

Figure 7.1   Anti-Racist Teacher Education: Key Agents and Context for Change

Alliance between parents, teachers and schools

> If we are to realize the goal for multiethnic Britain as a just society in which everyone has an equal chance to learn, live and work free from prejudice and discrimination and free from the fear of racial harassment and violence, we need to create the 'feel good factor', which comes from valuing people, as members of one race, the human race, in which we recognize differences and diversity, and the pain caused by oppressive and unfair treatment. We need people friendly policies and people focused programmes (Herman Ouseley 1994).

Both minority ethnic parents and teachers believe that a lot of White teachers hold stereotypical views of certain groups of minority ethnic children, which not only divides them from White children, but also from children of other Black communities. Minority ethnic parents have not uniformly found schools sufficiently friendly to wish to get involved with them as parents or as governors. They also believe that the school curriculum has tended to be epistemologically narrow and exclusively euro-centred. Swann and Scarman at some level acknowledged minority ethnic grievances and partly advised the state to heed them, but they also redefined them. Both Rampton and Swann linked the reasons of minority ethnic failure to inadequate provision at a preschool stage, lack of dialect appreciation, teacher expectations and inappropriate curriculum and examinations. They also believed that racism intentionally and unintentionally has a direct and important bearing on minority ethnic children's examination performance. They provided us with a text to legitimise racist state policies and to keep teachers and sociologists occupied for years to come, mostly trying to find out what they mean, and help continue the fiction that Britain has a balanced, liberal education system and an equitable legal one (Gurnah 1987).

The thus the coded message behind all this rhetoric of cultural diversity, language appreciation, and religious tolerance of the Swann Report was that the report accepted the failure of the school system as part of the balance. But it blamed and exonerated both White teachers and minority ethnic parents. To some extent the very existence of reports such as Swann and Scarman signifies the realisation of a balanced, fair, democratic and open society. What is important is not their content, but their hidden and symbolic meanings. They 'contain' public opinion by placating, reassuring, confusing, diffusing, legitimising and manipulating it. They do not resolve grievances but lubricate them and incorporate them in such a way that no action can ever result from them. Minority ethnic parents and teachers need to realise that there needs to be a large amount of political intervention to overcome discriminatory practices. They also need to realise that they need to build alliances with white parents and teachers who are genuinely interested in removing inequalities in education and in ensuring an anti-racist education for all their children. The problem is finding the political will and the organisational structures with adequate strategic concreteness and the flexibility to deal with specific problems and complexities of racial inequalities. Like the state sponsored inquiries, organisational structures in teacher education institutions and in schools are often very misleading.

The increasing autonomy of educational institutions, resulting from recent educational reforms, combined with increased powers of educational quangoes, with unelected and unrepresentative membership, means that the hidden brief of educational institutions, too, is not always open to question. But like the state-sponsored inquiries, we can't ignore them either, we need to study both of them in order to have a strategic response to them and secondly to construct an alternative strategy. Anti-racist teacher education cannot really be possible in a vacuum. Parents, children and the local communities need to have a direct access to, and influence on, what goes on in the institutions. The involvement of minority ethnic members on boards of governors and advisory committees has sometimes been productive, but only if such members are taken seriously and not marginalised. The tendency to ignore views that are uncomfortable or to choose members of minority ethnic groups, who fit 'the white mould', is all too common. Alliance between parents, teachers and schools with a shared agenda can indeed be very powerful.

Partnership between schools, LEAs and teacher-training institutions

If standards are to rise dramatically, the teaching profession needs to become more assertive, confident, and technologically competent. It also needs to be more open to new ideas, and accept and welcome accountability. In short it needs to be a learning profession. The schools and teacher education institutions, working together, can provide the foundation necessary for such a profession. It is clear that despite the Government's wish to make schools primarily responsible for training teachers, not many schools are willing to take on such a role, except of course in partnership with teacher education institutions. The recent proposals for the reform of teacher education are fraught with threats to equal opportunities in all its dimensions, and not least in its direct and indirect effects on the opportunities available to members of minority ethnic communities, both as teachers and as pupils. The present culture of teacher education is such that we need to create subversive spaces to introduce any kind of change. The national context of reduced funding, policy changes, and the weak status of Race Relations Act has almost ended the anti-racist campaign (Gilroy 1990). The reform of teacher education coupled with the Right-wing Think Tank's onslaught on to a slow moving anti-racist snail has almost crushed the movement.

   School-based teacher training, divorced from higher education, and where school mentors and very small departments are unable to provide students with a range of approaches and experiences, is only going to aggravate the lack of subject expertise noted by Ofsted (1993) in the Articled Teachers Schemes. If teachers go into schools without adequate knowledge of how children learn, it will be the children who will suffer most. Equally important is the effect that separation of teacher education from higher education will have on equality of opportunity in schools. Where teacher education institutions have developed effective equal opportunities policies and extensive programmes to implement such policies, the removal of teacher education from these institutions will lead to the impoverishment of student experiences and loss of important courses. A minority of schools may indeed be able to offer good models of equal opportunities in practice to support their understanding of the issues, but they may not be able to offer a basis for theoretical perspectives, and opportunities for reflection on practice. Graves (1990) argues that schools are not able to do so, because for teachers to become reflective practitioners, they need to understand what reflection-in-action means. 'The stress on practice does not necessarily provide skills, and it could in fact serve to de-professionalise, particularly black and women teachers' (Gundara 1993). Therefore, more practice without the opportunity to reflect and without an adequate intellectual framework to underpin their practice and reflection is not likely to lead to improved practice.

The use of Supply Teachers by schools and LEAs is another area where lack of experience and training opportunities can seriously hinder the performance of supply teachers. DfES has recently financed and supported the development of Self-Study Materials for Supply Teachers (2002) to support the work of supply teachers in schools. The five books cover a range of topics which will help raise supply teachers' awareness of recent developments in schools and include information on meeting the needs of all pupils and covers issues such as Inclusion, Special Educational Needs and EAL. It also includes a section on Professional Responsibilites and Legal Liabilities including information on Equal Opportunities. However, the use and effectiveness of these materials depends largely on schools and LEAs requiring their supply teachers to keep with the new developments and working with the Supply Teaching Agencies to ensure that they do so.

School-based training can only be effective if there is true partnership between schools and training institutions. It requires the abolition of boundaries, the capacity and will to understand each other's situation and perspective, to acknowledge each other's strengths and to construct a system of teacher education where joint appointments can make teaching and teacher education mutually dependent. CATE (1986) stressed this need for such partnership by stipulating that experienced teachers from schools should share responsibility with the training institutions for the planning, supervision and support of students' school experience and teaching practice, and be involved at some stage of the selection process. It also required that teacher trainers, concerned with pedagogy should be able to demonstrate and reinforce their own teaching effectiveness in schools.

The UDE case study demonstrated that it was even more crucial to ensure close and productive partnership for the training of minority ethnic teachers. For most of the time the bilingual students on the part-time PGCE course found themselves in schools where there were serious issues of conflict between head teachers and LEA advisers. The partnership worked best where the schools had been willing and prepared adequately to receive minority ethnic students as trainees, and where head teachers made an effort to ensure that student teachers were able to work with and learn from experienced and supportive class teachers. Minority Ethnic and Overseas Student Teachers in South-East England-an exploratory Study carried our as part of the National Partnership project (2003) by Stuart, Cole et al found that the time given to 'Equality and Equal Opportunities' education is inadequate to raise the general level of awareness about multi-cultural issues and racism. It found that the schools were not always willing or able to provide the necessary training and on-going support, so that the student teachers were often over-loaded. There was also evidence that most of the overseas teachers experienced considerable culture shock, compounded by the xenophobia and/or racism in the schools, which some were able to handle and some were not. For example, one Polish teacher found pupil behaviour quite shocking, 'at home a good teacher is one who can give knowledge; here it is one who controls well'.

Schools and training institutions need to collaborate in planning and implementing all aspects of assessment in order to ensure consistency and fair practice, including informing students of the criteria for assessment with opportunities for reasoned appeals and ethnic monitoring of assessment decisions. They need to recognise that levels of performance are context-related and may reflect discriminatory attitudes and cultures of schools. They also need to include, in the list of competencies to be assessed, the students' ability to deal with racism and the knowledge of race equality issues. Both, the trainers and student teachers, also need to recognise that the absence of evidence of racism is not necessarily an evidence of the absence of racism, 'in fact this may simply be due to the inadequacy of the system, given the highly complex, and sometimes subtle, forms of racism which many black pupils experience' (Gillborn & Drew 1992).

Equally important is the choice of schools for placement in terms of their ethos and commitment to promote issues of equal opportunities. Schools that encourage students to respect cultural diversity and to question the racist assumptions of many pupils and their parents also inspire confidence that they will ensure that prospective teachers do not suffer racial discrimination and racial harassment. Teacher education institutions also need to inspire that confidence and support students in situations where they are being harassed. They can only do that if they are sure that the tutors themselves are able to deal with issues of 'race' equality. It is therefore vital that both, the staff in teacher training institutions and in their partner schools, have a serious commitment to anti-racist education. The schools chosen for school experience and teaching practice need to be aware, sensitive as well as fully supportive, and act as equal partners in the process of training. It is also important that minority ethnic students are placed in schools with experienced and supportive teachers, who will enable them to perform and develop their skills at their optimum level, and benefit from their experiences in schools without fear of harassment and ridicule.

Collaboration between teacher training institutions and agencies for validation, accreditation and examination

Since the available evidence suggests that teacher education institutions have only made half-hearted attempts to tackle inequality, this has resulted in trainee teachers not being sufficiently equipped to tackle issues of inequalities within schools. The criteria for accreditation and validation of teacher education courses need to include, in the list of competencies, an extensive and continuous attention to issues of 'race' and culture. Teacher training institutions with a vague commitment to promote the development of anti-racist education need a steer, from their validating bodies and from CATE, to make multicultural concerns as a compulsory and integral part of the total teacher education curriculum. This also entails requiring school experience and teaching practice placements to provide an opportunity to work with children of diverse backgrounds.

When issues of 'race' and culture become a compulsory and integral part of a teacher education programme, examiners too would pay greater attention to the treatment of these issues in courses they examine. Similarly, internal course reviews should have these issues built in as part of a programme of quality assurance. Another significant point of intervention may indeed be the Ofsted Framework for Inspections of teacher education courses. Inspectors need to become aware that 'standards' are socially constructed, and have particular applications, functions, relevance, contexts and histories' (DTECC 1989), and that the vicious circle of Access, whereby entry to courses is allowed only to be neutralised by inappropriate curriculum and inflexible teaching and learning styles, needs to be broken. This is not an argument for rejecting Access courses or special initiatives. Teacher education institutions should neither abandon conventional routes nor oppose the development of alternative ones, but should develop, in conjunction with their validation and accreditation bodies, clearer criteria for assessing and monitoring new developments and studying the effectiveness of each route before abandoning them or adopting them as a blueprint.

The Ofsted Inspection Guidance (1995) does include issues related to equal opportunities, but there is little evidence of how much these inspections truly reflect the school policies on multi-culturalism, and how adequate the education of the minority ethnic trainee teachers really is. Minority ethnic students can become highly professional teachers, but a system of training that does not fully acknowledge and cater for the consequences of disadvantage and discrimination cannot be working in their favour. TTA surveys of trainees leaving ITT in the last 3 years have revealed that newly qualified teachers (NQTs) do not feel that they are trained and equipped to teach pupils from minority ethnic groups. Consequently TTA is in the process of setting up a national resource network for ITT providers. This is a welcome development and should contribute to the identification and development of good practice. The main task for the Teacher training Agency is to pool together the different strands, as in the work of the inspectors, and the policies of the higher education providers and the school mentors, and analyse their effectiveness within a rigorous framework of increased access and successful completion of training by a greater number of minority ethnic candidates.

Collaboration between the TTA, DfES, Ofsted, HEFCE and others responsible for funding, validation and accreditation

Institutions of teacher education and their courses are inspected, validated and accredited at regular intervals. Issues of 'race' and culture need to be included in all these processes as a mandatory part of all teacher education courses. HMIs inspect what they see, commenting on the quality of what they see and what has been included in the reports submitted by the institution. Some HMI reports do comment on issues of 'race' and culture but only if the institution concerned makes a reference to these in their policies and reports. HMIs need to adopt a more positive and pro-active stance by seeking to include in their remit attention to issues of 'race' and culture, as an integral part of all teacher education courses. The decisions about funding of teacher education courses are informed by these inspection reports. They are also influenced by reports of course validations and institutional accreditation. All these agencies need to work in tandem to ensure that issues of 'race', culture and anti-racist education are an integral part of the Quality Assurance Framework. We need to address the polarisation between quality and equality, which has been so skillfully manipulated by the far Right. Equality of educational opportunity, which embraces the concepts of equality of access, equality of treatment and equality of outcomes, can in no way be considered without reference to issues of quality. Some examples of recent developments and initiatives where these various agencies could have collaborated more are described below.

Green Paper 'Teachers meeting the Challenge of Change' (DfES 1999) set out detailed proposals for modernisation of the teaching profession. It contains some positive emphases in terms of valuing teaching as a profession. It also makes explicit references to the diverse society in which we live. 'Pupils need education for a multiethnic society in a world of rapid change in which both flexible attitudes and enduring values play a part.' It also describes the new era of education in terms of the school which takes responsibility for improving itself and which works with all pupils, irrespective of gender, ethnicity and social circumstance, to reach, even higher standards. An HEI is subject both to the QAA and to ITT criteria expressed in 'Framework for the Assessment of Quality and Standards in ITT' (Ofsted 1996a) developed jointly by Ofsted and TTA. Its aims are to provide a means of assessing the quality of ITT and the standards achieved, provide evidence to inform decisions on accreditation and allocation of student numbers, provide a means of identifying strengths and weaknesses in the training in order to help providers identify clear targets for improvement and contribute to raising standards in schools by improving standards in ITT. Ofsted claims that precepts of professionalism, fairness, integrity and co-operation underpin all inspection processes. Though there is broad agreement with the corporate goal of Improvement Through Inspection and the underpinning aspirations of objectivity, fairness, partnership, integrity and cost-effectiveness, the different emphasis placed by each of these agencies reflect their different location in the process.

HEFCE funded projects, as part of Special Initiatives to Encourage Widening Participation of Minority Ethnic Students in Teacher Education (Circular 9/93), were primarily concerned with a review and evaluation of existing provision for the recruitment of minority ethnic groups into the profession. Ten of the 16 projects had identified racism as one of the main concerns of students who had encountered overt or covert racism in schools and HE institutions. Black student teachers had also experienced isolation and intimidation from some White teachers.

Despite the specific intentions of these projects to address the issues of equality, the evaluation of HEFCE projects did not have a very specific framework so it was not possible to identify specific equality issues that need further attention. The emphasis within schools and hence within teacher education appeared to be more on implementation of the national curriculum and specific areas such as assessment rather than the experience of minority ethnic students. However, the projects indicated that change could be brought about if the funding bodies take the initiative and if money is attached to it. They have also demonstrated that if the issues covered in the projects are not made a part of the institution's culture, and properly monitored and audited, they could remain as interesting but passing phases in the context of multicultural education in Britain. Only one project (Kingston University) was aimed at identifying progression rates and support needs of trainee teachers from minority ethnic groups. More work needs to be done in this area to identify and analyse rates of progression and success of minority ethnic teachers. The reasons for any differential in progress and outcomes need to be further explored, as these could be of help in determining the level and range of learner support required for trainee teachers from minority ethnic groups.

Another example of lack of collaboration and a missed opportunity to address issues of equality is to be found in The Training Schools' Project that was proposed in the 1998 Green Paper 'Teachers: Meeting The Challenge Of Change'. It involved establishment of Training Schools, to develop and disseminate good practice in initial teacher training (ITT), train mentors and undertake relevant research. Schools that obtained Training School status were expected to have shown good practice already in teacher training, and they received funding to achieve specific objectives that they had identified in their bids to join the programme. An Evaluation of the Training Schools Programme (HMI 2003) included evidence of impact on quality and standards but made no reference to how Training Schools addressed issues of equality. Though there was some good practice in schools across the country with regard to successful teaching of children with special educational needs and of children from disadvantaged groups, this did not get mentioned in the HMI Report. This good practice needs to be harnessed for training future teachers, who do not always get sufficient training or opportunities to address these issues. Another evaluation of the project (Arora 2002) found that Training Schools have a tremendous potential for filling this gap and making issues of equality an integral part in the process of ITT courses as well as for those who are newly qualified. But this opportunity had been missed because the specification for Training Schools did not really include the issues of equality as one of the criteria to be addressed.

Training and Employment of Minority Ethnic Teachers

According to UCAS (1996) only 4.35 percent of Black and minority ethnic students were accepted on ITT courses. The TTA Corporate Plan (1996) included plans to increase the diversity of entrants to teaching and teacher training, consistent with maintaining quality, and stated, 'we also need to attract more men, people from ethnic minorities, and people with disabilities'. With many teachers leaving the profession due to low morale, poor public image and low salaries, and a general decline in recruitment onto teacher education courses, it will take a major effort of will, positive action and serious commitment for teacher education to attract suitably-qualified minority ethnic candidates into the profession. Again it will take a great deal of co-ordination at all levels to address the issues of recruitment to courses, relevance of curriculum and indeed opportunities for employment and career progression.

In effect the issue is circular, minority ethnic pupils may experience racial discrimination and harassment at school and often perceive their minority ethnic teachers to be similarly treated. They are reluctant to be teachers themselves, so institutions providing teacher education have few such students and may ignore any needs that they may have, leading to their isolation and a failure to consider the issue of race within the curriculum or in the institution generally. Thus White student teachers are not adequately prepared to counter racial discrimination, or to recognise the damaging effect of stereotyping and low expectations. And so the cycle is perpetuated. To break this cycle, it is not enough to be concerned about the lack of minority ethnic teachers in our schools. Concern without commitment can only raise expectations without addressing issues, thus aggravating the very problems they are designed to solve. Minority ethnic groups in this country need to know, that in addition to being welcome, they are also accepted and valued.

Teacher training institutions, in conjunction with their validating bodies, should make more positive and imaginative efforts to improve mechanisms for recognition of Overseas Qualifications. Overseas teachers especially those from the European Community and the Commonwealth have a great deal to contribute, not only as a means to tackling the domestic shortage of teachers but as part of international exchange schemes, and because they have something of quality to contribute to our education system. According to The National Academic Recognition Information Centre (NARIC), 'There is no 'official' recognition of overseas qualifications in the UK. British higher education institutions and professional associations remain autonomous and as such reserve the right to make their own decisions on the acceptability and recognition to be accorded to any overseas qualifications' (British Council 1993). But there is evidence that some teacher education institutions have been more sensitive and sympathetic than others in recognising overseas qualifications. It is therefore possible for training institutions to be more imaginative and take positive action, especially to improve their recruitment of minority ethnic students.

Teacher Training institutions could do that by marketing their courses in the minority ethnic media and target schools and colleges with a substantial proportion of minority ethnic groups. One example of good practice in this area can be found in 'Teachers For the Future' project at the University of Huddersfield (DFE funded programme of Taster Courses), This can help to introduce Black and minority ethnic people to teaching as a profession in a more positive context. A Recent report to the Teacher Training Agency (Carrington et al 2001) suggested several ways of improving the recruitment and supply of minority ethnic teachers including development of 'taster' courses and other opportunities for prospective entrants to gain experience of schools. The report recommended that:

- TTA to provide authoritative guidance on the assessment and comparability of overseas qualifications for admission to the PGCE.
- ITT institutions review their arrangements for staff training and development to ensure that matters relating to equity, social justice and citizenship are sufficiently covered.
- The issue of racial harassment needs to be addressed directly during staff development and mentor training sessions.
- Institutions should review the way they represent themselves to prospective ethnic minority students. This should encompass appropriate representation of ethnic minority trainees in publicity materials, an active presence in minority community settings including ethnic minority media, provision of facilities for religious and cultural observance etc.
- ITT institutions should pay particular attention to preparing and supporting their ethnic minority trainees for school placement. The TTA should promote this by providing guidance and examples of good practice.

Other ways of improving recruitment of minority ethnic teachers could also include:

- More LEAs to use GEST fund for training of mainstream bilingual teachers, and further Access provision to improve recruitment of minority ethnic students.
- Make teaching appear viable as a career to minority ethnic young people by increasing the number of minority ethnic teachers in schools, with a corresponding increase in promoted positions and by making teacher education programmes more reflective of diversity in Britain.
- Teacher training institutions could develop, implement and publicise their equal opportunities policies to assure minority ethnic students that they will receive fair treatment. The selection procedures need to be regularly monitored and scrutinised to ensure that direct or indirect discriminatory practices, which may serve to exclude minority ethnic groups from entering the profession, are not operating.

What Can Teachers Do?

'Teachers: Meeting the Challenge of Change' (1999) set out detailed proposals for modernisation of the teaching profession. It contains some positive emphases in terms of valuing teaching as a profession. It also makes explicit references to the diverse society in which we live and where pupils need education for a multiethnic society in a world of rapid change in which both flexible attitudes and enduring values play a part. It also describes the new era of education in terms of the school which takes responsibility for improving itself and which works with all pupils, irrespective of gender, ethnicity and social circumstance, to reach, even higher standards. Teachers have a responsibility to make this vision a reality. They also have a fundamental choice between accepting the system as it is, and work within it or to find ways of changing the whole system, overtly attacking all features manifesting or based on sexism, racism and class bias. This dichotomy is deliberately presented as if it was a simple choice. In reality, the choice is never simple. Preparation of teachers of the challenging kind necessitates mechanisms to ensure awareness of anti-racist issues not only amongst all staff involved in teacher education, but also amongst staff in partner schools. Such awareness needs to be informed by 'Black perspective', which in many cases requires a consistent presence of minority ethnic staff. Sometimes it is possible to achieve this effectively by one-off inputs from visiting lecturers or by offering optional courses, but only when these happen in the context of a strategy of 'permeation' of the whole training course with an anti-racist perspective. Such an approach, if it works, is the most convincing demonstration of the central importance of an anti-racist perspective.

Some teachers dismiss the notion of racism as a marginal matter compared with other forms of disadvantage in our school system. The construct of 'under achievement' is used to distract attention away from institutional structures, from the school, the curriculum, the assessment procedures and most of all from the teachers. The focus seems to be mostly on the under achievement of children, but almost never that of the school or the teachers. I do not wish to suggest that all teachers are incompetent. On the contrary, I prefer to believe that many teachers, despite their inadequate initial training, are very aware of their individual and collective values and attributes and that others are beginning to examine the effects on children's achievement of unintentional racist practices in schools. Undoubtedly all this requires enormous courage, sensitivity and tact to deal with entrenched fears, ignorance and prejudice that is the bedrock of racism in our society. More than that it requires, amongst teachers, an agreement and a common concern to counter racist practices and racist attitudes, and the inequalities and discrimination that result from them. Those who believe in the 'Treat them all the same', 'They are all children', 'Don't notice their colour syndrome' often feel proud that they don't operate any kind of conscious discrimination. In practice it often means that children are treated as if they are all 'white' British. It is also used as a reason for not changing the curriculum. But treating the children in the 'same' is in no way treating them 'equally' or with the same consideration to their needs as individuals or as members of communities that are significantly different from their monolingual counterparts.

For example, the disadvantage of a bilingual child or a non-English speaker, as s/he is usually referred to, is one imposed by teachers and schools. Lack of English or inadequate English does **not** mean that the child is linguistically deficient like a child whose first language is English, but who has problems with reading or writing.

By confusing linguistic difference with linguistic disadvantage, thus relegating learners of English as a second language to remedial classes, schools undermine the self-confidence of these children and then blame them for having a low self-image. The problem here is with the teachers rejection of children's languages caused by their lack of linguistic discrimination between 'linguistic difference' and 'linguistic deficiency' and not with the children who speak languages or dialects other than English. The rejection of a child's first/home language is one of the many ways in which educational inequalities operate within our schools. Even where schools have taken on board the main recommendation of the Bullock Committee (1975), 'No child should be expected to cast off the language and culture of the home as he crosses the school threshold, nor to live and act as though school and home represent two totally separate and different cultures which have to be kept firmly apart' and partially accepted the value and use of Asian community languages, similar consideration is seldom shown to West Indian pupils, whose use of dialect and Creole is regarded as a sub-standard form of English.

The obsession with conformity is not limited to the requirements of school rules and curriculum but to all kinds of expectations about individual behaviour and interactions with other people. Those who don't conform are rejected as bad pupils and bad parents, whilst non-conforming behaviour is deemed as bad behaviour and non-conforming language as bad language. The so called obedient, docile and co-operative children from Asian families may appear to be conforming more readily than children of Afro-Caribbean origin, who are often regarded as having a 'chip on their shoulders'.

Schooling in Britain is intentionally divisive. The assessment system eventually segregates pupils into those with opportunities open to them and those to whom many doors are closed. Teachers almost always act as gatekeepers who only open the gates to pupils who conform to their requirements and those of the schools. The notion of 'standards' in schools, whether it relates to examinations, curricula or social behaviour, tends to conform with teacher expectations about children's performance. The educational and vocational aspirations of children from minority groups are frequently rejected by teachers as unrealistic or over ambitious. This rejection is further compounded by selective procedures within the process of schooling, where pupils are allocated to different 'sets' or 'bands'. Here racial inequality operates visibly, though teachers strongly deny that their selection procedures are discriminatory. The criteria used may appear objective but, if based on the results of an inappropriate or biased test and also affected by social judgments of individual teachers, the outcome can and does mark the beginning of a vicious cycle and perpetuate racial stereotypes, as it happened in the allocated of West Indian pupils to ESN schools (B. Coard 1971). These are only some of the ways in which institutional racism serves to perpetuate the educational inequalities in our schools. The professional expertise of teachers, their social attitudes and beliefs and their expectations of pupils are fundamentally important if the process of schooling with all its curriculum, classroom interaction, allocative procedures and rules and rituals is to counter the tide of racism and reduce the effects of social inequalities on all our children.

Final Comments

In the absence of clear criteria that identify and recognise anti-racist practice, reports of inspection, of accreditation and of validation are only likely to continue to perpetuate inequalities. On the other hand, by requiring institutions to focus on practices that take account of the wider implications of multicultural society, inspectors, validators and accreditors will make a significant contribution to promoting anti-racist education. But that can only happen if there is collaboration between teacher training institutions and those responsible for inspection, validation, accreditation and examination of courses. Teacher-training institutions, including those with clear policies for equal opportunities, will only begin to take these issues seriously in practice, if their partner schools and other local employers and LEAs will share that commitment. The commitment of these schools in turn depends to a large extent on greater alliance and co-operation between parents, schools, governors and LEA advisers.

Teacher-training institutions will need to research and develop effective collaboration not only with their own professional associations and trade unions, but also with anti-racist agencies outside their immediate domain, for example with associations of Black teachers and other Black professionals, voluntary groups, such as Anti-Racist Teacher Education Network, National Anti-Racist Movement in Education, Anti-Racist Alliance and Race Equality Councils. The guiding principle of such collaboration must always be that it is of reciprocal nature and each organisation participates on an equal footing. Such collaboration should ensure a consistent and professionally appropriate pressure to be maintained at all the key points in the system. There is also a strong need for national alliance of academics from Blacks and other minority ethnic communities to provide a forum for discussions, and to cultivate collaborative links with local, regional and national anti-racist organisations and community networks. ARTEN, in particular, has a responsibility to provide assistance to mobilise specific demand articulation and positive action policies. It needs to work closely with minority ethnic groups and other anti-racist organisations, to liaise with key agents and make constructive interventions, to secure minority ethnic participation in the decision-making processes within teacher education.

Finally, I believe that if the teacher education institutions could match the determination of their minority ethnic students, and persevere in their attempts to get the balance right in their courses, we can look forward to a competent profession. I have found that if there is a single theme that runs through this book, and through all my work with minority ethnic teachers, it is the determination of very large numbers of people from minority ethnic groups to persevere with their education in the hope of obtaining their desired occupations.

Bibliography

Books, Chapters in Books, Articles in Journals and Periodicals, Research Reports, Conference Reports and Working Papers

Alexander, R., Craft, M., Lynch, J. (1984) *Change in Teacher Education: Context and Provision since Robbins*. London: Holt, Rinehart and Winston.

Alexander, R., & Harris, P. (1977) *The Evaluation of New Courses in College of Education*, Manchester (Reprinted **in** Original Resources in Ed. (1981) Vol. **5** (3)).

Alexander, R & Wormald, E. (1983) *Validation in Teacher Education* **in** Practice and Perspectives in Validation, (ed) Church, Guildford, SRHE.

Alexander, R., Rose, J., Woodhead, C. (1992) *Curriculum Organisation and Classroom Practice and Primary Schools*: A Discussion Paper, London: DES.

AMMA (1983) *Our Multicultural Society: The Educational Response*, London.

AMMA (1987) *Multi-Cultural and Anti-Racist Education Today*, London.

Arora, R. (1985) 'Preparing Teachers for Power' **in** Multicultural Teaching, Vol. **3** (3) Arora, R. (1986) 'Initial Teacher Training: A Decade of Change in Bradford'; **in** Arora, R. & Duncan, C, (eds) Multicultural Education, Towards Good Practice, London: RKP.

Arora, R. & Duncan, C. (1986) *Multicultural Education: Towards Good Practice*. London: RKP.

Arora, R. (1989) 'DTECC Course Evaluation', quoted in Arora, R. (1994) *Teacher Education and Ethnic Minorities in Britain*, references section (DTECC 1989b) Ph.D Thesis, Bradford University.

Arora, R. (1989) 'Evaluation of Part-time PGCE Course' at UDE, Manchester.

Arora, R. (ed 1991) *Teacher Education and Ethnic Minorities*, The Race Relations Research Unit, Bradford: BICC.

Arora, R. (1994) 'Teacher Education and Ethnic Minorities in Britain' Ph.D Thesis, Bradford University.

Arora, R. (2002) 'Evaluation of the Training Schools Project', Unpublished Report for the DFES: London.

ARTEN (1987) Occasional Papers 1, 2 and 3. Glasgow: ARTEN.

ARTEN (1988) *Permeation: The Road to Nowhere*, Occasional Paper 4, Glasgow.

ARTEN (1989) Head Count Survey of Black Lecturers in Teacher Education Institutions.

ARTEN (1990) Occasional Paper 5, Glasgow: ARTEN.

ARTEN (1993) 'Response to the DES Consultation Document for The Reform of Initial Teacher Training', Glasgow: ARTEN.

Ashton, P. & Henderson, E. (1989) *Teacher Education Through Classroom Evaluation. The Principles and Practice of IT- INSET*. London: RKP.

Baker, J. (1987) *Arguing for Equality*, London: VERSO.

Ballard, R. & Vellins, S. (1985) 'South Asian Entrants To British Universities: a comparative Note' in New Community **12** (3).

Banks, J. (1984) *Multicultural Education and its Critics, Britain & the USA*, The New Era.

Barrett, E. et al (1992) 'Report of Modes of Teacher Education Project', in *Initial Teacher Education in England and Wales*, London: Goldsmith College.

Beane, J. (1990) *Towards Democracy, Dignity and Diversity*, New York/London: Teachers College Press.

Ben-Tovim, G & Gabriel, J. (1979) *The Politics of Race in Britain*, in Sage Race Relations Abstracts **4** (4).

Bhattacharyam, G. et al (2003) Minority Ethnic Attainment and Participation In Education And Training, University of Birmingham.

BICC (1988) *Asian and White Perceptions of The Teaching Profession*, A Summary Report of Research into Ethnic Minority Young People and Entry to Teacher Education, Bradford: BICC.

Birley High School. (1980) 'Multicultural Education in the 1980s', A Report of Teachers' Working Party, Manchester.

Blake, M. & Blake, D. (1990) 'Practitioner Involvement in Initial Teacher Training', in JFHE, Vol. **14** (2).

Bolton, E. (1979) 'Education in a Multi-Racial Society' in Trends in Education: No **4**.

Bourne, J. (1980) 'Cheerleaders and Ombudsmen: The Sociology of Race Relations in Britain', Race and Class, Vol. **21** (4).

Boxall, W. & Burrage, H. (1989) 'Recent, Relevant Experience, How CATE Legitimates narrowly defined concepts of Education' in JFHE Vol. **13** (3).

Brandt, G. (1986) *The Realization of Antiracist Teaching*, UK: Falmer Press.

Brittan, E. (1983) *Education for a Multiracial Society: an Evaluation*, London: The Schools Council.

Bullivant, B. (1981) *The Pluralist Dilemma in Education*, London: Allen & Unwin.

Carby, H. (1982) 'Schooling in Babylon', in *The Empire Strikes Back*, CCCS, London: Hutchinson.

Carrington, B. et al (2001) 'Ethnicity and the Professional Socialisation of Teachers' Report for the TTA, London.

CCETSW (1991) *Antiracist Social Work Education, Setting The Context for Change*, London: CCETSW.

Chambers, P. (1981) 'Teacher Education for a Multicultural Society', Courses at Bradford College in Megarry J, Nisbet S. and Hoyle E. *Education of Minorities*, *World Yearbook of Education* 1981, London: Kogan Page Ltd.

Clay, J., Cole, M., Hill, D. (1990) 'Black Achievement in Initial Teacher Education: How do we proceed into the 1990s?' in Multicultural Teaching, Vol **8** (3).

Clay, J., Gadhia S., Wilkins, C. (1991) 'Racism and Institutional Inertia: A 3D Perspective of Initial Teacher Education', Multicultural Teaching, Vol. **9** (3).

CNAA (1982) Working Group on Multicultural Education, London, CNAA.

CNAA (1985) Notes on 'Multicultural Education and the Professional Preparation of Teachers', London: CNAA.

Coard, B. (1971) *How the West Indian Child was made Educationally Sub-Normal*, London: New Beacon.

Cohen, L. (1989) 'Ignorance not Hostility' Student Teachers Perceptions of Ethnic Minorities in Britain', in Verma, G. (ed) *Education for All*, London: Falmer Press.

Cohen, L. & Manion, L. (1983) *Multicultural Classrooms*, London: Croom Helm.

Collins, H. (1992) *The Equal Opportunities Handbook: A Guide to law and best practice in Europe*, Oxford: Blackwell.

Connor, H. et al (1996). *Minority ethnic Graduates Differences by Degree*, IES Report 309 in Research Review.

Conrad, J. (1994) 'A Discussion of the Concept of Quality in Relation to Educational Planning', Conference paper.

Craft, M. (1981) *Teaching in a Multicultural Society: The Task for Teacher Education*, UK: Falmer Press.

Craft, M. (1986) *Teacher Education in a Multicultural Society*, University of Nottingham: School of Education.

Craft, M. & Atkins, M. (1983) *Training Teachers of Ethnic Minority Community Languages*, University of Nottingham School of Education.

Craft, M. & Craft, A. (1983) 'The Participation of Ethnic Minority Pupils in Further & Higher Education', Educational Research **25** (1).

Davies, G. (1981) 'Multicultural Education: Some Assumptions underlying Current Practices', Paper for Research Seminar at the Institute of Education, London.

Derbyshire College of HE (1987) B.Ed. Submission document, CNAA.

De-Souza, P. (1991) 'Review of the Experiences of Black Students in Social Work', Quoted **in** *One Small Step Towards Racial Justice*, London: CCETSW.

Dhondy, F. (1978) 'Teaching Young Blacks' **in** Race Today, May/June 1978, London.

Dominelli, L. (1988) Anti-Racist Social Work, BASW, Macmillan.

Dorn, A. (1980) *Review of Doing Good by Doing Little*, **in** Multicultural Education Vol. **9** (1).

Downs, S. (1993) Work Placement Project Special Interest Groups, Luton College of Higher Education.

Dunn, D., Eggleston, S., Purewal, A. (1981) 'Inservice Education for the Teaching of Minority Groups in England and Wales' **in** Meggarry, J., Nisbet, S. and Hoyle, E. *Education on Minorities, World Yearbook of Education 1981*, London: Kogan Page Ltd.

Ealing Educational Service (1973) Extract from Education Vol. **12** pp364-377.

Ealing, London Borough of (1988) *Ealing's Dilemma, Implementing Race Equality in Education*, London: Ealing LEA.

East, M. (1992) 'Equal Opportunities in Higher Education, Black Access into Initial Teacher Training', unpublished M.A. Dissertation, London, Institute of Education.

Eggleston, J. (2000) Review of *Educational Inequality: Mapping Race, Class and Gender* by Gilborn and Mirza, in MCT **19** (1).

Eggleston, J. et al (1986) *Education for Some*, Stoke-on-Trent: Trentham Books.

Epstein, D. (1991) 'Inservice fairy tales? The role and limitations of antiracist INSET', **in** Multicultural Teaching, Volume **9** (3).

Fisher, S. & Hicks, D. (1981) World Studies 8-13, London: Schools Council.

Foster, P. (1990) *Policy and Practice in Multicultural and Antiracist Education*, London: RKP.

Foster, P. (1991) 'Case Still Not Proven', reply to Wright, C. **in** British Educational Research Journal, Vol. **17** (2).

Foster, P. (1992) 'Some Problems in Establishing Racial/Ethnic Equality or Inequality in Schools', *Unpublished Paper*.

Fuller, M. (1992) 'Teacher Education programmes and Increasing Minority School Population: An Educational Mismatch?' **in** C. Grant (ed) *Research and Multicultural Education*, London: Falmer Press.

Furlong, J. et al (1988) *Initial Teacher Training and the Role of the School*, Milton Keynes: O.U.P.

Garg, S. (2002) 'The Race Relations (Amendment) Act 2000 – a renewed opportunity to promote race equality in schools' in MCT **20** (3).

Gibbs, N. (1980) The Society of Immigrant Teachers, London.

Giles, R. & Cherrington, D. (1981) *Multicultural Education in the UK* (unpublished).

Gillborn, D. (1990) *Race, Ethnicity and Education*, London: Unwin Hyman.

Gillborn, D. (2001) 'Racism, Policy and the (mis)education of Black Children' in R. Majors (ed) *Educating Our Black Children: New Directions and Radical Approaches*, London: Routledge-Falmer.

Gillborn, D. & Drew, D. (1992) 'Research in Teacher Education', **in** New Community, **18** (4).

Gillborn, D. & Drew, D. (1993) 'The Politics of Research: Some Observations on 'Methodological Purity', in New Community, **19** (2).

Gillborn, D. and Mirza, H S. (2000) 'Educational Inequality: Mapping race, class and gender; a synthesis of research evidence'. London: Ofsted.

Gilroy, P. (1980) 'Managing the "underclass": a further note on the Sociology of Race Relations in Britain', Race and Class, Vol. **XXII** (1).

Gilroy, P. (1990) 'The End of Antiracism', **in** New Community Vol. **17** (1).

Gokulsing, K. (1999) 'From the respected to the reviled: Teacher Education and the Training of Teachers in Contemporary England and Wales', paper for the 19th Annual Seminar of International Society for Teacher Education, England: UEL.

Graham, J. (1999) 'Improvement Through Inspection?' in Asia Pacific Journal of Teacher Education & Development, Vol. **2**, No.(2).

Grant, C. & Millar, S. (1992) 'Research and Multicultural Education', **in** Grant, C. *Research & Multicultural Education*, London: Falmer Press.

Graves, N. (1990) 'Thinking and Research on Teacher Education' **in** *Initial Teacher Education*, Chapter 4 London: Institute of Education.

Grinter, R. (1985) 'Bridging the Gulf: The need for Antiracist Multicultural Education' in Multicultural Teaching, Vol. **3** (2).

Grosvenor, I. (1990) Education, Racism and the employment of black teachers in MCT **8** (2).

Gurnah, A. (1987) 'Gate Keepers and Caretakers: Swann, Scarman and the Social Policy of Containment,' **in** B Troyna (ed) *Racial Inequality in Education*, London: Tavistock.

Gurnah, A. (1991) 'Professional foul or own goal, where is the problem?' **in** Multicultural Teaching, Vol. **9** (3).

Gundara, J. (1993) 'Changing Ways', A review of Siraj-Blatchford (ed) *Race, Gender and Teacher Training*, TES, Dec 3.

Hall, S. (1977) 'Pluralism, Race and Class in Caribbean Society', **in** Race and Class in Post Colonial Society, Paris, UNESCO.

Hall, S. (1980) 'Teaching Race', **in** James, A. and Jeffcoate, R. (eds) (1981), *The School in the Multicultural Society*, London: O.U.P. and Harper Row.

Halsey, A. (1972) 'Political Ends and Educational Means', **in** Educational Priority, Vol. **1**, London: HMSO.

Halsey, A. (1975) 'Sociology and the Equality Debate in School and Society', **in** *School and Society: A Sociological Reader*, London: RKP and OUP.

Hardy, J. & Vielder-Porter, C. (1992) 'Race, Schooling and the 1988 Education Reform Act', *in* Flyde, M. and Hamper, M. (ed.), *Racism & Education - Structures & Strategies*, London: OUP.

Hargreaves, D. et al (1989) *Teacher Supply and Teacher Quality*, Cambridge Education, Paper I, Cambridge University.

Hatcher, R. (1985) 'Education for Racial Equality' **in** Multiracial Education, Vol. **13** (1).

Hatcher, R. (1989) 'Two Perspectives for Change', **in** Ed. Troyna, B. *Racial Inequality in Education*, London: Tavistock.

Hatcher, R. & Shallice, J. (1983) 'The Politics of Antiracist Education', **in** Multiracial Education, Vol. **12** (1)

HEFCE (1995) Special Initiatives to Encourage Widening Participation of Students from Minority Ethnic Groups in Teacher Training, Bristol: HEFCE.

Hexall, I., Lawn, M., Sidgwick, S., Walker, S. (1991) *Imaginative Projects: Arguments for a New Teacher Education*, London: Goldsmiths College.

Hill, D. (1991) 'What is left in Teacher Education', *in Changing the Future*, London: Tufnell Press.

James, A. (1981) 'Education for a Multicultural Society in Education', Education 3-13, Vol. **9** (1).

James, A. (1982) 'What's Wrong with Multicultural Education?', **in** New Community, Vol. **X** (2)

James, A. & Jeffcoate, R. (eds). (1981) *The School in the Multicultural Society*, London: Harper and Row.

Jeffcoate, R. (1979) *Positive Image Towards a Multicultural Curriculum*, London: Chameleon Press.

Jeffcoate, R. (1982) *Ethnic Minorities and Education*, London: OUP.

John, G. (1976) Quoted in British Council of Churches, 'The New Black Presence in Britain, A Christian Security', London: BBC.

Jones, K. (1990) 'Equality and the National Curriculum', **in** MCT, Vol. **8** (3).

Joseph, K (Lord). (1984) 'Speech at the North of England Education Conference', Sheffield, on 6th January, **in** Oxford Review of Education, **10** (2).

Kelly, E. & Cohn, T. (1988) *Racism in Schools - New Research Evidence*, Stoke-on-Trent: Trentham Books.

Kibble, N. (1991) 'The Performance of Non- Traditional Students on Law Degrees and on the Professional Courses at South Bank Polytechnic', London.

Kirp, D. (1978) *Doing Good by Doing Little*, U.S.A.: University of California Press.

Lawler, S. (1990) Teachers Mistaught: Training in Theories or Education in Subjects, London: Centre for Policy Studies.

Lawrence, E. (1981) 'White Sociology, Black Struggle', **in** Multiracial Education, Vol. **9** (3).

Lawrence, E. (1982) 'In the Abundance of Water the Fool is Thirsty, Sociology and 'Black' Pathology' **in** C.C.C.S., *The Empire Strikes Back*, London: Hutchinson.

Little, A. & Willey, R. (1983) *Studies in the Multiethnic Curriculum,* London: Schools Council.

Lucas, P. (1988) 'An approach to Research based Teacher Education through collaborative enquiry', **in** Journal of Education for Teaching **14** (1).

MacDonald, I., Bhavnani, R., Khan, L., John, G. (1989) *Murder in the Playground: The Report of the MacDonald Inquiry into Racism and Racial Violence in Manchester Schools*, London: Longsight.

Mac an Ghaill. (1988) *Young, Gifted and Black*, Milton Keynes: O.U.P.

McLennan, S. & Seadon, T. (1988) 'What price School-Based Work'? in Cambridge Journal of Education, Vol **18** (3).

McNamara, D. (1982) 'Research in Teacher Education: The past Decade and Future Trends', in *Change in Teacher Education*, Chapter 14.

McNamara, D. & Ross (1982) 'The B.Ed. Degree and its Future', Lancaster School of Education, University of Lancaster.

Menter, I. (1992) 'The New Right, Racism and Teacher Education', in Multicultural Teaching, Vol **10** (2).

Menter, I. & Branunholtz, R. (1991) 'Antiracism in Teaching and Professionalism' in Multicultural Teaching **9** (3).

Milner, D. (1983) *Children and Race Ten Years On*, London: Ward Lock.

Mortimer, T. (1985) 'Recruitment and Employment of Ethnic Minority Teachers', in Multicultural Teaching, Vol. **3** (2).

Mullard, C. (1981) 'Multiracial Education in Britain', in Tierney, J. (ed.) (1982) *Race, Migration and Schooling*, London: Holt Rinehart and Winston.

Mullard, C. (1982) 'Multiethnic Education, A Historical Overview' in Multiethnic Education Review, Vol. **2** (2).

Mullard, C. (1984) *Antiracist Education: The Three Os*, Walsall: NAME.

National Advisory Body for Higher Education. (1989) Action for Access. London: NAB.

NAME (1984) 'Teacher Education', Walsall: NAME.

NAME (1985) 'NAME on Swann', Walsall: NAME.

NATFHE (1982) 'Multicultural Education, Evidence to the Swann Committee', London: NATFHE.

NATFHE (1983) 'Teacher Education: Current Issues', London NATFHE.

NATFHE (1992) 'Response to the Secretary of State's proposals re ITT changes', London: NATFHE.

Naylor, F. (1989) *The School Above the Pub*, London: The Claridge Press.

Nightingale, P, and O'Neil, M. (1994) *Achieving Quality Learning in Higher Education*. London: Kogan Page.

Nixon, J. (1981) 'Multiethnic Education in Inner London', in New Community, **IX** (3).

N.U.T. (1982) 'Education for a Multi-Cultural Society' (Evidence to the Swann Committee), London: NUT.

N.U.T. (1983) 'Combating Racism in Schools', a union policy statement, London: NUT.

O'Hear, A. (1988) *Who Teaches the Teachers?* London: Social Affairs Unit.

O'Keefe, D. (ed). (1986) *The Wayward Curriculum*, London: Social Affairs Unit.

O'Keefe, D. (1990) *The Wayward Elite*, London: The Adam Smith Institute.

Osler A. & Morrison M. (2000) 'Inspecting Schools for Race Equality: Ofsted's Strengths and Weaknesses', Trentham for the CRE.

Palmer, F. (1987) *Antiracism: an Assault on Education and Value*, Sherwood Press.

Parekh, B. (1981) 'Exercising the Imagination' in *Multicultural Education :Views From The Classroom*, London: BBC.

Phillips-Bell, M. (1981) 'Multiracial Education: What is it?' in Multiracial Education, **10** (1).

Preen, D. & Collier, G. (1987) 'Beyond CATE: A Future for the PGCE', in Higher Education Quarterly Vol. **41** (2).

Ranger, C. (1988) *Ethnic Minority School Teachers*, a CRE survey of eight LEAs, London: CRE.

Raynor, R. (1981) *Teachers for the Inner City*, The Gulbenkian Foundation.

Reid, K. & Patrick, H. (1980) 'The Structure and Process of Initial Teachers Education within Universities in England and Wales', **in** *Development in PGCE Courses*, ed. Alexander, R. & Whitaker, Guildford: SRHE.

Rex, J. & Tomlinson, S. (1979) *Colonial Immigrants in a British City - A Class Analysis*, London: RKP.

Richardson, R. (2002) 'Changing Race Relations: Education and the New Legislation' in MCT **20** (2).

Rooney, B. (1980) *Active Mistakes - A Grass Roots Report in Multi-Racial Social Work*.

Rose, E. & Associates (1969) *Colour and Citizenship: A Report on British Race Relations*, London: Oxford University Press.

Rowe, D. & Newton, J. eds. (1994) *You, Me, Us: Social and Moral Responsibility for Primary Schools*, London: Home Office.

Runnymede Trust (1993a) *Equality Assurance in Schools*, London: Runnymede Trust.

Rushdie, S. (1982) 'The New Empire Within Britain', **in** New Society, 9 December, (Also a TV broadcast 'Opinions').

Sarup, M. (1986) *The Politics of Multiracial Education*, London: RKP.

Scruton, R. (1986) 'The Myth of Cultural Relativism' **in** Palmer (ed) *Anti-Racism: An Assault on Education and Value*, London: Sherwood Press.

Shah, S. (1989) 'Effective Permeation of Race and Gender in Teacher Education Courses' in Gender & Education **1**.(3).

Shiner, M. & Madood, T. (1994) Minority ethnic groups and Higher Education: why are there differential rates of entry?, London: PSI.

Siraj-Blatchford, I. (1990) '*Positive Discrimination*: The Underachievement of Initial Teacher Education', **in** Multicultural Teaching, Vol. **8** (2).

Siraj-Blatchford, I. (1991) 'A Study of Black Students' Perceptions of Racism in Initial Teacher Education', British Educational Research Journal, **17** (1).

Siraj-Blatchford, I. (ed, 1993) *Race, Gender and The Education of Teachers*, Milton Keynes: O.U.P.

Sivanandan, A. (1976) 'Race, Class and the State: The Black Experience in Britain', Race and Class, Vol. **XVII** (4).

Sivanandan, A. (1983) 'Challenging Racism Strategies for the 80s', **in** Race and Class, Vol. **XXV** (2).

Smith, D., Tomlinson, S. (1989) *The School Effect: A Study of Multi-Racial Comprehensives*, London: Policy Studies Institute.

Stitt, S. Dr. (1997) 'Suffer Little Children Unto School: Democracy and Education', Paper for Conference at The University of Hertfordshire.

Stuart, Cole et al (2003) 'Minority Ethnic and Overseas Student Teachers in South-East England'- an exploratory Study (part of the National Partnership project).

Stubbs, M. (1985) *The Other Languages of England: Linguistics Minorities Project*, London: RKP.

Tatum, D. & Lane, H. ed. (1989) *Bullying in Schools*, Stoke-on-Trent: Trentham Books.

Taylor, M. (1981) *Caught Between*, Windsor: NFER-Nelson.

Taylor, M. & Hegarty, S. (1985) *The Best of Both Worlds*, Windsor: NFER-Nelson.

The HEIST Project (1995) 'Higher Education: The Minority Ethnic Experience', Leeds Polytechnic. Unpublished.

Tickle, L. (1987) Learning Teaching: A Study in Partnership in Teacher Education, London: Falmer.

Tierney, J. (ed). (1982) *Race, Migration and Schooling*, London: Holt, Rinehart and Winston.

Tomlinson, S. (1987) 'Towards A D 2000, the Political Context of Multicultural Education', **in** New Community Vol. **14** (12).

Townsend, H. (1971) *Immigrant Pupils in England: The LEA Response*, Windsor: NFER-Nelson.

Townsend, H. & Brittan, E. (1972) *Organization in Multiracial Schools*, Windsor: NFER-Nelson.

Townsend, H. & Brittan, E. (1973) *Multiracial Education: Need and Innovation*, Schools Council Working Paper 50, London: Evans/Methuen Educational.

Tracy, M. (1986) 'Initial Teacher Training and Multicultural Education', in Journal of Further and Higher Education, Vol. **10** (3).

Troyna, B. (1982) 'The Ideological and Policy Response of Black Pupils in British Schools', **in** Hartnett, A (ed.) *The Social Sciences in Educational Studies*, London: Heinemann.

Troyna, B. (1987) 'Beyond Multiculturalism: Towards the Enactment of Antiracist Education' **in** *Policy, Provision and Pedagogy*, Oxford Review of Education, Vol. **13** (3).

Troyna, B. & Williams, J. (1986) *Racism, Education and the State*, London: Croom Helm.

University of Huddersfield (1994) *Teachers for the Future*, DFE funded programme.

Vellins, S. (1982) 'South Asian Students in British Universities: a Statistical Note' in New Community **10** (2).

Voluntary Colleges (1984) Guidelines for the Voluntary Colleges for 'Teachers and Higher Education in a Culturally and Racially Diverse Society' (Working Party Report).

Wadsworth, A. (1994) 'Review of the Promotion of Teaching as a Career', report by for the TTA, unpublished.

Whitty, G. (1991) *Next in line for the treatment: Education Reform and Teacher Education in the 1990s*, London: Goldsmith College.

Whitty, G. & Menter, I. (1989) 'Lessons of Thatcherism - Education Policy in England and Wales 1979-88', **in** Journal of Law and Society, Vol. **16** (1).

Williams, I., Cocking, I. & Davies, L. (1989) Words or Deeds? A Review of Equal Opportunities Policies in Higher Education. London: CRE.

Willis, M. (1987) 'Report on Handling Race Issues' at Birmingham Polytechnic, unpublished.

Willey, R. (1983) 'Training All Teachers For a Multiracial Society', **in** Primary Education Review, No. **16**, London: NUT.

Willis, P. (1977) *Learning to Labour: How Working Class Kids Get Working Class Jobs*, Aldershot: Gower (first published Saxon House).

Wright, C. (1986) 'School processes - an ethnographic study', **in** Eggleston, J. Dunn, D. & Anjali, M. (1986), *Education for Some*, Stoke-on-Trent: Trentham Books.

Wright, C. (1987) 'Black Students, White Teachers' **in** Troyna, B. (ed), *Racial Inequality in Education*, London: Tavistock.

Young, K. & Connelly, N. (1981) *Policy and Practice in the Multiracial City*, London: Policy Studies Institute.

Zec, P. (1980) 'Multicultural Education: What kind of Relativism is Possible'? in Journal of the philosophy of Education, Vol. **14** (1).

Government Publications and Semi-official Reports

ACSET (1983) 'Criteria and Mechanisms for the Approval of Initial Teacher Training Courses', London: DES.

CATE (1986) CATE NOTE 4: 'Links between Initial Teacher Training Institutions and Schools', London: DES.

CATE (1991) 'Membership of Local Committees', Annex 1, Para. 8. London: DES.

Cockcroft Report (1982) *Mathematics Counts*, London: HMSO.

CRC/ATCDE (1974) *Teacher Education for a Multicultural Society*, London: CRE.

CRE (1985) 'The Swann Report, a response from the Commission for Racial Equality', London: CRE.

CRE (1985) *Referral and Suspension of Pupils in Birmingham*, London: CRE.

CRE (1988a) *Learning in Terror*, London: CRE.

CRE (1988b) *Medical School Admission: Report of a formal investigation into St. Georges Hospital Medical School*, London: CRE.

CRE (1992) 'Response to the DES Consultation on Proposals for Reform of Initial Teacher Training', London: CRE.

CRE (1992) *Set To Fail*, London: CRE.

CRE (1992) *Secondary School Admissions*, London: CRE.

CRE (2000) *Learning For All: Standards For Racial Equality in Schools*, CRE: London.

DES (1965) *The Education of Immigrants, Circular 7/65*, London: HMSO.

DES (1969) Select Committee on Race Relations and Immigration '*The Problems of Coloured School Leavers*', London: HMSO.

DES (1971) *The Education of Immigrants, Education Survey 13*, London: HMSO.

DES (1972) *The James Report: Teacher Education and Training* (Report by a Committee of Inquiry under the Chairmanship of Lord James of Rusholme), London: HMSO.

DES (1973) 'A Report by the Select Committee on Race Relations and Immigration' (Sessions 1972-73), London: HMSO.

DES (1974) *Education and Disadvantage and the Educational Needs of Immigrants*, London: HMSO.

DES (1975) *The Bullock Report: A Language for Life*, London: HMSO.

DES (1977) The Curriculum, London: HMSO.

DES (1977a) *Education in Schools: A Consultative Document*, London: HMSO.

DES (1978) *Primary Education in England: A Survey by HM Inspectors of Schools*, London: HMSO.

DES (1980) *A View of the Curriculum, HMI Series: Matters for Discussion 10*, London: HMSO.

DES (1981) *The Rampton Report, West Indian Children in Our Schools*, London: HMSO.

DES (1981a) *The School Curriculum*, London: HMSO.

DES (1982a) *HMI series: Matters for Discussion 5*, London: HMSO.

DES (1982b) 'Racial Disadvantage, The Government Reply to the Fifth Report from the Home Affairs Committee', London: HMSO.

DES (1982c) *The New Teacher in School*, London: HMSO.

DES (1983) Circular 8/83, which replaced circular 11/73, concerned with the qualification of teachers, London: HMSO.

DES (1983a) *Teaching in School; The Contents of Initial Training*, HMI discussion paper, London: HMSO.

DES (1983b) *Teaching Quality*, London: HMSO.

DES (1984) *Initial Teacher Training: Approval of Courses* (Circular 3/84), London: HMSO.

DES (1985) *The Swann Report: Education for All*, Committee of Inquiry into the Education of Children from Ethnic Minority Groups, London: HMSO.

DES (1985b) Consultation paper *Increasing the supply of Ethnic Minority Teachers*, London: HMSO.

DES (1985c) *The Curriculum from 5 to 16* (HMI Series: Curriculum Matters 2) London: HMSO.

DES (1985d) *Better Schools*, London: HMSO.

DES (1987) *Quality in Schools: The Initial Training of Teachers, HMI Survey*, London: HMSO.

DES (1988) *Initial Teacher Training in Universities in England, Northern Ireland and Wales*, (Education Observed 7), London: HMSO.

DES (1989) *Ethnically Based Statistics on School Teachers*, Circulars 8/89 & 12/89, London: HMSO.

DES (1989a) *The National Curriculum, From Policy to Practice*, Circular 5/89 London: HMSO.

DES (1989b) *Future Arrangements for the Accreditation of Courses of Initial Teacher Training*, A Consultation Document, London: HMSO.

DES (1989c) *Standards in Education, 1987-1988*, The Annual Report of HMI Senior Chief Inspector of Schools, London: HMSO.

DES (1989d) The Education (Teachers) Regulations 1989. Circular 18/89 (on Licensed Teachers) London: HMSO.

DES (1989e) *Initial Teacher Training Approval of Courses*, Circular 24/89. London: HMSO.

DES (1990) *Standards in Education 1988-89*, The Annual Report of HM Senior Chief Inspectors of Schools, London: HMSO.

DES (1991) The Education Teacher Regulations, Circular 13/91, London: HMSO.

DES (1991) Circular 11- *Linguistic Diversity and the National Curriculum*, London: HMSO.

DES (1992) *Choice and Diversity: The White Paper*, A New Framework for Schools, London: HMSO.

DES (1992a) Reform of Initial Teacher Training. A Consultation Document, London: HMSO.

DES (1992b) Press Notice: 'Patten announces expansion of School Based Teacher Training', London: DES.

DES (1992c) Letter from the Minister of Education, John Patten, to the Chair of CATE, appended to DES (1992b).

DES (1992d) *Initial Teacher Training, Secondary Phase*, (Circular 9/92) London: HMSO.

DfEE (1993) Circular 14/93, *The Initial Training of Primary School Teachers: New Criteria for Courses* (England), London: HMSO

DfEE (1993) 'The First Wholly School Based Teacher Training Project', announced, (67/93) John Patten, 4th March 1993, reported in Cambridge Journal of Ed. **18** (3).

DfEE (1998), *Teaching: High Status, High Standards*, Circular 4/98 (Annex A) London: HMSO.

DfES (1999) *Teachers: Meeting the challenge of change* (Green Paper, Cm 4164). London: The Stationery Office.

DfEE (1999) *Learning To Succeed: A New Framework for Post-16 Learning*, White Paper HMSO: London.

DfES (2001) Schools Achieving Success, White paper, London: HMSO.

DfES (2002) Self-Study Materials for Supply Teachers, London: DfES.

EOC (1989) *Formal Investigation Report on Initial Teacher Training in England and Wales*, Manchester: EOC.

GTTR (1989) Annual Report Table 16, Gloucestershire: GTTR.

GTTR (1992) Annual Report Table ET1 and 2, Gloucestershire: GTTR.

HEFCE (1993) *Special Initiatives to Encourage Widening Participation*, Circular 9/93, London: HEFCE.

H.M.I. (1987) *Primary Schools: Some Aspects of Good Practice*, London: HMSO.

H.M.I. (1988) *The New Teacher in School* - A Survey by HM Inspectors in England and Wales, London: HMSO.

H.M.I. (1989) 'Responses to Ethnic Diversity in Teacher Training', London: HMSO.

H.M.I. (1990) Report of Hertfordshire Action on Teacher Supply (HATS).

H.M.I. (1991) *School-based Initial Teacher Training in England & Wales*, London: HMSO.

H.M.I. (1992) *Report on School Based Teacher Education*, London: HMSO.

H.M.I. (1992) *Annual Report on Education in England*, London: HMSO.

H.M.I. (1992a) *Framework for the Inspection of Schools*, London: HMSO.

HMSO (1973) Select Committee on Race Relations and Immigrant Education, A Report on Sessions 1972-73, 3 Vols, London.

HMSO (1988) *The Education Reform Act*, London: HMSO.

Home Affairs Committee (1981) *Racial Disadvantage*, Vol. **1** Para 138-142, London: HMSO.

Home Office (1989) *Report of the Inter Departmental Racial Attacks Group*, London: HMSO.

Kingman Report (1988) *Report of The Committee of Inquiry into the Teaching of English Language*, London: HMSO.

Labour Party (1991) *Investing in Quality: Labour's plans to Reform Teacher Education and Training*, London: The Labour Party.

Little, A. & Willey, R. (1981) *Multiethnic Education: The Way Forward*, Schools Council Pamphlet 18, London: Schools Council.

Macpherson, W. (1999) *The Stephen Lawrence Enquiry*, Report of an Enquiry by Sir William, London: The Stationery Office.

NAB (1988) *Action for Access: Widening Opportunities in Higher Education*, London: DES.

NCC (1990) *The National Curriculum and the Initial Training of Student, Articled and Licenced Teachers*, York: NCC.

NCC (1990a) *Curriculum Guidance 3: The Whole Curriculum*, York, NCC.

NCC (1991) National Curriculum Council Newsletter.

NFER (1991) *Evaluation of the Articled Teachers Scheme*, Slough: NFER.

Office of National Statistics (2001), The United Kingdom Population by ethnic group.

Ofsted (1992) *Report of The Licence Teacher Scheme* (Sept. 1990-July 1992) London: HMSO.

Ofsted (1993) *The Training of Primary School Teachers*, London: HMSO.

Ofsted (1996) *The Annual Report of Her Majesty's Chief Inspector of Schools*, London: HMSO.

Ofsted (1996) *Guidance on the Inspection of Nursery and Primary Schools*, London: HMSO.

Ofsted (1996a). *Framework for the assessment of quality and standards in ITT*, London: Ofsted and TTA.

Ofsted (1996b) *Making the most of inspection: A guide to inspection for schools and governors*, London: Ofsted.

Ofsted (1998). *Framework for the assessment of quality and standards in ITT* London: Office for Standards in Education/Teacher Training Agency.

Ofsted (1998). *The annual report of Her Majesty's Chief Inspector of Schools 1997-8.* London: The Stationery Office.

Ofsted (1999) 'Raising the Attainment of Minority Ethnic Pupils; school and LEA responses' London: The Stationery Office.

PCAS (1992) Annual Report.

Pearce, S. (1985) 'Education and the Multicultural Society', Monday Club, Policy Paper.

QCA (2003) *Respect For All* - QCA Website, Resource for Teachers.

Runnymede Trust (1992) *Choice, Diversity and Racial Equality*: Response to the White Paper: Choice and Diversity, London: Runnymede Trust.

Schools Council (1981) *Education for a Multiracial Society: Curriculum and Context 5-13*, London: Longmans.

The National Commission on Education (1993) *Learning to Succeed*, London: Hamlyn.

TTA (1995) School-centred Initial Teacher Training Scheme: Notes for guidance, London: HMSO.

TTA (1995) Corporate Plan 1995, Promoting High Quality Teaching and Teacher Education, London: TTA.

TTA (1996) Corporate Plan: Promoting Excellence in Teaching, London: HMSO.

TTA Corporate Plan (1999-2002), London: TTA.

TTA (1999) *Initial teacher Training Performance Profiles*, London: TTA.

TTA (1999) 'Recruitment and Retention of Teachers from Ethnic Minority Communities', Report by Wolverhampton Race Equality Council Consortium for the TTA.

TTA (2000) *Raising the Attainment of Ethnic Minority Pupils*, London: TTA.

UCAA (1989-90) Statistical Supplement to the 28th Report. Table 11c.

UCCA (1993) 'Annual Report of Universities Council for Central Admissions'.

UCET (1990) Press statement on Teacher Education, UCET.

Extracts from Newspapers, Speeches and Correspondence

Alexander, R. (1991) 'The Primary Needs Independent Evaluation Project', Reported in Times Educational Supplement (TES) 2nd August 1991.

Bolton, E. (1992) Extract from a speech at CLEA Conference on 23 July, published **in** Education Vol. **180** (4).

British Council. (1993) Extract from a leaflet by the National Academic Recognition Information Centre, (NARIC) London: British Council.

Clarke, K. (1992) Speech in The House of Commons 9 June.

Cox, C. (1989) Unqualified Approval, **in** TES, 6 January 1989, London: TES.

Daily Mail (1988) Quote from the Secretary of Professional Association of Teachers.

Dore, A. (1993) 'On Patten's Mum's Army Recruitment Plan', **in** TES, June 18, London: The Times.

Education Guardian (1992) Comments from Julian Debnam from Dartford in Kent and Barry Thompson from Bedford.

Education Guardian (1992) 'License Allows Break Through', Reported by Berliner,W. on 24th Nov., London: The Guardian.

Education Guardian (1993) 'Motivated Mums are the new Primary Teachers', Patten, J., 11th June.

Education Guardian (1993) 'The High Court dismissed the appeal by Bangladeshi Parents in Bradford against the Bradford Council's decision not to allocate places in upper school according to parents' choice', 11th September, London: The Guardian.

Howard, M. (Rt. Hon), (1994) Extract from a Keynote address at a conference on the 'Future of Multi-ethnic Britain', in Reading on 23rd Sept.1994, Runnymede Trust.

Jenkins, R. (Rt. Hon), (1966) Address given by the Home Secretary to a meeting of Voluntary Liaison Committee: NCCI.

Joseph, K. (Lord). (1984a) Letter in response to an inquiry by Arora, R. (a lecturer at BICC).

Kane, I. (1989) Extract from an article in Times Educational Supplement, 20 October.

Lawlor, S. (1990a) 'Something is Wrong in the Classroom', London: Daily Telegraph, 11 June.

Major, J. (Rt. Hon). (1992) Extract from a speech at a Tory Party Conference in Brighton.

NUT (1993) Comments on Mum's Army **in** Education Journal, June 1993.

Ousley, H. (1994) Extract from a Keynote speech at a conference on the 'Future of Multiethnic Britain', Reading 23-24 Sept. Runnymede Trust.

Pugh, G. (1993) Comments of an Articled Teacher in Wales, TASC Bulletin 16, Spring.

TES (1985) 'Asian biased head suspended', Sept. 13, London: The Times.

TES (1985) Extract from an article about the closure of Teacher Education, 1st Nov.

TES (1985a) Head in Grievance row over parents in staff-room, August 1985, London: The Times.

TES (1989b) Comment by McAvoy, D. of the NUT, 19th May, London: TES.

TES (1990) Caroline Cox on O'Keefe, D. (1990) in *Initial Teacher Education*, ed. Graves, N., London: Institute of Education.

TES (1990) News item about Hertford Action on Teacher Supply, December.

TES (1991a) The High Court ruled that a parent's right to choose a school overrides the Race Relations Legislation (Runnymede Trust Bulletin 251), TES 13th December.

TES (1991b) 'Asian Head who dares and wins', 10 May, London: The Times.

TES (1991c) German Teacher, who left after an unpleasant experience in the U.K.

TES (1992) 'A Long Journey to Contentment. Teaching Dynasties', 12th June, London: The Times.

TES (1992a) Comments about Brigitte Peyrac, with a degree in French and experience of teaching adults, TES 7th February.

TES (1993) 'Mum's Army demobbed' in TES 26th November.

TES (1993a) Comment by TACTYC (Tutors of Advanced Courses For Teachers of Young Children).

Thatcher, M. (Lady) (1987) Extract from a speech at a Tory Party Conference.

The Independent (1989) 'Baker Opens Schools in Britain to EEC Teachers', 12 May.

THES (1986) News Item on CNAA paper for Multicultural Education, 14 March.

THES (1991) 'DES Upset as School Based Training fails', London, Times Higher Educational Supplement.

Index